P9-CDB-734

THE BIG BOOK OF

FLY FISHING TIPS & TRICKS

501 Strategies, Techniques, and Sure-Fire Methods

C. BOYD PFEIFFER

First published in 2013 by MVP Books, an imprint of MBI Publishing Company, 400 First Avenue North, Suite 300, Minneapolis, MN 55401 USA

Material from the book originally appeared in the works *Complete Photo Guide to Fly Fishing* and *Complete Photo Guide to Fly Tying*, Creative Publishing international, Inc., published in 2006.

Library of Congress Cataloging-in-Publication Data on file

Editor: Josh Leventhal
Design Manager: Brad Springer
Designer: Simon Larkin
Layout: Kazuko Collins
Cover designer: Simon Larkin

Printed in China

NOTE: For visual clarity, some photos may show flies larger than normal or line/leaders that are thicker diameter than normal and/or artificially colored.

All photographs are by the author except: front cover, pages 113, 114, 138, 146, 166, and 176, photos by Creative Publishing international, Inc.; pages 1, 2, 5, 6, 9, 10, 15 bottom, 18, 25, 30 bottom, 37, 40, 48, 50, 55, 56, 60, 68, 76, 78, 82–83, 86, 88, 96–97, 104, 106 bottom 111, 117, 145, 156, 161, 170, 180, 184 left, 200, 203, 207, 215, photos courtesy shutterstock.com.

Contents

Introduction 6

Part I: General Fly Fishing Tips 8

Chapter 1 Tackle and Tackle Rigging: Making the Most of Your Equipment 10
Chapter 2 Getting Ready: Preparation and Other Essential Gear 40
Chapter 3 General Fly Fishing: Basic Tips and Strategies 56
Chapter 4 Casting: From Line Control to Mending to Retrieving 68
Chapter 5 Freshwater Fly Fishing: Working Streams and Rivers 76
Chapter 6 Saltwater Fly Fishing: Reading Water, Locating Fish, Choosing Flies 84
Chapter 7 Fly Fishing from Boats: Tactics for Anchors, Drifting, Line Tangles 88
Chapter 8 Care and Cleanup: Keeping Equipment in Prime Condition 98
Chapter 9 Travel with Fly Tackle: On the Road and in the Air 104

Part II: Fly Tying Tips 112

Chapter 10 Getting Started with Fly Tying 114
Chapter 11 Tools and How to Use Them 122
Chapter 12 Thread: Tying On and Tying Off 138
Chapter 13 Handling Hooks and Making Weed Guards 146
Chapter 14 Making Legs, Adding Eyes, and Tying on Tails 166
Chapter 15 Tying Bodies, Heads, and Ribbing 176
Chapter 16 Working with Cork, Foam, and Balsa 188
Chapter 17 Tying Fly Wings: Wet, Dry, Streamer, Saltwater, Bass 196
Chapter 18 A Few Miscellaneous Tips 204

Final Words 216
Further Reading 218
Index 220
Acknowledgments 224

Introduction

Think of a tip as a shortcut or improved way to accomplish something. In the case of fly anglers, tips and tricks are those concise tidbits of information that lead to a simpler, better, faster, cheaper, more effective, more organized, or more efficient way of doing something connected with fly tying and fly fishing. That "something" might be dealing with tackle, rigging your fly outfit, fighting a fish, landing a fish, casting under difficult conditions, cleaning your gear, fly fishing from boats, solving stream fly fishing problems, releasing fish, unsnagging flies, tying flies, and more. These tips can save you minutes or hours of time over a fishing career and in the process help you have more fun with your favorite sport.

Tying flies can be a consuming off-season hobby with the promise of fun to come as you devise, create, and tie flies for specific fish and fishing situations. Learning how to effectively and quickly tie such flies makes this hobby both more fun and more productive toward the goal of filling a fly box.

In some cases, a fly tying tip can be as simple as substituting clear nail polish for the head cement typically recommended to seal the final thread wrap of a fly. In other cases, it might be a simple way to add tungsten powder to epoxy sealer for saltwater flies to make them heavier and sink more quickly to the best fishing zone.

Fly fishing tips can include the best ways to control fly line when casting from the bow of a flats boat. Or it might involve using side pressure to turn and control a giant catch that could otherwise threaten to break off or spool your reel.

This book is a collection of 501 of the very best tips for fly fishing and fly tying. They address all aspects of freshwater and saltwater fishing, boat fly fishing, tying flies, gear, care of flies and tackle, protecting yourself from the elements, traveling with fly tackle, using lines and leaders, fly storage, and much more.

Some of these tips have been originated by the author while others are a compilation of the best ideas learned over the years from other experts in fly fishing and fly tying. You will find some old standards here, but you might also find some new tips, which hopefully will produce a more successful and enjoyable experience with fly fishing and fly tying.

In this collection, the most commonly known tips and tricks have largely been omitted, since most would be learned by the time you read this book. Similarly, tips and tricks that would only be used for highly specialized fishing or fly tying are not included.

I have divided the tips into sections so that you can go to a specific concern and find an answer to a vexing problem. In some cases, there might be only one solution—or one solution presented here and the only one that I know—to solve a specific problem. In other cases, you might have several choices from which to pick the tip or solution best suited to your fly fishing.

When I learn new tips and tricks, I try them to prove (or sometimes disprove) their efficacy. Those that don't work, I discard. And what I do learn in tips, tricks, wrinkles, and methods of doing something, I try to pass along. This, then, is a gathering of those tips, some developed by me, but many learned from others and some just common sense. This is an effort to share these ideas more widely to make the sport of fly fishing a little more fun and a little less work. Enjoy, learn, experience—and pass along your knowledge to others.

PART 1

GENERAL FLY FISHING TIPS

CHAPTER 1 TACKLE AND TACKLE RIGGING

Making the Most of Your Equipment

1 PRESOAK FLIES

Fluffy and wool-material flies are difficult to sink, and often require a couple of casts to soak completely and get down to the fish. There is an easy way to solve this problem. If you know that you are going to fish these flies, carry a small zipper-seal plastic bag, add a little water, and soak the flies. Make sure that once you finish fishing you remove the flies from the bag and allow them to dry thoroughly before returning them to your fly box.

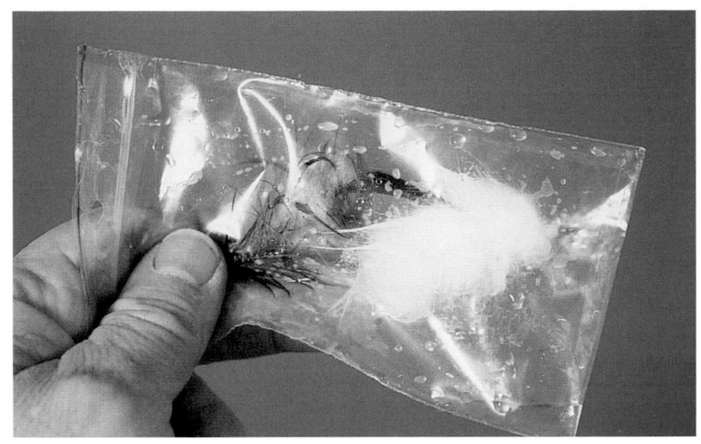

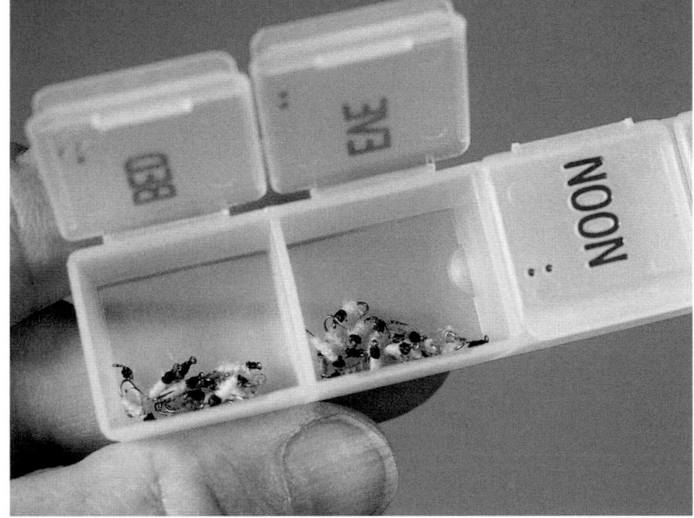

2 FLOATING FLIES

Many emerging flies (mayflies, caddis flies, and stone flies) float in the water film, rather than on top of it as do the mature dry spinner forms and the dry flies designed to imitate them. To simulate a struggling fly, take some of your darker colored dry flies and use scissors to trim along the bottom of the fly. That way, the tail, body, and hackle float in the surface, rather than riding high. In essence, you are transforming standard dry flies into flies that float in the surface film as do the specially designed comparaduns.

3 STORING SMALL FLIES

Small flies, size 18 and smaller, have a habit of getting lost, getting mixed up with other flies, or escaping from their compartments in standard fly boxes. To prevent this, use a special box for small flies. Actually, make up several boxes, since the individually lidded compartment pillboxes are best for these small flies.

You can get two styles—one with four compartments for daily dosing, and one with seven compartments for weekly dosing. The big advantage is that each style of box has individual compartments with separate lids, and that lid has internal ridges around all four sides to prevent even the smallest flies from escaping. An added advantage of these is that with only one compartment open at a time, you are less likely to lose flies should you drop the box or the wind gusts unexpectedly.

4 ALTERNATIVE WEED GUARD

Unless you tie a fly with a weed guard built in, you can't add one later—unless you are using large flies. Lure anglers use clear, short lengths of soft plastic that are fitted over the eye of a jig and then threaded onto a hook point to protect it.

Do the same thing with flies by threading your fly tippet through the end of the soft plastic weed guard, tying on the fly, and then rigging the weed guard over the fly point. Since these are not small, this is best with streamer or long-shank flies in about size 6 and larger. You can also use them on popping bugs and sliders. These are available from regular tackle shops and catalog houses—not fly shops.

You can do the same thing by dividing or splitting a clear plastic worm lengthwise into four sections, then cutting to length for use as a weed guard. There is no hole through which to thread the leader, so you have to carry a needle to thread the tippet through the end of the weed guard. An easy alternative is to push the head of the fly through the soft plastic and then tie the leader to the fly.

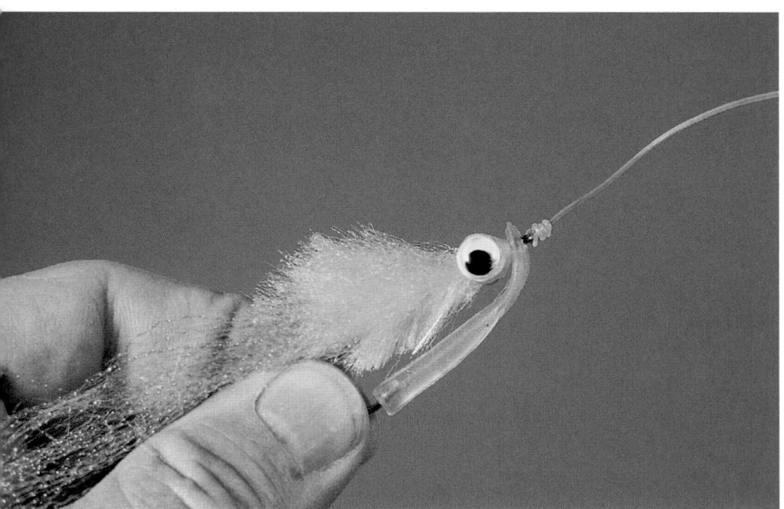

5 WEEDLESS FLIES FOR SNAGS ▲

Weedless flies are not only for weedy situations. They are also great when fishing around snags, through brush piles, over logs, or around docks or any other structure that can hang up a fly. The best weed guard on flies is the double-mono-loop style that covers both sides of the hook and protects it even when snaked on its side over a log.

6 SPLIT SHOT AND SMALL SHOT

To use split shot effectively to sink your flies, use several small split shot instead of one or two big split shot. Position the split shot along the leader several inches apart to spread out the weight so that there is less likelihood of bottom snags or rocks catching the weight. This also allows for a more lifelike movement of the fly in the water.

7 SIMULATING BAITFISH

Pick streamers that simulate local baitfish when choosing streamer flies. Thus, for freshwater trout fishing, pick patterns such as the Black Ghost, Black Nose Dace, and White Marabou that simulate dace and small freshwater minnows. For inland striper fishing, pick slab-sided flies that simulate shad that are food for these game fish. For bass and other warm-water fishing, pick fat and dark brown flies such as Muddler Minnows and similar patterns that simulate sculpins and mad toms.

In saltwater, choose large flies such as white and tan Deceivers that simulate mummichogs or killifish, bright-sided patterns that imitate glass minnows or silversides, or very slim, long flies that look like sand lance or eels. Simulating the local baitfish populations is the same as matching the hatch with insects to give the fish what they are used to seeing and eating.

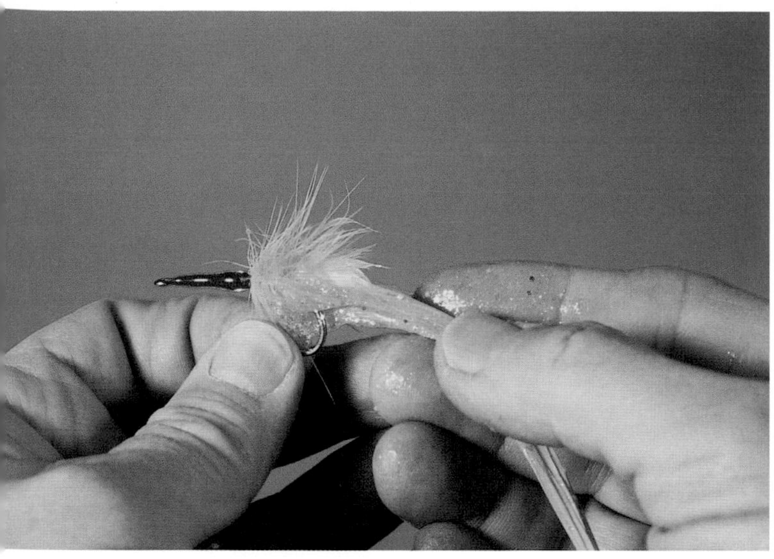

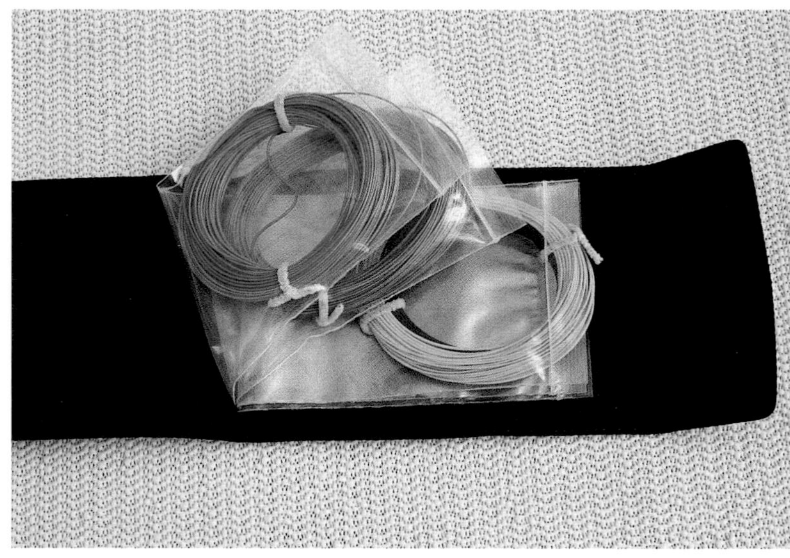

8 ADDING FLASH

You can add flash easily to any streamer fly while on the water. Carry some of the glitter gel that women use on their bodies for fun and evening wear. Use a small dab rubbed into the wing of any streamer fly to add flash. The gel will wash off as the fly is used, but this also spreads the glitter in the water to simulate scales, thus adding to the attractiveness of the fly. You can also make your own concentrated glitter by mixing fine or coarse glitter from a craft store in a clear gel, such as that used for hair. Store the glitter in a small jar or bottle for instant use in the field. Make sure this is not illegal where you fish.

9 EMERGENCY TIP-TOPS

Even if you do not carry a full field tackle repair kit, it makes sense to carry a spare tip-top, along with a tube of heat-set glue, in your fly vest. That way, if you do unfortunately break a tip section of your rod, you can glue on the spare tip-top and continue fishing. Make sure that the tip-top you carry is a size or two larger than your tip end, since breaking a tapered tip section will require a larger tube than the one mounted on the rod. Carry a few matches or a small lighter to melt the glue, then smear it on the broken rod tip end and slide the spare tip-top in place.

10 CASE FOR SPARE LINES

Spare lines are easy to install if you use the loop-to-loop connections of line/backing previously described. But you have to carry them some way. The best way is to coil up each line, use a string-tag label to mark the line weight and other characteristics (the marking system described on page 34 for weight and sink rate should suffice), and store them in a case. Try a nylon-fabric CD case, often available on sale for a few bucks from discount stores. Store each line in a separate plastic sleeve. You can carry up to half a dozen lines in one of these cases. If carrying this on the stream, slip it into the rear pocket on your fishing vest.

11 TESTING FLY HOOKS FOR SHARPNESS

To test fly hooks for sharpness, hold the fly in one hand and rest the point on the thumbnail of the opposite hand. Without applying any pressure, pull the fly across the nail. If the fly hook catches in the nail, the point is sharp. If it slides, the hook needs sharpening. Do not use pressure when doing this—you want to see if the fly hook catches without pressure, not drive the hook through your thumbnail!

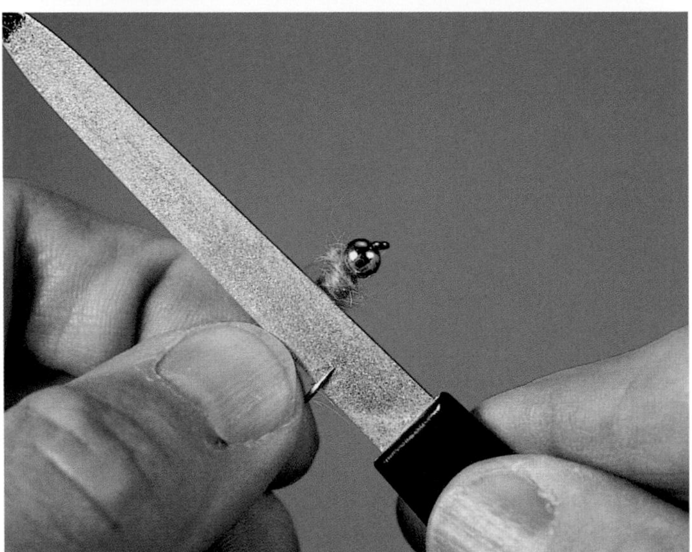

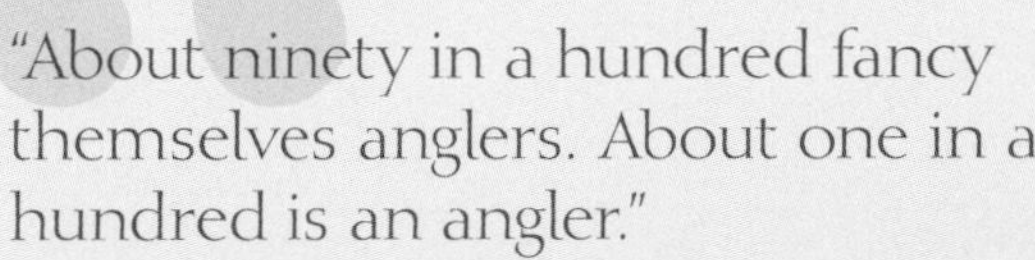

"About ninety in a hundred fancy themselves anglers. About one in a hundred is an angler."

—*Col. Peter Hawker,* Instructions to Young Sportsmen *(1814)*

12 SHARPENING HOOKS

Because they are smaller, fly hooks can sometimes be more difficult to sharpen than hooks used in other fishing circumstances. The best way to sharpen any hook is with a diamond hone. When picking a diamond hone for hook sharpening, pick one that is slim enough or small enough to work on fly hooks.

For very small flies, run the sides of the hook point on the hone, and then touch it up along the bottom area of the point. For larger hooks, run the hone at an angle over the sides of the hook point and then touch it up along the point bottom.

Diamond dust fingernail files, available in drug stores, are easy and inexpensive hook hones for flies. They are very thin, so they can work easily in the gap of fly hooks to triangulate the point. Buy several and keep one in each fishing vest, fanny pack, shoulder pack, leader wallet, or wader pocket. Use these often to touch up flies.

13 FLY HOOK DAMAGE

Check your fly hooks for damage while fishing. This is especially true after snagging something, or if your fly ticks something on the backcast. Flies break when they hit rocks. Check for dull flies by touching the point to your thumbnail and sharpening if necessary.

14 HOOK GAP

Most flies have a good hook gap—the distance between the shank and the point at which a fish is well hooked. Carefully check flies with full bodies or those with deer-hair-spun bodies, such as many bass bugs. These flies, if the deer hair is incorrectly trimmed, may have enough of a hair body to block part of the gap and prevent good hooking. To correct flies that have a blocked gap, use trimming scissors to cut away materials in the gap area. Make sure you do not cut the fly-tying thread as you do this.

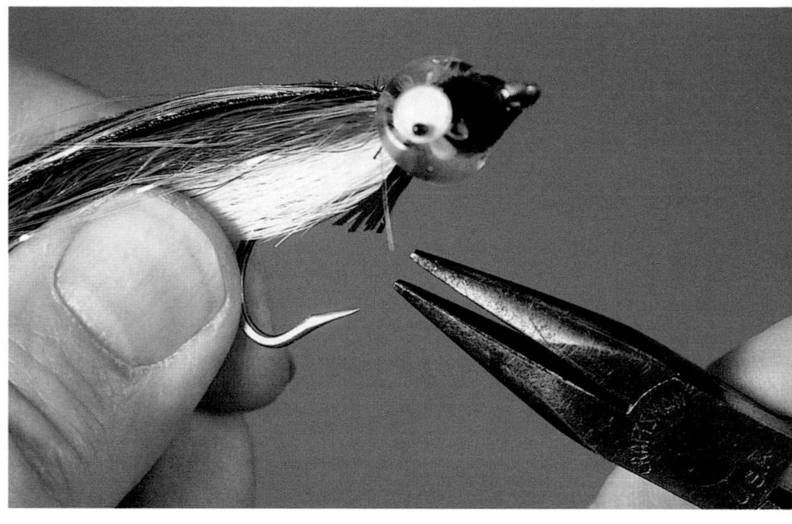

15 PINCH DOWN HOOK BARBS

The barbs on hooks designed to keep fish from becoming unbuttoned are not as important as we think. To make unhooking fish easy, pinch the barbs down with pliers. Use a flat-nose pliers held in line or on the axis with the hook point. This also makes it quick and easy to remove a fly should you hook yourself or a companion.

Some fly fishing areas have regulations that require fishing only with barbless hooks. Be sure to check your local regulations before heading out.

16 SNELLED HOOK HOLDERS

Fishing large saltwater flies requires a heavy shock, or bite, leader tippet. To keep a fly and short tippet ready rigged, use one of the two types of snelled hook holders used by saltwater surf anglers when bait fishing. One type is a round plastic tube with notches around the opening at one end (for hooks or flies) and a round rubber flange with cuts at the other to hold the mono snell or fly shock leader. You can use these to hold either wire or heavy mono bite leaders.

The other type of snelled hook holder is a flat bracket with openings for the hooks (flies) at one end, and tension spring clips at the other for the snelled leader loop. You can do the same thing with short bite leaders for fly fishing, forming a loop connection in the end of each bite leader. Possibilities for mono include a perfection loop knot, figure-eight knot, or surgeon's loop. For saltwater or warm-water fishing, use the above or a crimped-leader sleeved loop in braided wire or haywire twist in monel wire. These are not leader stretchers, but can hold several rigged flies, ready to have the bite leader tied to the tippet.

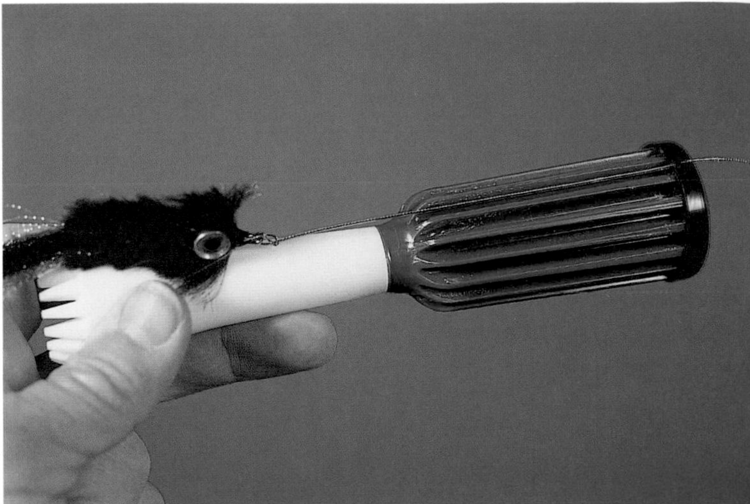

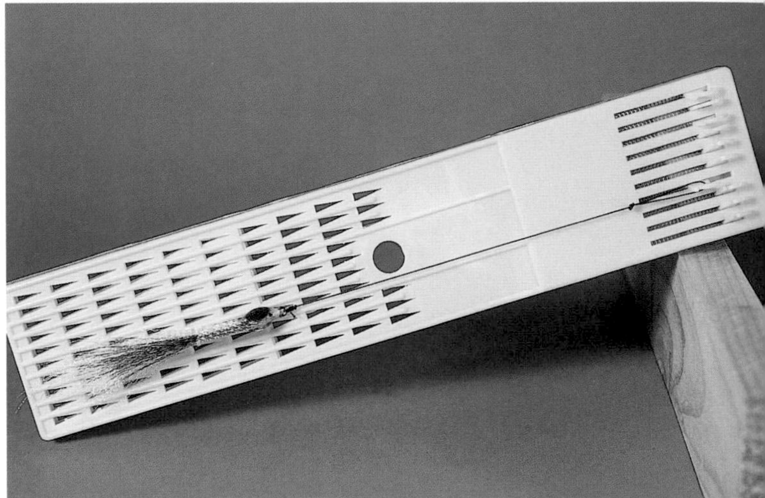

17 RATTLE FLIES

Fly anglers argue over rattles in flies. Many anglers swear by them, especially when fishing for species such as pike, redfish, stripers, and largemouth bass. They can attract fish, since bait makes noise that attracts game fish. Crayfish, for example, make clicking noises with their claws as they move or when they feel stressed or threatened. In all cases, rattles may not help, but they certainly do not hurt.

Situations where rattle flies shine include fishing deep and fishing in muddy, or murky, water. Often these flies are at their best when visibility is limited. The best way to fish these flies is with a series of slight twitches to cause the rattles to make continuous noise. The best flies are head-weighted so that each twitch throws the rattle to the back of the chamber to make noise and each pause causes the rattle to slide forward as the head of the fly sinks first.

18 GEL-SPUN VERSUS DACRON BACKING

Gel-spun lines are being used more frequently as fly backing, and they offer several advantages for fly fishermen. The braid is similar to the Dacron used for most backing, is very strong for a given diameter, and has little stretch (less than Dacron).

The disadvantage of the gel-spun lines is that most of them are very abrasive and have to be handled carefully. If used wrong, they can cut you; this can be particularly dangerous with line running out of the reel. You cannot hold the line or wrap it around your hand to break off a snag—it will cut you. Used carefully, however, a gel-spun line can offer more line capacity with greater strength backing than Dacron.

19 BACKING SIZE

Generally, anglers consider 20-pound (9.1-kg) Dacron backing the standard for most fly fishing. Those after big fish (sharks, large tarpon, billfish, or large snook) or fishing in snaggy areas choose 30-pound (13.6-kg) Dacron. Some fly anglers after tuna use 50-pound (22.7-kg) Dacron backing because of the possibility of the tail of a tuna hitting, abrading, and breaking lighter backing. If after fish no larger than 20 pounds (9.1 kg) under normal fishing conditions, choose 20-pound-test (9.1-kg) backing. If after larger fish, choose 30-pound (13.6-kg) Dacron backing.

As mentioned on the previous page, gel-spun lines are an alternative that provides you with stronger backing and increased line capacity.

20 MORE BACKING CAPACITY

Need more backing on your fly reel? You can get some by cutting back the rear portion of any weight-forward line that you are using and using the added space for backing. This is easy to do the next time you change lines or do reel maintenance. Note you can only do this with level or weight-forward lines—you do not want to cut back a double-taper line. Cutting back the fly line usually makes little practical difference to your fishing, while adding backing insurance. Most lines are about 90 to 105 feet (27.4 to 32.0 m) long.

If you don't cast the entire line, it becomes unnecessary bulk on the reel. For example, if your maximum casting range is about 60 feet (18 m), cut back the line to 70 feet (21.3 m) [keep 10 feet (3.0 m) of line for insurance] and use the rest of the reel capacity for backing. Note that you must cut the line from the rear—the running portion only! Then follow the tips for adding any fly line and backing (see Adding Backing to the Reel, above right) to fill the reel properly and completely.

21 ADDING BACKING TO THE REEL

To correctly add backing to the reel, first tie an arbor knot, then place a piece of tape over the loop knot to secure the line to the arbor. Next, secure the reel on a rod and crank the line onto the reel, running the line through a heavy work glove or clean rag. Note that fly reels do not have a level wind as do bait-casting reels, nor the reciprocating shaft of spinning reels, both designed to place the line evenly on the spool.

Use the little finger of your glove/rag hand to control the line and guide it side-to-side on the reel for neat, even spooling. By spooling the line tight on the reel, you reduce the chance that the line will dig into previously spooled layers of line when a fish makes a run, causing a break-off as the line pinches. This system is best for all backing lines and is very important if you are using gel-spun lines for backing.

An alternative to this method is to spool the line on extra tightly, using one of the newer line spooling machines designed for all reels and spools, such as the Cyclone Line Winder from Pure Fishing.

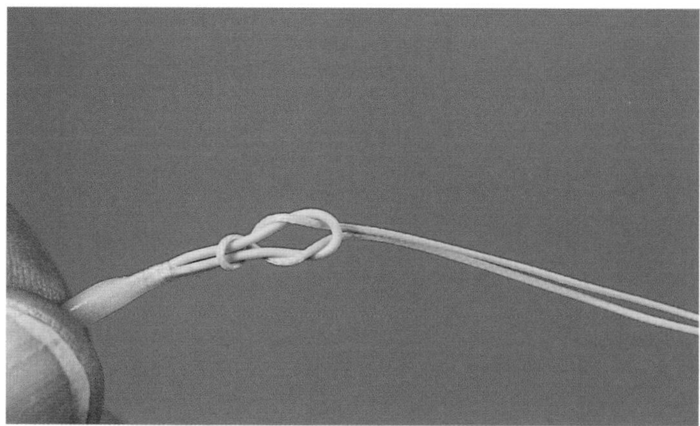

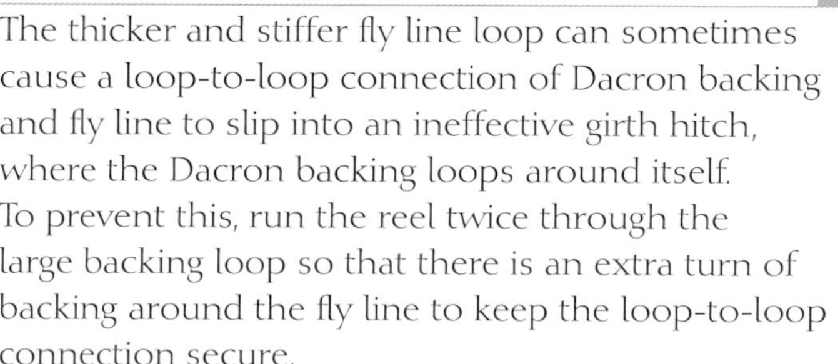

22 DOUBLE LOOP OF BACKING

The thicker and stiffer fly line loop can sometimes cause a loop-to-loop connection of Dacron backing and fly line to slip into an ineffective girth hitch, where the Dacron backing loops around itself. To prevent this, run the reel twice through the large backing loop so that there is an extra turn of backing around the fly line to keep the loop-to-loop connection secure.

23 MAINTAINING REEL DRAG

Drags work differently in different reels. Some manufacturers seal them and, therefore, the drags do not need lubrication or maintenance. Some drags have special washer materials and require special lubricants or must be used "dry." Many drags have a large cork washer. This creates a braking force when it rubs against the reel spool or a metal plate attached to the spool. You must lubricate these, preferably with neat's-foot oil. You can get kits for this, like the Abel kit containing sealed metal reservoirs of oil, grease, and neat's-foot oil.

24 CHANGING REEL DRAG

The best drag setting on a reel is a light drag. Too heavy a drag will break off a fish, since the water resistance of line is often enough drag to keep a fish from coming unbuttoned. One way to check a drag directly off of the reel is to hold the leader in your mouth and pull out line with your lips until you can no longer pull line. This will usually be a drag of 1 or 2 pounds (0.5 or 0.9 kg).

There are several ways to increase drag. One is to palm the reel on those reels (most of them) that have an external palming rim. The next best way is to raise the rod to about a 45-degree angle. This increases the functional drag (not the drag off of the reel) through the friction of the line going through the guides. Note that water resistance on the thick line also creates drag on any run.

Use all three of these methods. An added advantage of raising the rod to 45 degrees is that the limber rod provides insurance against the leader tippet breaking.

25 RIGHT- OR LEFT-HAND RETRIEVE

Anglers debate about whether to rig reels to retrieve line with the casting hand or the opposing line hand. If you are not after big fish, it doesn't matter much, provided that you are happy with your rig. Many experts agree that if you are after big fish that run out a lot of line or you are making long casts that require frequent lengthy reel retrieves, it is best to have the reel handle on the "rod casting" side. Thus, for big fish, always set up your reels so that you switch hands to fight the fish and retrieve with the dominant (casting) hand.

Reasons for this include: your dominant hand has more strength for long retrieves; your dominant hand can retrieve in small circles (spinning, with which this is often compared, requires large hand-turning circles); and your dominant hand has finer control if you must use a palming technique to exert drag pressure on the reel. Remember to fish the system with which you are most comfortable.

26 UP-LOCKING/DOWN-LOCKING REEL SEATS

Fly rod reel seats have knurled locking collets to secure the sliding hood onto the foot of the reel. These are available as up-locking (with the sliding hood and collet nut at the bottom) or down-locking (with the collet nut and threads at the top). The best for most fishing is the up-locking style, since this provides for a slight "extension butt." This protects the reel from damage when resting the rod on the ground, or allows you to rest the rod against your body to better fight big fish without the reel tangling in your clothing.

27 DIRECT-DRIVE VERSUS ANTI-REVERSE REELS

Fly reels come in two basic styles, direct-drive (left) and anti-reverse (right) models. Direct-drive models are just that—the handle is attached to the spool so that turning the handle turns the spool. There is no slippage, no braking action, and no drag as long as you have your hand on the reel handle. Anti-reverse reels have a separate plate or bar to which the handle is attached. The spool slips with the drag setting of the reel when a fish takes line, without the handle turning or moving backward.

Most freshwater and light-tackle inshore anglers use direct-drive reels while some offshore anglers like anti-reverse reels. But reel choice is not that simple. For example, if using a reel set with a very light drag while using a very light tippet, the anti-reverse reel has minimal advantage, since it is easily possible to turn the reel handle as the drag slips without moving or tiring the fish. Thus, the anti-reverse reels are best when using stouter tippets (big game fishing) and heavy drag settings that allow reeling in line when you turn the handle.

If you can't reel in line, the heavier force required to reel alerts you to this. Direct drive is best for light tippets, but has the disadvantage of the reel handles spinning anytime a big fish takes line. Thus, you have to release the handle on a direct-drive reel when a strong fish takes line or risk a break-off and/or hand injury.

28 CONVENTIONAL VERSUS LARGE-ARBOR REELS

Large-arbor reels are sometimes rated as "better" than conventional reels in that they supposedly retrieve more line with each turn of the handle, retrieve line more quickly, reduce stress, reduce fatigue when reeling, etc. That is true if you are choosing a large-arbor reel that has a larger overall diameter than the reel that you would otherwise use. It is not true if you are buying a large-arbor reel that is the same or very close to the diameter of the conventional reel you are replacing. Pi in physics remains constant, and a large-arbor reel of the same diameter as a conventional reel has no advantages. It only becomes a "reduced-line-capacity" reel. Of course, both reels must have the same spool width to make comparisons equal.

29 EXTENSION BUTTS

In the past, many fly rods for large fish had long extension butts of up to 6 inches (15.2 cm) in length. These caused more problems than they cured. While they did allow some separation of the fly reel from the angler's body, they also often caught loops of fly line on the cast, causing break-offs. To prevent this, use an up-locking reel seat with a very short extension butt of no more than 2 inches (5 cm). You still get enough separation of the fly outfit from your body and clothing, but will reduce the risk of catching the fly line.

30 SECURING LOOSE REELS

Sometimes, reels will be slightly loose on a reel seat. This can be as a result of the reel seat having too long a barrel for the short reel foot, having thin reel foot ends that are loose under the hoods, or reel feet not wide enough to fill the reel seat hoods. To prevent the resulting reel seat wobble, wrap a rubber band around the non-threaded part of the reel seat barrel. Make sure that you have several turns of the rubber band and that they do not overlap each other. Then, when you slide the reel foot into the fixed hood, the rubber band will create extra pressure and space on the reel seat/reel foot area to keep the reel from sliding around.

If you want a permanent solution, get a wide rubber band and glue one or more sections of it to just the reel seat area where the reel foot touches the reel seat.

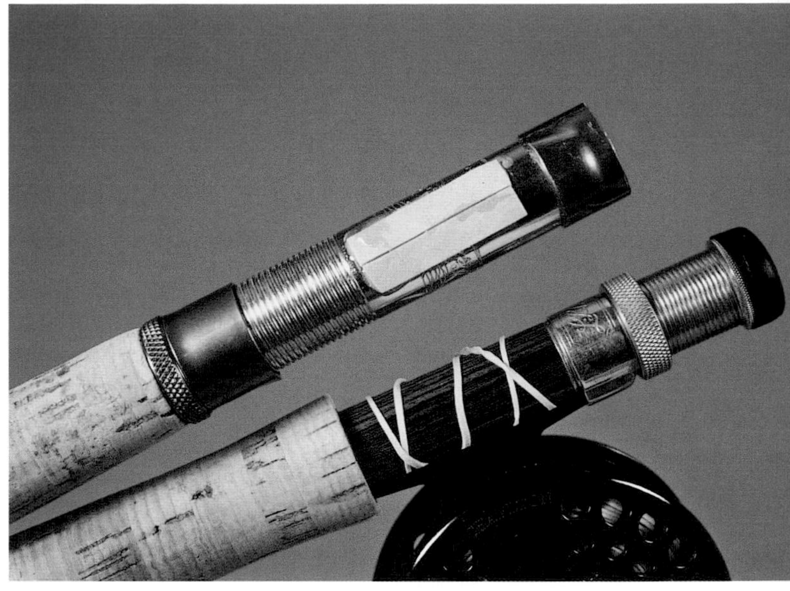

31 SECURING A SLIDING HOOD

Reels that have a single collet nut and a sliding hood can become loose while fishing. To prevent this, get an O-ring from your hardware store that will stretch over the rod butt and is no larger than the diameter of the collet nut. Slide this in place between the collet nut and the sliding hood. When you tighten the collet nut, the neoprene O-ring creates constant pressure on the hood and nut to prevent slippage and loosening.

32 EXTRA SPOOLS

Lots of fly reels today are expensive, but a simple way around both the cost and multi-line problem is to buy spare spools for different fishing situations. Spools are less expensive than a new reel and most reels allow easy spool exchange with a flip lever on the front of the spool. Thus, you can change to the line of choice before each trip, or carry a spare spool in your vest to switch from floating to sinking-tip to sinking lines or shooting heads. Just make sure that the spools you buy are an exact fit for the reel, and that the spool holds both the line and necessary backing for the fishing you plan to do.

33 MARKING FLY SPOOLS

Mark your fly reels with the line size and any other particulars of the line (tropical or cold weather, sink rate, etc.). Do this on the side plate of the reel with a small self-stick label or with a label maker. Protect the label with a covering of clear tape. You also can do this on the outside or the inside of the reel spool. If placing the label on the inside of a spool, make sure that it doesn't interfere with any of the pawls, gearing, or drag mechanisms of the reel as the spool turns. Many manufacturers sell fly lines with self-stick markers for this purpose.

34 CONTROLLING LEADERS AND LINES

You can control coiled leaders and lines and keep them untangled by several means. One way is to use short twist ties, like those used for trash bags. You can also use chenille-type pipe cleaners, cut in half. A third way is to use rubber bands. By looping a rubber band around the coil and then through itself, you can cinch up the rubber band until it is tight and stays tight on the line/leader coil. For best results, secure at three different spots around the perimeter of the coil. It also helps to label the line or leader so that you know what you have when you use it the next time.

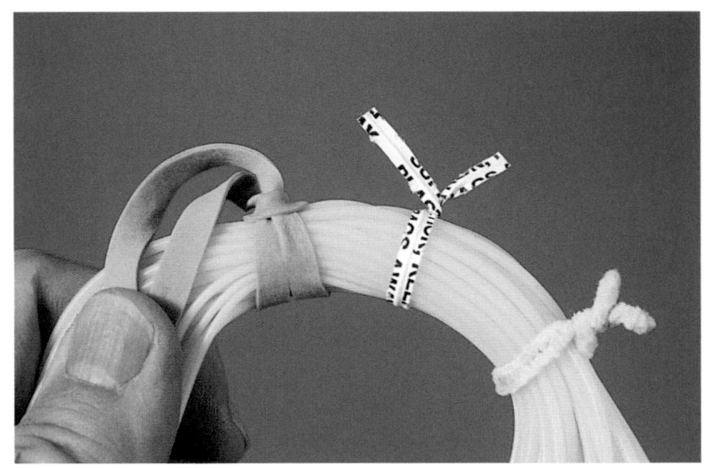

35 REMOVING LEADER COILS

Leaders coil up when stored on the reel or in a leader wallet. To straighten them for fishing, pull on the leader material with your hands or let the leader material slide through your hands as you pull on it. Use tension to create friction through your hands so that the slight heat helps straighten the leader. Make sure that you use less pressure as you progress from the heavy butt section to the lighter taper and tippet. Do not use a rubber patch as was done in the past, since this can create enough heat to harm the mono. Some patches of synthetic rubber also soil the mono. If fishing mono, it helps to store leader coils with a little moisture in a sealed plastic sandwich bag.

36 CUTTING MONO

An easy way to cut mono leader material is with a nail clipper. To make this simple to use, remove the lever arm and bar from the clipper and use your finger and thumb to press the edges together to cut mono. Strung from a loop of cord, this makes it easy and convenient to cut and adjust leaders and to trim knots. Hang it from a button or "D" ring on your vest.

37 REMOVING LINE COILS

Most fly lines retain some coiling when stripped from the reel for casting. This can impede casting, particularly when shooting line for a long cast. To prepare a line for fishing, stretch it to remove any coiling. This is particularly important in cold weather.

To do this, have an angling buddy hold the loop of line while you hold the end and the reel after you spool out a cast-length of line. Have him or her hold the line at this loop while you pull on both ends. Then return the favor for him with his fly line. If by yourself, loop the line around a tree limb, side mirror mount on your car, or similar structure to pull on the line to remove stretch. Just make sure that any structure used does not have any sharp edges, points, or rough spots that can damage the fly line finish. Round posts or tree limbs are best for this. If all else fails, remove large coils and stretch the line gently but firmly between your hands, a 6-foot (1.8-meter) section at a time. Repeat until you have stretched all the castable line and it is straight for casting.

38 SPOOLING LINE

You don't want to underfill or overfill your fly reel. But it is difficult to tell how much backing any reel takes if you put the backing on first. To fill a reel properly, first spool on the fly line, front end first, then connect and tie on the backing, and continue to fill the reel with the backing until within about 1⁄8 inch (3.175 mm) of the spool capacity. Reverse all of this onto another reel of equal or larger capacity. This does not have to be a fly reel; it can be any large spool to hold the line temporarily. Then spool the line again onto another large reel, and finally back onto the original reel. This switching of the line will put the backing on first, followed by the fly line, all with the right amount of line to properly fill your reel.

39 THREADING YOUR ROD

Run the line through your fly rod by first doubling the line and using this doubled end to thread each guide. That way, if you slip and drop the line, the doubled end catches in the next guide down so that you do not have to completely rethread the rod. Also, once the doubled end clears the tiptop, flipping the rod will pull out the rest of the line and the leader.

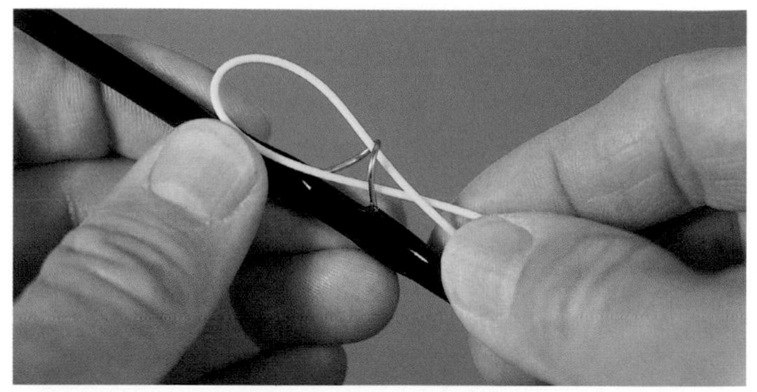

40 PREVENTING LINE SLIP

With today's highly polished reels, the backing arbor knot can slip on the reel if a fish takes enough line to run the end of the backing close to the reel spool arbor. If this happens, the line may slip, making it impossible to retrieve line. To prevent this, run the backing line around the spool arbor twice and then make a slipknot around the standing line with the tag end. Pull tight. Finally, add a small piece of masking tape over the line connection and arbor knot to prevent slippage. The subsequent line wrapped over this piece of tape prevents the tape from coming off or the line from slipping.

41 FLOATING LINES

To get just under the surface, fish a sinking or lightly weighted fly with a floating line. The floating line will suspend the fly while the lightly weighted fly will sink and fish the upper part of the water column. For this, you can use any floating line and should use a long leader of 7½ to 9 feet (2.3 m to 2.7 m) or longer. The length and retrieve speed along with the weight of the fly controls the depth of the fly fished.

When picking a fly, make sure that you choose one with only a little weight so that it does not cause the floating line to sink unnecessarily. The best flies are those with only a few wraps of lead on the forward part of the hook shank, or with a metal bead or dumbbell eyes for a little weight. Front weighting the fly helps to give it more movement when you work in a twitching retrieve.

42 SINKING SHOOTING HEADS

Most shooting lines are sinking style. You can also make your own from lead or lead-free trolling line. Realize that the strength of a lead-core trolling line is in the braided sleeve. To get maximum sink rate of the line, use as light a line as possible, since most lines use the same-diameter lead or non-lead product, and the thinner diameter of the light line creates less water resistance and sinks faster.

To make the line attachment to the running line, fold over the end, wrap it tightly with fly-tying thread, add a whip finish, and seal it with Pliobond or Ultra Flex. Make a similar loop in the front end for attaching a short leader with a loop-to-loop connection. Splice, or tie, a similar larger loop on the end of the braided running line, or make a wrapped, whip-finished loop if using level fly line for the running line. Make a similar loop in the other end of the running line for loop-to-loop attachment to the fly line backing. Spool all the parts on the reel—backing, 100 feet (30.5 m) of running line, and 30 feet (9.1 m) of shooting head—and you are ready to fish.

43 ALTERNATIVES TO LEAD

Because lead is toxic to all living things, many anglers are concerned about using lead fishing products, and more and more states, Canadian provinces, and regulated areas are banning lead in fishing equipment. This ban also often includes brass products, since lead is a component of brass. Most lead in fly fishing tackle is found in lead-core lines used for making sinking shooting heads, in split shot and other sinker choices, in lead wire wrapped onto a hook for weight when tying a fly, and lead dumbbell eyes used for the same purpose.

Substitutes to lead-based products include products of tungsten, bismuth, and tin. Check your local regulations about use of lead, and contact your local fly shop for lead substitutes.

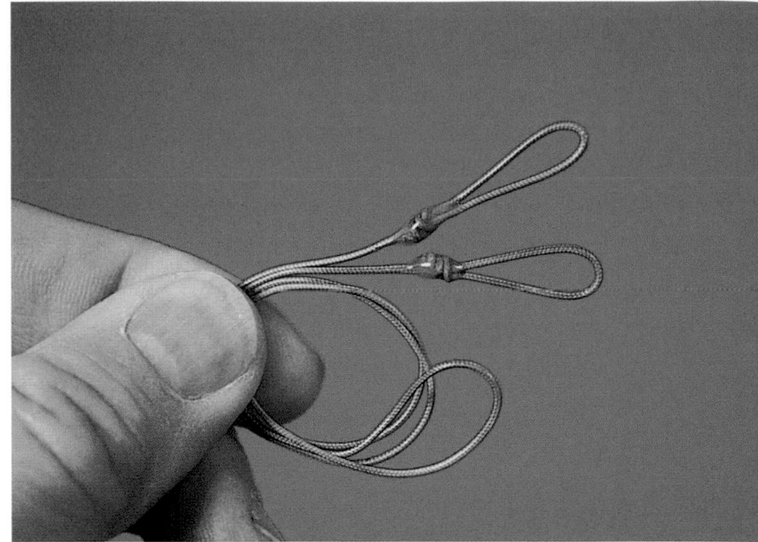

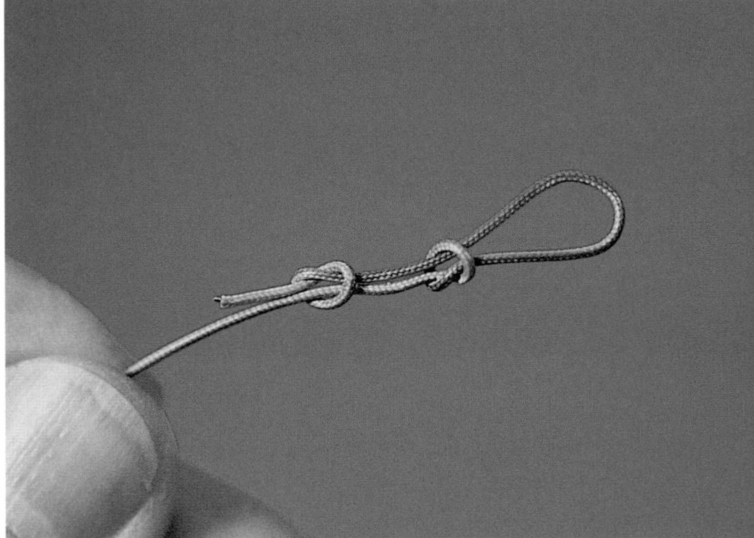

44 MINI LEAD HEADS

If you don't want to buy a sinking or sinking-tip fly line but still want to fish deep, there is an easy solution. Use "mini lead heads," as I call them, which are nothing more than short lengths of lead-core (or non-lead-core) line with a loop in each end to attach into your loop-to-loop system between the line and the leader or in the middle of the leader. If you do attach these in the middle of the leader, you must use loops between your butt leader section and the tapered leader portion. You can buy these mini lead heads (Orvis, Cortland, and Gudebrod, among others, make them) or you can make them using lead-core trolling line. You can also use lead-free trolling line, which is available from several manufacturers, including Gudebrod. The commercial mini lead heads are 2- to 6-feet (0.6- to 1.8-m) long, and have neat braided loops on each end. To make your own, use 27- to 30-pound-test (12.2- to 13.6-kg) lead-core line. Cut the mini head to the length that you want. I like 2-foot-long (0.6-m) lengths, which can be used individually or looped together to make longer lengths for deeper fishing or heavier outfits.

Fold over the ends to make a loop and whip-finish it with fly-tying thread (see Loop-to-Loop Connections on page 31 for details), or make a simple Homer Rhode knot in the end. In either case, seal the knot or the loop wrap with a flexible glue or cement. (See Sealing Fly Line Loops on page 31 for details.)

45 LEADER FORMULA 50/30/20

One simple formula for fly leaders is the 50/30/20 formula, which makes the butt section of the leader 50 percent of the leader length, the tapered portion 30 percent of the length, and the tippet 20 percent of the total length. This means that with a heavy, 10-foot-long (3.0-meter) saltwater leader with a 12-pound-test (5.4-kg) tippet, you would use 5 feet (1.5 m) of 40- to 50-pound-test (18.1- to 22.7-kg) butt section, 3 feet (0.9 m) of tapered section of about 30- to 15-pound-test (13.6- to 6.8-kg), three sections of 1 foot (0.3 m) each of 30-, 20-, and 15-pound-test (13.6-, 9.1-, and 6.8-kg) and 2 feet (0.6 m) of 12-pound-test (5.4-kg) tippet.

Use blood knots for all of these leader section connections. If using a loop-to-loop connection with the line, tie a surgeon's, figure-eight, or perfection loop knot. All ensure that the loop stays aligned with the leader.

Other factors can be colors of monos, which (when mixed) might alert fish to something unnatural tied to your fly. In standard leader kits, all the monos included are the same brand and type. If you do use different brands of mono, use the stiffer one for the butt section and the limp one for the tippet.

> "Never throw with a long line when a short one will answer your purpose."
>
> —*Richard Penn (1833)*

46 WEIGHT-FORWARD VERSUS DOUBLE-TAPER LINES

The argument used to be (and sometimes still is) that a double-taper line provides a more delicate presentation of the fly than any of the weight-forward lines. This is not true, although there are a few exceptions. Manufacturers base presentation on the degree or length of the front taper of the line, from the belly to the very short level section at the end. Line manufacturers debate this, citing mass/air-resistance ratios, floating versus sinking lines and their respective diameters, etc., but it basically comes down to front taper length. Many weight-forward lines available today have a front taper that is as long as or longer than that of most double-tapers.

There are exceptions, with the so-called "bass bug tapers" usually having a shorter front taper than that of double-tapers. But with that exception, most weight-forward tapers give you as, or more, delicate a presentation than double-tapers, along with the advantage of the front-weighted belly that makes them easier for distance casting.

The main advantage of a double taper is that you can reverse it when the one end wears out to get double the fishing time from one line. If you never cast long distances, consider this. Otherwise, opt for a weight-forward taper after checking the specs of the respective front tapers of the line brand you choose to make sure that you are getting the line that performs best for your fishing.

47 STUFF THAT IS BAD FOR YOUR FLY LINE

We all know that monofilament is impervious to almost anything, except battery acid. Long exposure to sun and heat also degrades it. Avoid products that can impart a scent to the line. (A possible exception is WD-40, which some anglers use to spray lures and baits, stating that it attracts fish.) But fly lines are different in that they are made (most of them, anyway) of a PVC coating over a mono or braided core. The PVC coating is susceptible to some degree of damage from a number of things, including a long list of outdoor and personal products, such as DEET insect repellent, some perfumes, sunscreens, oil, gasoline, fly sinks and floats, alcohol-based products, and petroleum-based demoisturizing agents, such as WD-40.

This last one has always loomed large on the radar screen of fly fishermen, since it seems to make it impossible to spray your reel with this protective petroleum product without hitting the fly line, unless the fly line is removed. Anglers name WD-40 as particularly bad for fly lines—some even suggest it will dissolve lines in short order.

In one test of the reported damaging properties of WD-40, a length of fly line was left soaking in a can of WD-40 for a period of months and checked periodically. After nearly a year in the can, the fly line was found to have stiffened very, very slightly, perhaps a result of the WD-40 removing some of the solvent in the fly line and slightly stiffening the remaining PVC coating. However, the result was still a fly line that could be used with little noticeable effect on the practical fishing properties of the line.

One solution to the problem of protecting fly reels is to spray fly reels with WD-40 and then add the backing and fly line. At the end of each season, strip off the fly line and spray the reel. According to line manufacturers such as Gudebrod and similar petroleum-based products, those products will not affect Dacron line or fly line backing.

48 CHOOSING LEADERS AND TIPPETS

Today, fly fishing leaders and tippets are getting simpler. There used to be many formulas for these, but most experts now agree that simple is better. Typically, one simple leader formula of 50 percent butt section, 30 percent tapered section, and 20 percent tippet is right for most cases. And this usually works for any length of leader for different fishing circumstances.

Even level leaders work for most fishing, particularly if you do not need a fine tippet, as for trout. Thus, for bass, pike, carp, and many saltwater species, a single length or 15- to 20-pound test mono works fine as a leader. Tie a loop for line attachment at one end and tie the fly to the other end and you are ready for fishing. Naturally, for some fish such as tarpon you might want a heavy mono end and for pike or musky a short wire leader to prevent cut-offs.

Fluorocarbon for leaders has had a lot of hype, but for the most part it is not necessary for much fishing. Fluorocarbon is less visible in the water, has more abrasion resistance, does not weaken by absorbing water, sinks faster, and is stiffer. It also has a lower tensile strength per diameter, thus reducing the purported advantage of less visibility if you need a certain tensile strength leader or tippet. It is stiffer and thus more difficult to use when tying knots and for fly movement in the water. For fishing deep, fluorocarbon does sink faster, which is an advantage, but a disadvantage when fishing on top. The cost of fluorocarbon is also higher, and it does not break down as mono does if lost as litter.

49 TIPPET SIZE

One way to minimize drag in any fly fishing situation is to use a very long, fine tippet. Make sure that you are using very flexible tippet and leader material that can drift with the current and not stiffen to cause the fly to drag. By using a long tippet, you have the maximum flexibility possible to prevent drag from affecting the fly. By using the finest tippet you dare, you have minimal possible chance of the fish sighting your leader or you and the maximum flexibility in the tippet section.

This same solution applies when sight-fishing in very shallow water for fish like bonefish and permit and on some clear river trout situations.

50 SLIP STRIKE WITH LIGHT TIPPETS

Striking a fish when using a very light tippet may break the tippet if you are not careful. To guard against this, use a "slip strike." For this, don't hold on to the line when you strike. Instead, allow the line to slip through your fingers and rod guides as you make a striking twitch with the rod. This exerts enough pressure on the hook to bury it in the fish, while allowing the line to slip so that you do not overtax the leader and break the tippet. It is a simple technique that takes some time to get used to by allowing the line to slip or slide as you twitch the rod on a strike. Practice this, since it seems foreign to our natural tendency to set the hook with a hard strike.

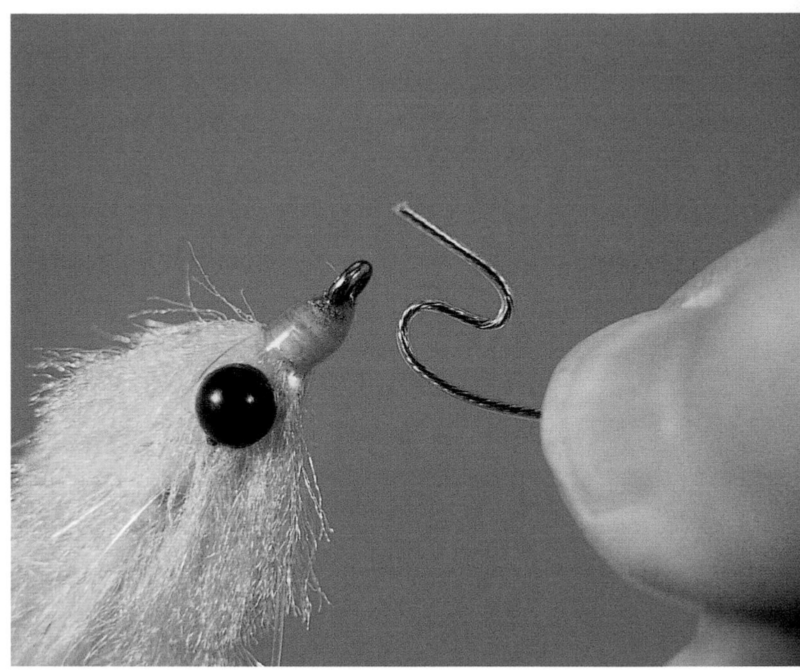

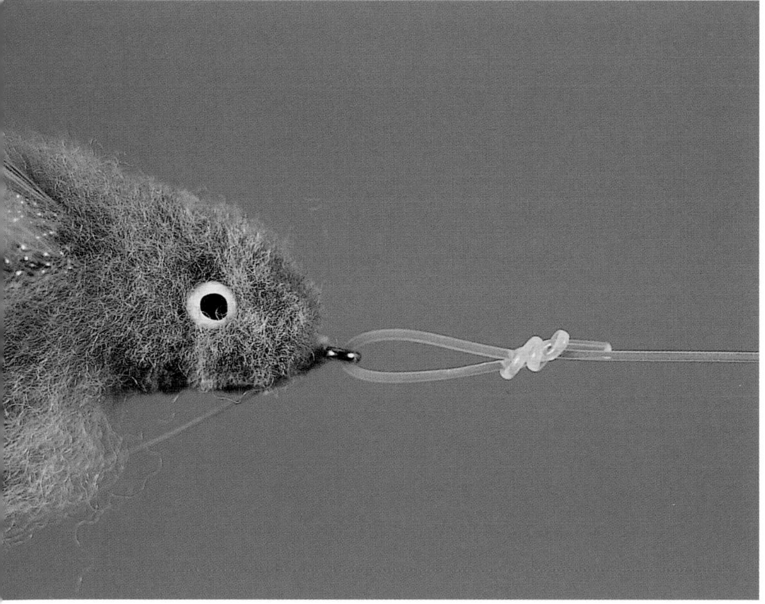

51 HEAVY SHOCK LEADERS

If you use a heavy shock leader of mono tied with a clinch knot against the fly, the fly may have little action as a result of the stiff mono. To give the fly action, use a loop knot. The best is the Homer Rhode loop knot, which is simple to tie with heavy mono. It does not have the best knot strength, but when used with a heavy shock or bite leader, this makes no difference. The advantage is that the fly can swing, swim, twitch, and suspend independently of the heavy mono bite leader to have maximum action in the water.

52 BRAIDED WIRE LEADERS

Wire leaders are needed when fishing for toothy critters, such as pike, muskie, barracuda, bluefish, and the like. An easy way to attach a fly to a braided wire leader is to thread the wire through the fly eye, then around the wire and back through the formed loop in the opposite direction. Tighten by pulling the tag end of the wire. This also makes it easy to replace flies, since you can back out the tag end, remove the fly, add a new fly, and repeat the tie without cutting the knot. Just make sure that you use this only with standard braided wire.

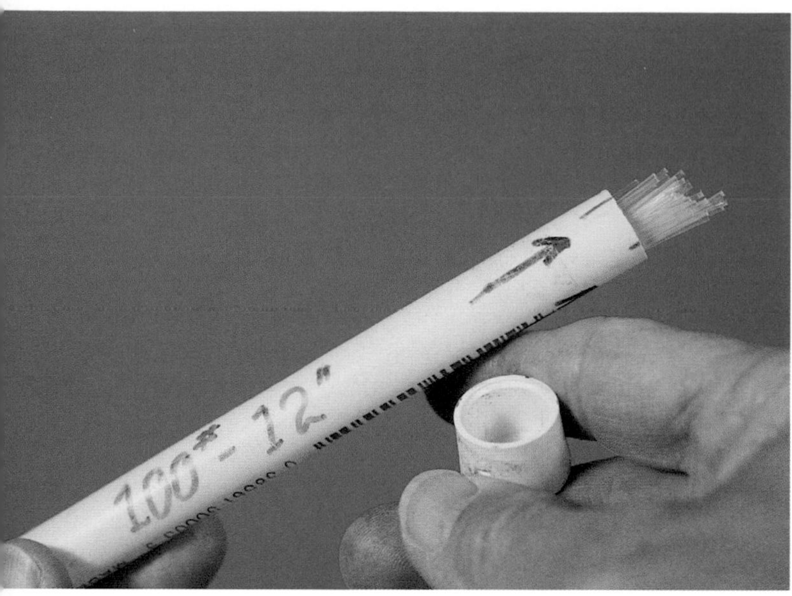

53 STORING LEADERS

To store mono in 50- to 200-pound-test (22.7- to 90.7-kg) lengths for shock tippets, make a leader section case. For this, get a length of ½-inch (13-mm) PVC pipe, glue and cap one end, and buy a second slip-on friction cap for the other end. Make the case about ½ inch longer than the lengths of mono stored. Use a permanent felt-tip marker to mark the pound-test measurement of the mono stored inside and the length of the leader material. Mark the slip-on cap end so you know which end to remove.

54 PREPARING LEADERS

For some fishing (tarpon and big snook), you will need a heavy shock or bite leader between the fly and the tippet. Something from about 50- to 200-pound-test (22.7- to 90.7-kg) is standard. The problem is that when fishing, it is almost impossible to stretch this heavy leader material to make it straight. One solution is to cut a board the length you want the leader sections, and notch it at both ends. Wrap the chosen mono tightly around the board lengthwise. Then "cook" the mono for a few minutes in a pot of boiling water.

If you do not have a big enough pot, make a dipping tank from a length of 2-inch (5-cm) PVC pipe, glued and capped at one end. Secure this upright, add the mono-wrapped board, and pour in the boiling water. (If holding the PVC, use a funnel to pour the water and hold it with a potholder to prevent burns.) Allow the mono to sit in the boiling water for a few minutes, then remove the mono board and immediately place it in ice-cold water.

The boiling water "relaxes" the mono into a stretched, straight length, while the cold water "sets" it in this state. Once the mono is set, remove it from the cold water, cut off the ends where it went around the board, and save it in straight lengths to use as a shock tippet.

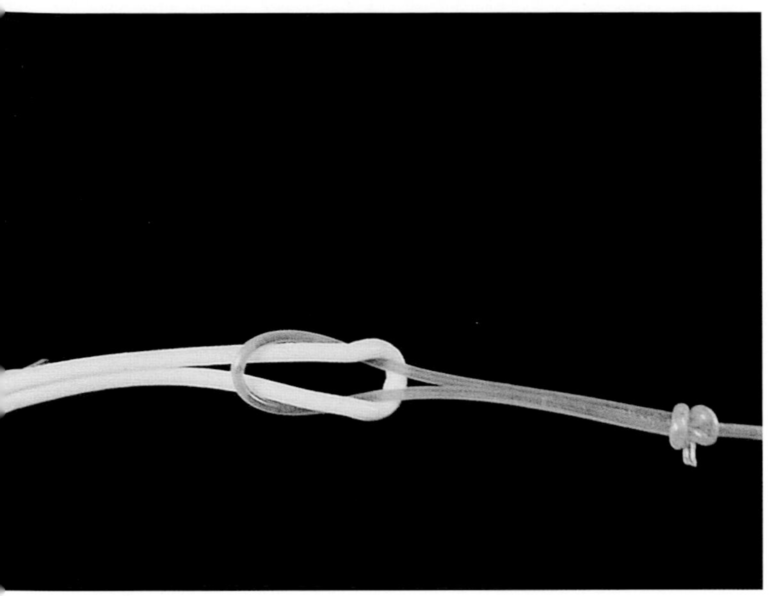

55 LOOP-TO-LOOP CONNECTIONS

Nail knots used to be very popular for line and leader or backing connections. Today, consider the advantages of the loop-to-loop connection. If you have a spliced or knotted loop in your backing, a loop in each end of your fly line, and a loop in your leader butt, you can easily change anything, anytime you wish. This allows you to change lines from a floating to sinking or sinking-tip while fishing, to change complete leaders, or to add some mini lead heads between the line and the leader to help sink the fly.

There are many ways to do this, including braided loop sleeves, tied-on mono loops, etc., but the best way to add a loop in your fly line is to fold over and wrap the end of the line itself. This eliminates other weak links in the chain. To do this, fold over the end of the fly line, hold the folded end with some fly-tying thread on a bobbin, and twirl the bobbin around the folded line while holding the loop end with the other hand. After wrapping the loop with fly-tying thread, make a whip finish in the line to complete it. Clip the excess thread and then seal the wrap with flexible glue, such as Ultra Flex, as described in the next tip.

56 SEALING FLY LINE LOOPS

Seal fly line loops to protect them by using flexible glue, such as Pliobond, Ultra Flex, or similar flexible cement. If the glue is too thick, consider diluting it with a solvent. Check the label for the correct thinning solvent or call the manufacturer (most manufacturers list a toll-free number on the glue container that you can call for information). Once the glue is diluted to the proper consistency, apply it to the wrapped section of the fly line only, using a bodkin or small disposable brush. If you are using the popular Ultra Flex to seal your fly line loops, you can use acetone fingernail polish remover for dilution. It is similar to MEK (methyl ethyl ketone), the basic solvent for this glue.

57 TURLE KNOT

The Turle knot is an old knot, but still a good one for tying your leader tippet to your fly. Anglers most often use Turle knots with dry flies, but you should only use it with flies tied on hooks with turned-up or turned-down eyes. This is because the leader goes through the eye of the hook with the knot tied around the hook shank/head of the fly in back of the eye. Thus, tying this on a straight eye hook results in the leader tippet adversely kinked up or down.

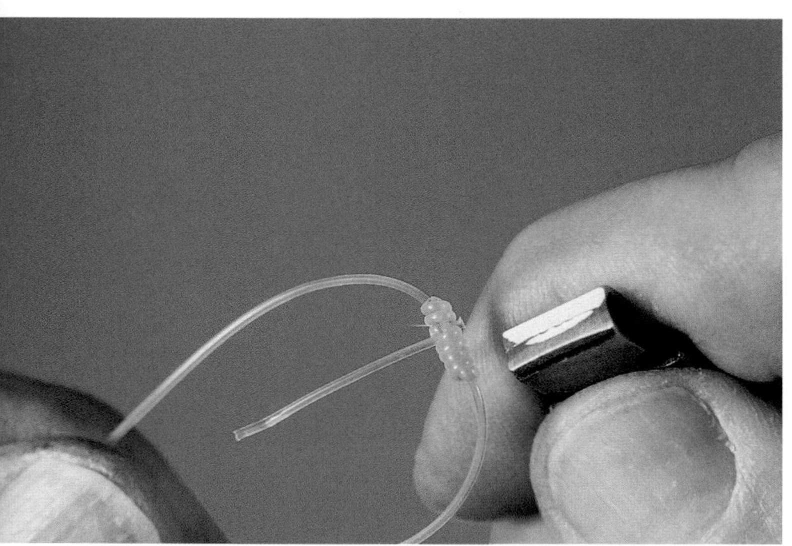

58 TRIMMING KNOTS

When tying knots and pulling them up securely, make sure that you trim the knot properly. To do this, use nippers or nail clippers to cut the tag end of the line close to the knot. The cutters on most pliers are seldom good for this, since they often do not allow close cutting. If you leave an extended tag end, the knot is no stronger, and you'll catch more algae or cause a sinking leader to float longer. Remember, tighten securely, and then trim closely.

59 CUTTING KNOTS

"Wind knots" are overhand knots that occur in fly leaders while casting. While we call them wind knots, really they are the result of poor casting (perhaps a gust of wind now and again) that causes the leader to wrap and knot around itself. If the wind knot is loose, it is easy to untie it, straighten the leader, and keep on fishing. If the knot is tight, break or cut it and retie the leader, using a five-turn blood knot. Trim the knot ends closely. A tip from Chuck Edghill is to use two hook points (two flies) to pull apart a loosened knot.

60 LUBRICATING KNOTS

When you pull a knot tight in monofilament, it creates friction. Friction creates heat, which can be damaging to line and knot strength. To prevent this, and to ensure tight and secure knots, lubricate the loose knot with saliva, and then pull the knot tight. This both lubricates the knot to prevent friction and heat and also allows you to pull the knot very tight. Also, experts say saliva masks odors that might scare fish.

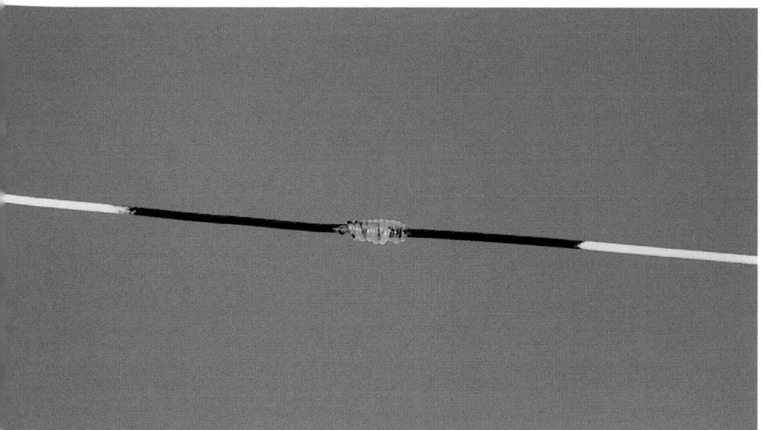

61 MARK LINE FOR PICK-UP

Years ago, Scientific Anglers introduced a line that had a slightly swollen area for several inches at the point where you should pick up the line for the next backcast. The purpose was to give fly anglers a tactile signal where to pick up a given fly line off the water for the next cast. While it was designed with the beginner or inexperienced fly angler in mind, it was handy for any angler. This great idea remains in the Scientific Anglers' beginners Headstart lines with the Telecast bump, but you can do the same thing on any fly line using one of two methods.

One method is to mark the fly line for an inch or two (2.5 to 5 cm) along this "sweet spot," using a permanent felt-tip marker. While it is not tactile, you can see this marked part of the line coming into the guides to signal when to pick up for the next cast. The other method is to tie a long nail knot around the line at this spot using 10- to 20-pound-test (4.5- to 9.1-kg) mono. Clip the tag ends short. You can feel this pick-up point as the line runs through your hands. To determine this spot, rig your rod complete with a practice fly (no hook) and practice over water to find the best spot to pick up the line considering your fishing and casting ability. Then mark the line at this point.

Do this with each outfit, since it varies with the weight and type of line used. You can also combine these methods, marking the line for a visual signal as well as wrapping it with mono for a tactile signal, or combine both with a wrap of bright fluorescent mono. You can do this only on floating or sinking-tip lines, since sinking lines must be retrieved most of the way in and pulled out of the water to make an aerial roll cast.

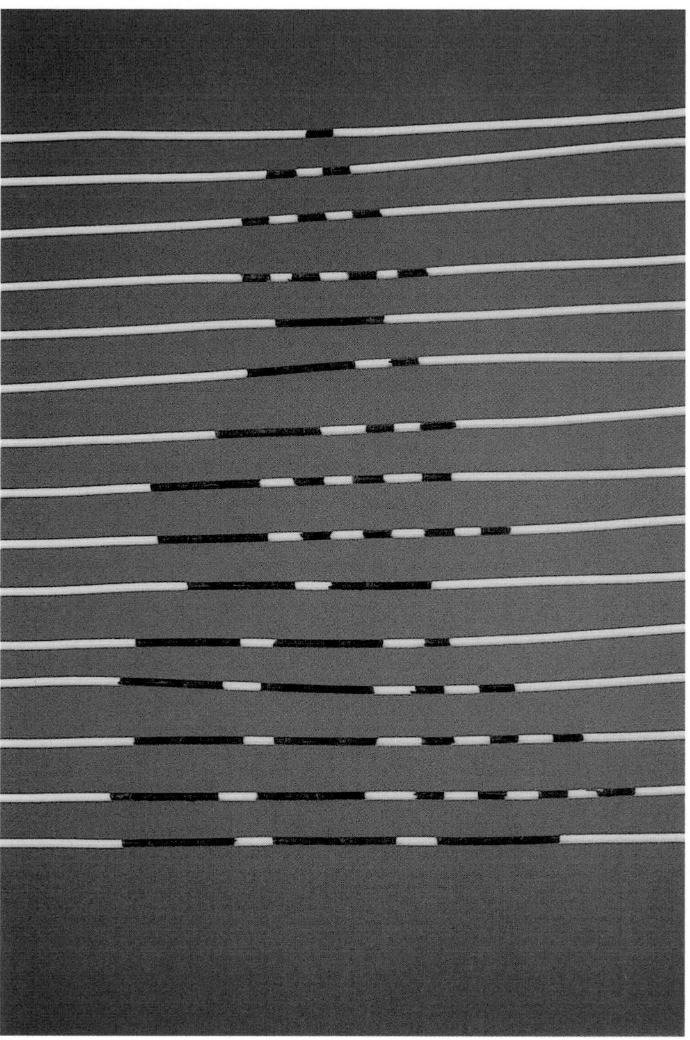

62 NUMBERING FLY LINES

To keep track of which fly line is on which reel, mark all your fly lines. This is particularly important to prevent line mix-up if you use the loop-to-loop connection system. Do this with a system of small marks (bands) to indicate "1," and a wider mark or band to indicate "5." That way, you can mark all lines simply and easily. One wide mark and three small marks is an 8-weight line, a 3-weight line will be three small marks, and a 12-weight line will be two wide marks and two small marks. Do this by using a permanent black felt-tip marker on light colored line and mark a few inches from the line end.

Use a razor to split lengthwise the felt tip on a wide felt-tip marker (about ¼-inch/6-mm) width, then secure or have someone hold the marker while you rotate the line in the slot to mark it. Make two marks close together and then connect them to make the wide "5" mark.

63 MARKING SINKING LINE SINK RATES

To mark the line weight of sinking or sinking-tip lines (which are usually black or very dark) or any dark line, use bright or white fabric paint. This thick paint is water-based acrylic, but it becomes waterproof when cured for 24 hours. Mark the lines the same way you would mark floating lines with the wide and narrow bands for "5" and "1" respectively. The marking diminishes in time but is easy to restore using the same steps above.

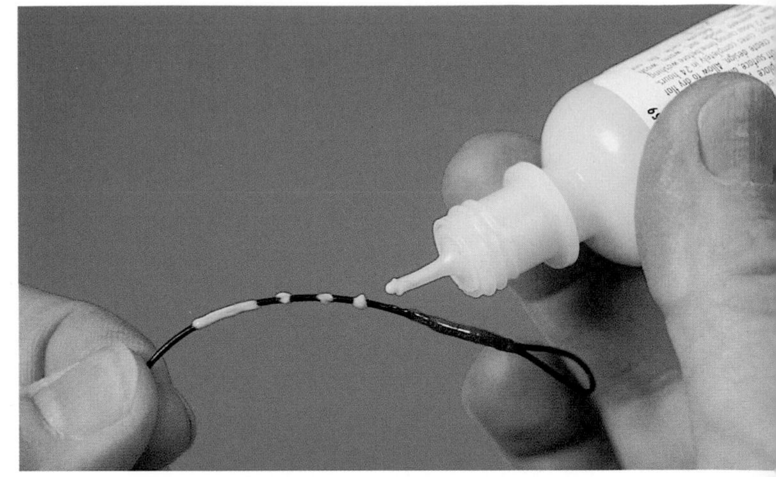

64 CAMOUFLAGE YOUR LINES

It goes without saying that trout spook easily. They even spook with the solid color of fly line in the water. To camouflage your line, strip it from the reel, wrap it around your hand or a large box (a cereal box is ideal), and then randomly mark the line with different-color, permanent felt-tip markers. Good colors are black, green, brown, blue, gray, and tan. Neatness does not count here, since any random coloring keeps the line from looking like a straight stick of color and thus makes it less visible to fish.

65 ROD TUBES

Aluminum rod tubes are great for protecting your rods, but the caps are easily lost. To prevent this, tie the cap to the top of the rod tube. There are two ways to do this. One is to use heavy mono, nylon cord, or scrap fly line to tie securely around the top of the rod tube, then extend the end of the cord through the hole in the middle of the cap and tie a knot to prevent the cord from pulling through the hole. If the hole is too large for a knot, add a small bead or button to the cord before making the knot.

You can also drill a small hole in the top side of the rod tube (remove the rod first, for obvious reasons!). Drill a hole in the center of the cap (if it lacks one) and then thread cord through the two holes, knotting as shown to keep the cap in place and attached to the tube.

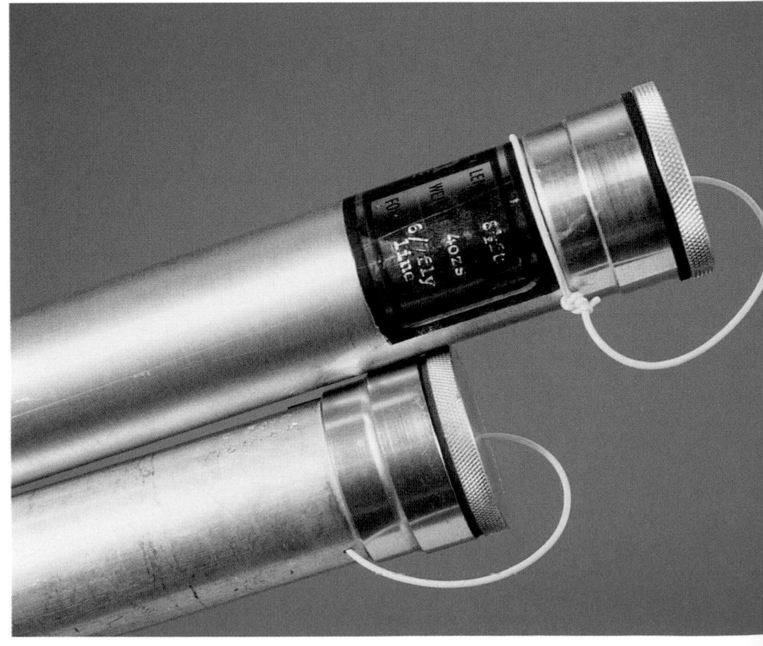

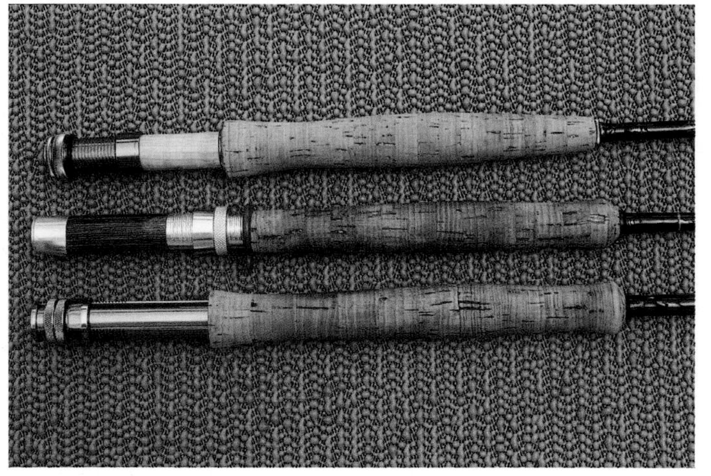

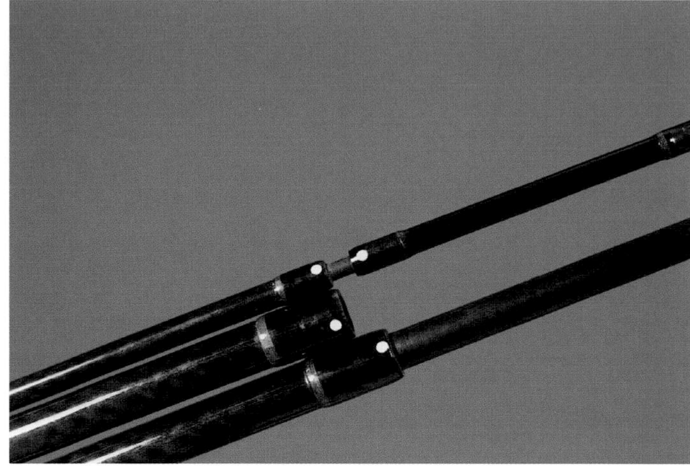

66 ROD GRIP

When buying a fly rod, make sure that the grip is comfortable. If you want a certain brand of rod, you may not have a choice, but if you are open to several brands, there are options. While cigar-shaped grips are popular for most small rods, some rod companies use a Half Wells grip, with the Half Wells put on in reverse so that the thin tapered end is at the front. This makes the rod more aesthetically pleasing, but far less functional. And form should follow function.

Many rod manufacturers use the same reversed Half Wells on larger rods. This is wrong, since anything over a size 6-weight rod, or any rod that you use for long casts, should have a Half Wells put on correctly (swelled end at the front) or fitted with a Full Wells (swollen at both ends). This swollen end makes a good thumb rest and makes it easier to punch out a long cast than with a cigar grip, reversed Half Wells, or other slim grip.

67 MARKING ROD SECTIONS

Many rod manufacturers make similar-size fly rods on the same blank and then through an external grinding process adjust the blank weight and action to the desired line weight. This makes it almost impossible to ever get the right rod sections back together if you mix up several three- or four-piece travel rods of the same brand. To prevent mix-up of rod sections, mark each section with a dot of colored paint that can help line up the guides as well as identify the rod sections.

Use different-color dots for different rods and double dots if you have a lot of rods and run out of colors. For best results, use a waterproof enamel, lacquer, or acrylic-based paint. To mark the rod, touch a pin or finishing nail head to the paint, and then touch it to the rod at the ferrule location and in line with the rod guides.

> "To the fisherman born there is nothing so provoking of curiosity as a fishing rod in a case."
>
> —*Roland Pertwee, "The River God" (1928)*

68 ROD BAGS

Why have a fly rod bag when the rod came with a rod case? More and more rods come in cases that have attached partition bags—that is, they are part of the case and do not come out, as did the separate bags in aluminum cases of the past.

Many fly rod bags from manufacturers have a tie cord at the top; some also have a tie cord in the middle. If you use these, make sure that you tie loosely to prevent the rod from bending or warping during storage in the rod tube. Use a very loose bowknot in these situations or just wrap the ends of the cord around the top of the bag after folding over the end flap.

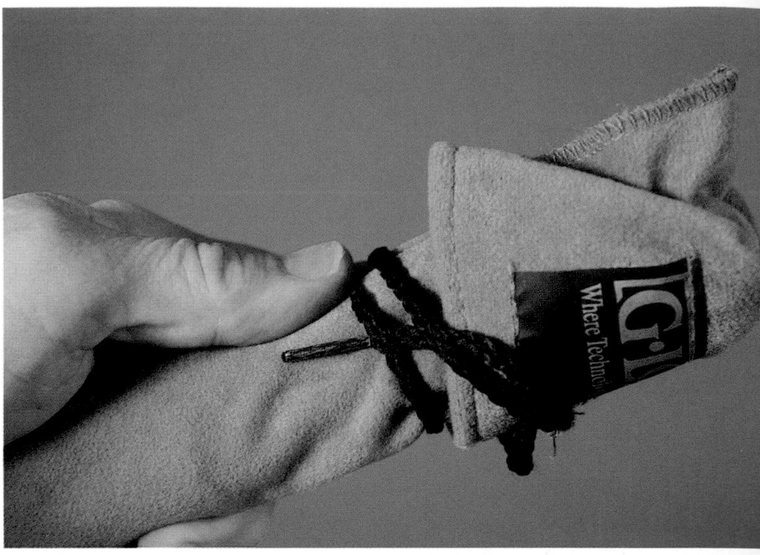

69 MAKING ROD BAGS

You can buy fly rod bags or you can make your own. I make them from remnants of flannel cloth sold inexpensively at fabric stores.

Be sure to buy enough material to make the style and number of bags that you want. If you are working with three- or four-piece rods, you can get by with 1 yard (0.9 m) to make several bags. If you have two-piece 9- to 10-foot (2.7- to 3.0-meter) rods [half the rod measures 4½ to 5 feet (1.4 to 1.5 m)], you will need 2 yards (1.8 m) of material, unless the material is wide enough. Fifty-four inches (137.2 cm) is about the maximum width of most materials and some are only 36 inches (91.4 cm) wide.

To make a bag, fold over a piece of cloth to make the bag the right length and diameter for your rods. For four-piece rods, 9 feet (2.7 m) long, make the bag about 10 inches by 32 inches (25.4 cm by 81.3 cm). For two-piece, 9-feet-long (2.7-m) rods, make bags 5 inches (12.7 cm) wide by 59 to 60 inches (149.9 to 152.4 cm) long. The extra length in each of these allows the top flap to fold over. The width varies on these cases, since travel rods require four slots; two-piece rods require only two slots. Make the bags wider on rods that have extra-large grips, extension butts, or large stripping guides.

70 LABELING ROD BAGS

Mark all rod bags, commercial or homemade, with pertinent information. You might choose to mark the line weight, rod length, brand, or something else. Mark the bag at the top flap with a permanent felt-tip marker. With black or very dark bags, sew on a strip of white cloth and mark the cloth with the information. This helps when getting ready for any trip to prevent taking the wrong rod and not realizing it until too late. You don't want to pull out your 3-weight when getting to Alaska expecting to find a 10-weight for big king salmon.

71 LEARNING SIMPLE KNOTS

It is far better to know a few knots very well than to try to learn all the knots in the knot book yet have difficulty tying most of them. For most fly fishing, you need only a few knots. These include the following:

- a simple arbor knot to attach the line to the reel;
- a loop added to a fly line for loop-to-loop connections;
- a nail knot for the line/leader connection, if you are not using the loop-to-loop method;
- a mono loop knot for leader ends (with loop-to-loop connections), such as the perfection loop knot, figure-eight loop knot, or surgeon's loop knot;
- a blood knot to make and retie leader sections;
- a fly-eye knot, such as a Palomar or improved clinch knot;
- a Bimini to make a long loop in your backing if not tying directly to the fly line.

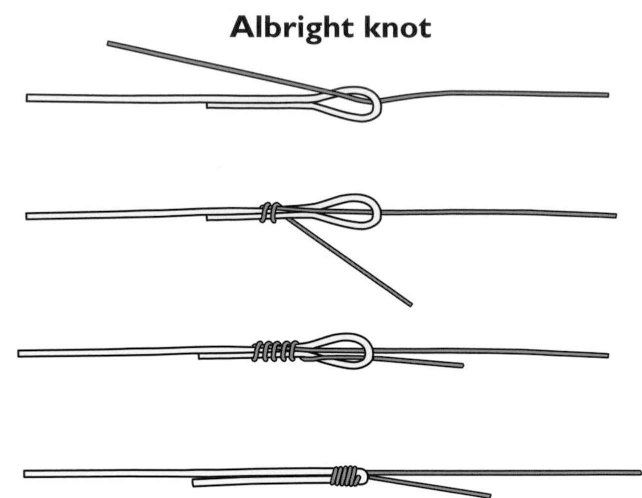

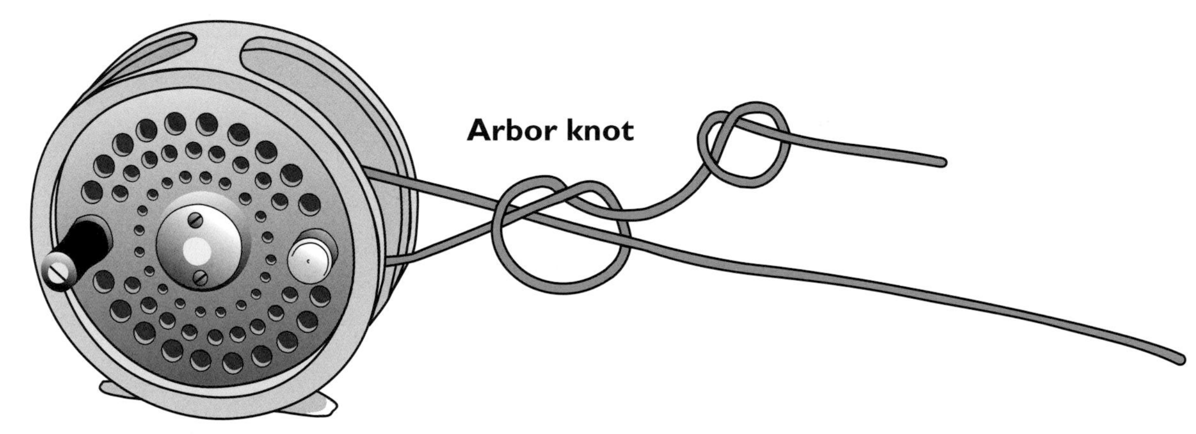

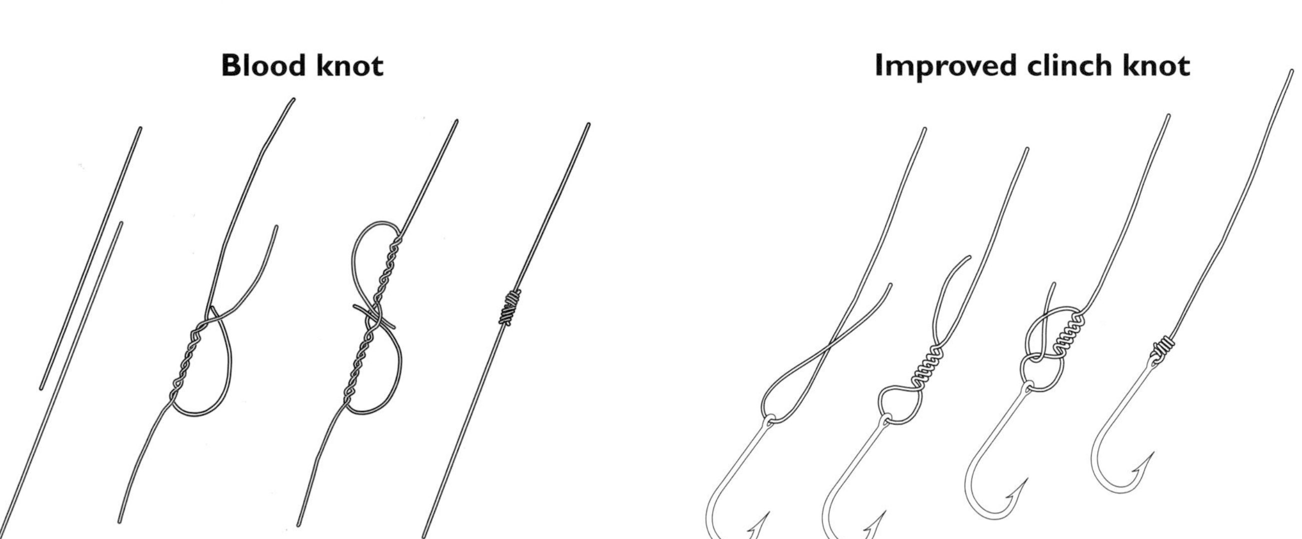

If you do specialized fly fishing using wire or fishing the tropics, it also helps to know the following:

- a figure-eight knot for braided wire when fishing for toothy fish, such as bluefish, barracuda, and pike;
- an Albright, for tying a heavy bite leader to a light tippet section or backing to a fly line; and
- a Homer Rhode loop knot for tying heavy bite mono to a fly.

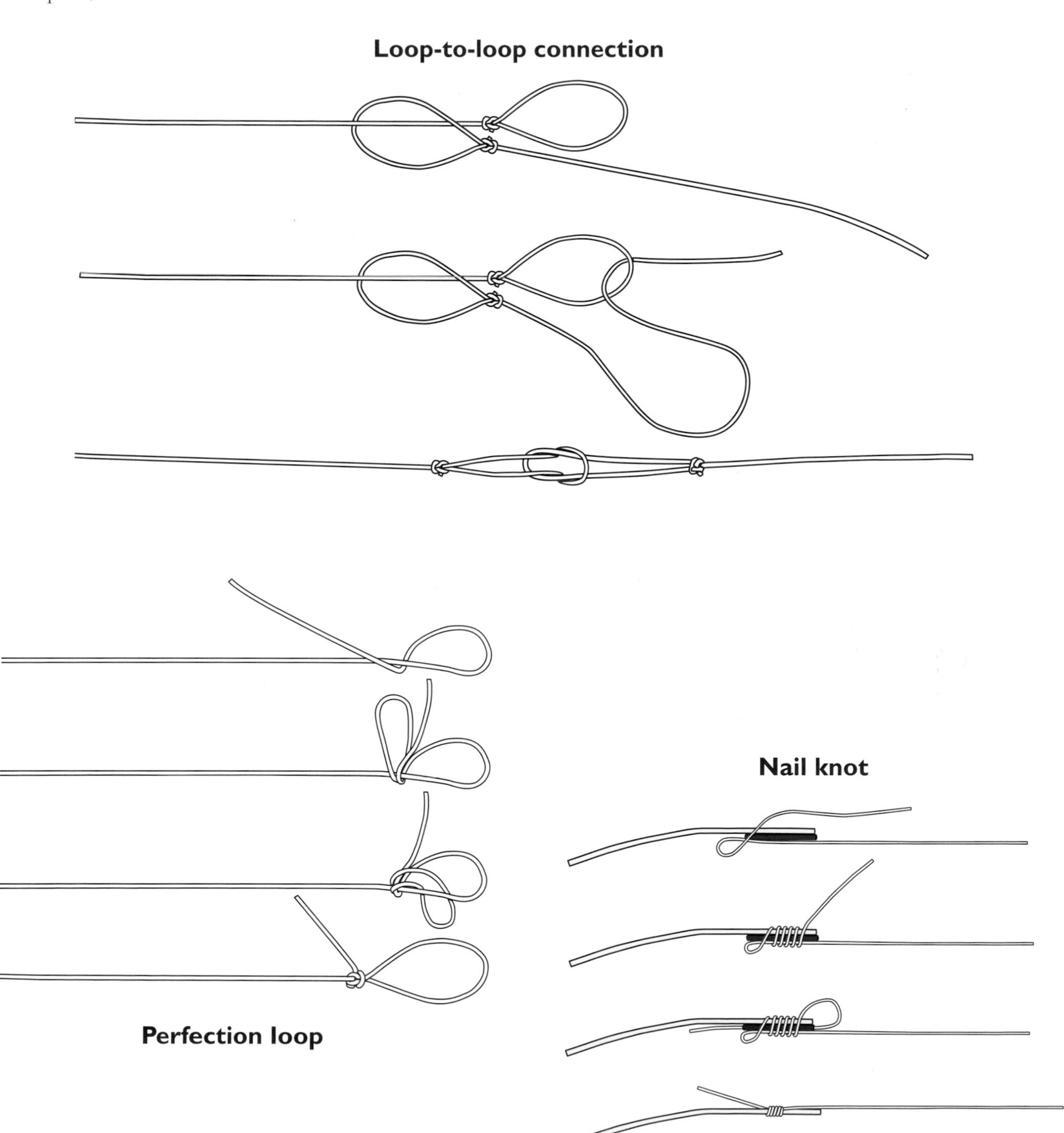

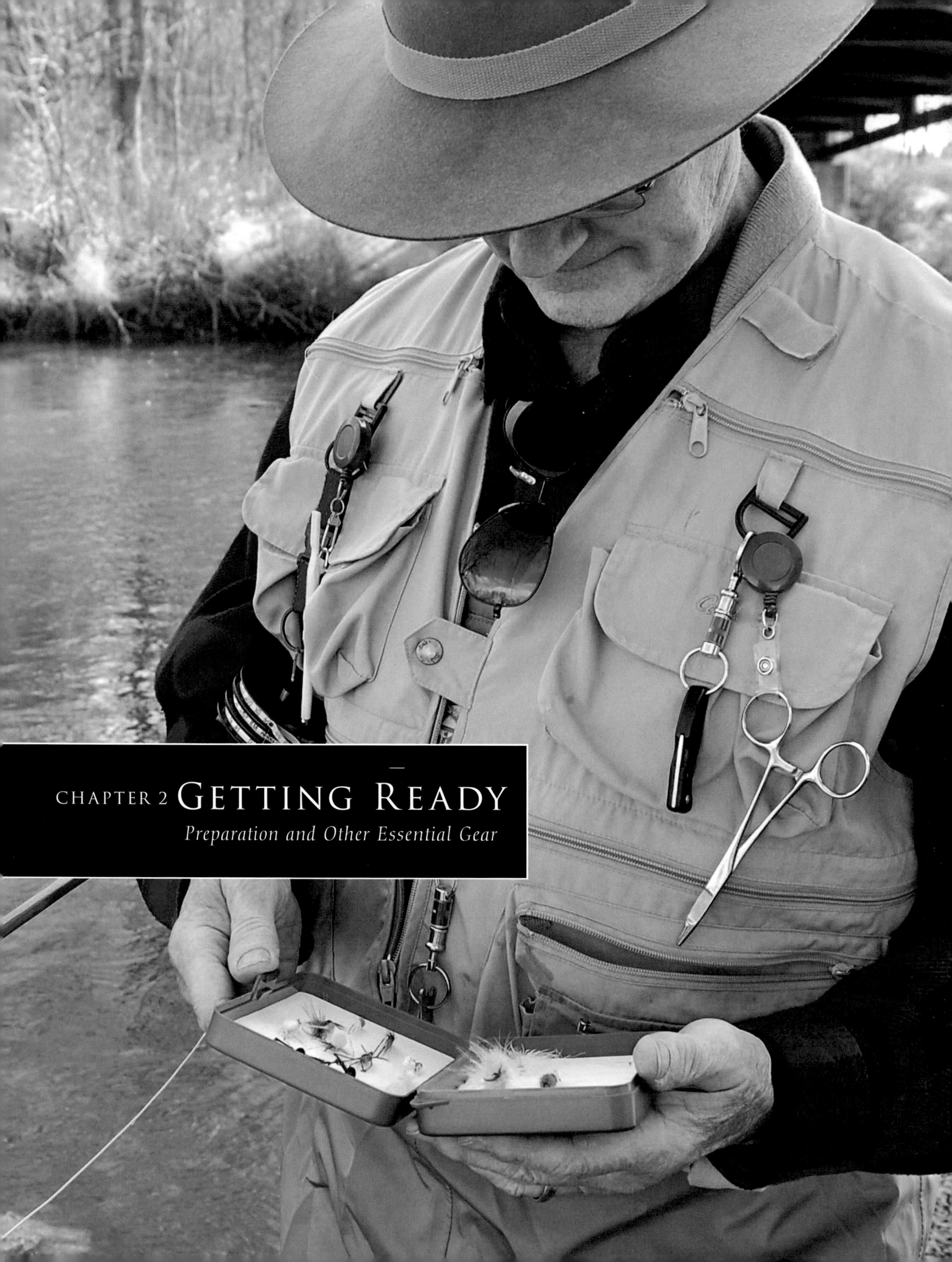

CHAPTER 2 GETTING READY

Preparation and Other Essential Gear

72 WADING STAFFS

Wading staffs are great when you need them and a nuisance when you don't. You need them when you get too deep into a stream, get into fast water, or are carrying a camera. Other times, they can get in the way and even trip you.

The easy solution is to carry a folding wading staff in a holster on your wader belt. Several are available on the market, varying in lengths suit any angler. All have an internal bungee cord, so when you pull the staff out of the holster by the handle, the rest of the wading staff springs and locks into a sturdy staff. The sections will not stay joined if the tip of the staff gets stuck in the mud, but that is a minor inconvenience.

An inexpensive but still effective approach is to buy used ski poles, frequently found at flea markets and garage sales. You can use the poles in one of two ways, depending on the terrain. For wading on sandy or mucky bottoms, you can keep the ski pole as is, with the webbing (usually plastic) near the base serving as a "snowshoe" to prevent the pole from sinking too deep into the bottom. Alternatively, you can remove the plastic webbing (with wire cutters or a hacksaw) to make a straight pole for rocky streams. Add a lanyard that you can attach to your bootstrap or fishing vest to prevent loss of the recycled wading staff.

73 LANYARDS AND RETRACTABLE REELS

To avoid losing gear, use lanyards or retractable pull cords that are stored in small reels. Often these are generically called "zingers." Lanyards are good for fishing pliers, wading staffs, clippers, nippers, dry fly dressing bottles, nets, and similar gear. Small ones for nippers and clippers are available from all fly shops. Larger, heavy-duty models are necessary for holding pliers, landing nets, wading staffs, etc. The best of these currently available are the Hammerhead Gear Keepers, which come in many styles, different attachment methods, and also different strengths and pull tensions.

> "Perhaps the greatest satisfaction on the first day of the season is the knowledge in the evening that the whole of the rest of the season is to come."
>
> –*Arthur Ransome, "The First Day at the River,"* Rod and Line *(1929)*

74 MAKING A SIMPLE LANYARD

You can make a simple lanyard for pliers by using a plastic coil-spring key chain, usually available for a few bucks at most discount stores. To do this, use the split ring end to attach to the pliers, and attach a clip or snap on the other end to your fishing vest or wader belt. You can use these, which stretch several feet, without risking loss. They also work with nets and other gear.

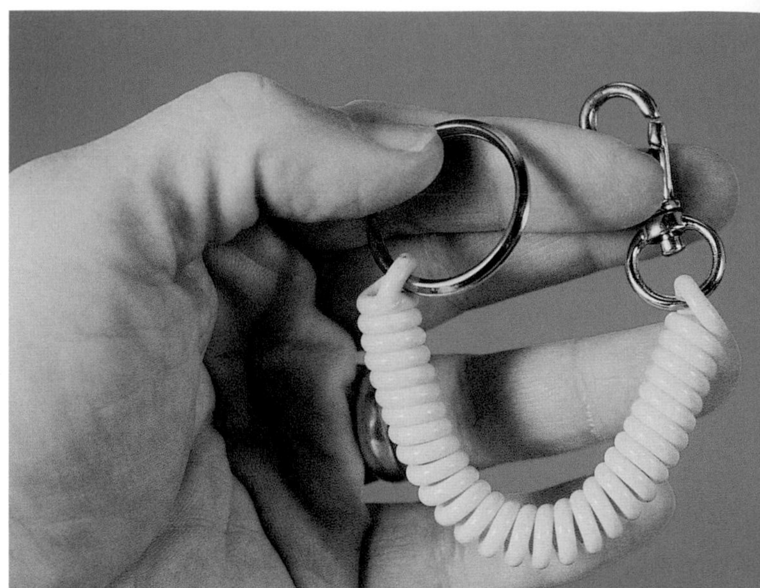

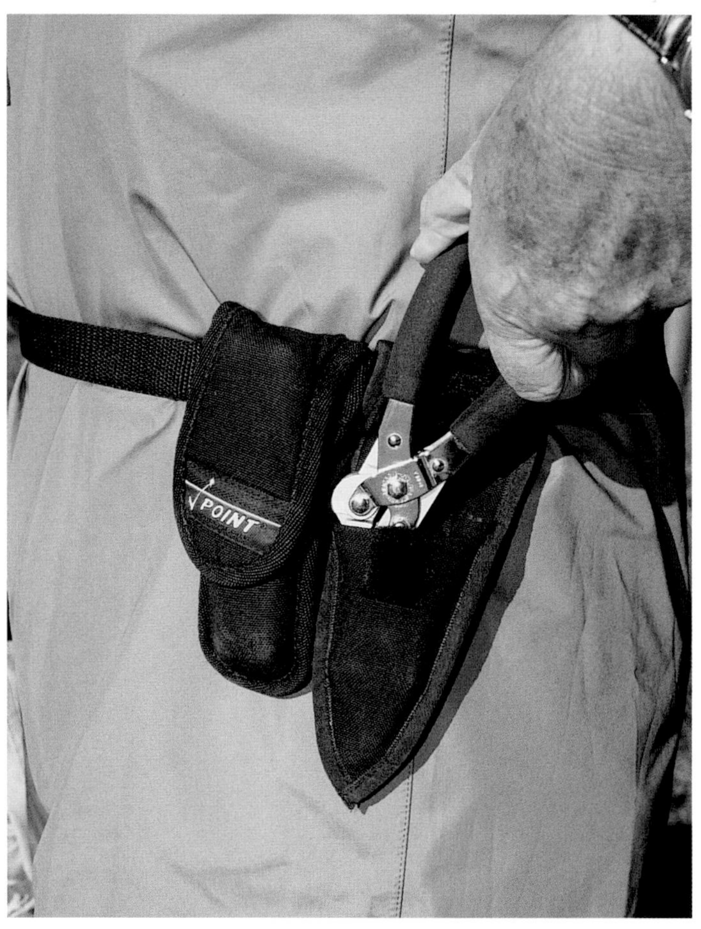

75 PLIERS

Most anglers carry sheathed fishing pliers at all times. The easy way to carry pliers is on your wader safety belt. If fishing in saltwater, nylon sheaths are better than leather sheaths. Wash out nylon sheaths as required. Leather sheaths soak up and hold salt, which can be detrimental to any equipment.

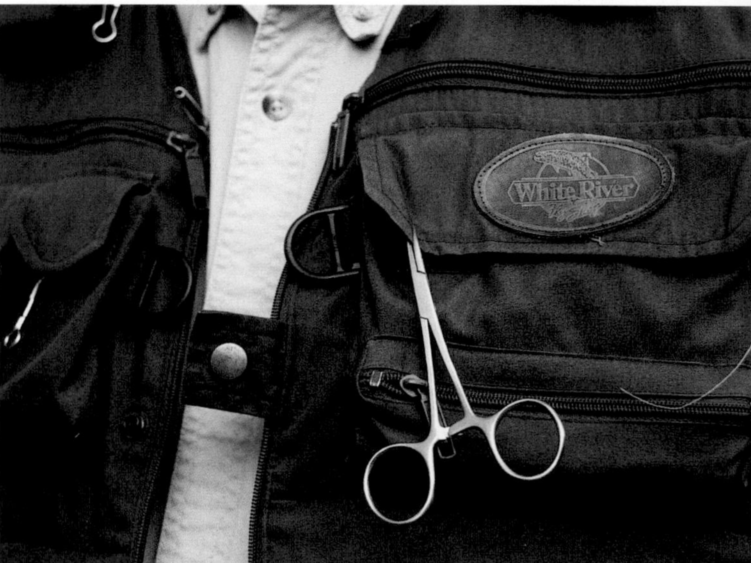

76 HEMOSTATS

Surgeons use hemostats, or clamping forceps; fly anglers do, too. They are handy for holding small flies when tying knots and especially to remove flies from landed fish. Forceps allow careful clamping and holding of a fly hook so that you can remove the fly from the fish's jaw with minimal damage and handling of the fish. As such, they are ideal for catch-and-release fishing.

To keep them with you, clamp the jaws onto a pocket flap of your fishing vest, pack, or shirtfront.

77 CLOTHING FOR FISHING

Most fishing vests are tan, gray, or green. You will seldom find large blocks of one solid color in nature, and such vests might spook trout in shallow-water streams. To camouflage yourself while fishing, wear a camouflage shirt or lightweight jacket, similar to what hunters wear. But for best results, wear the jacket *over* your fishing vest to disguise and hide that solid color. You can leave the jacket open in front to easily get flies and other necessities from your pockets, while the mixed pattern of the jacket or shirt hides you from the trout.

Choose the pattern of camouflage to match the woods where you will be fishing. Available camouflages include spring woods, fall trees, large trees, winter with snow, barren areas, and others. A spring (green pattern) woods look is best for most early season trout fishing.

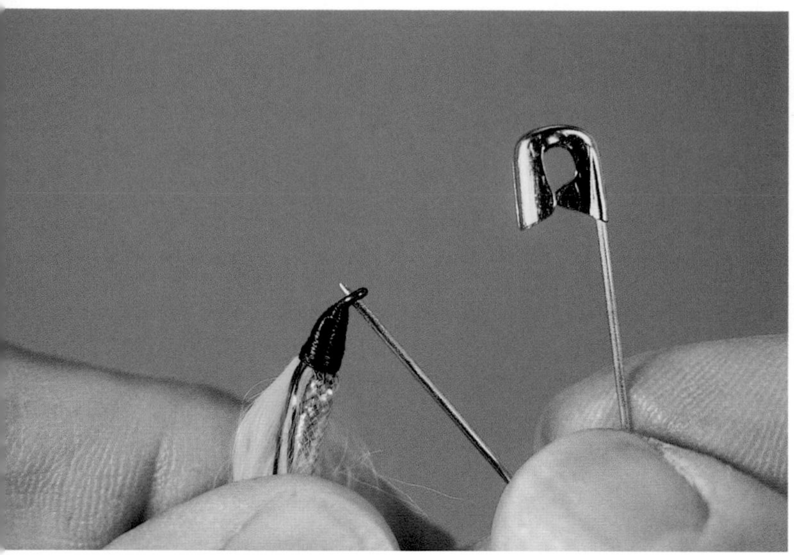

78 PINS IN YOUR FISHING VEST

Stick a few different-size safety pins into your fishing vest. They are handy for clearing the head cement out of flies. Different sizes make this task easy on various-size flies. They are also handy if something breaks on a strap or other part of your gear, to be used for a quick, temporary repair.

79 VEST LENGTH

If you wear chest-high waders and often fish deep, get a "shorty" fishing vest to prevent the vest from getting wet. If you are fishing in hip boots, a full-length vest gives you more room and pockets. An alternative to the shorty vest for deep-wading fly anglers is to wear a long vest, but wear it inside your waders if there is enough room.

80 ATTACHING NETS TO VESTS

Attach a landing net to the D-ring located on the back of all fishing vests. This is the best way to carry a landing net while stream fishing. (If your vest does not have a D-ring, you can add a key-style split ring to the strap or use a short cloth strap to sew a D-ring in place.) Buy a French snap from a hardware store and attach it to the end of the landing net. These snaps are unlike dog leash snaps in that you operate them by squeezing the two arms or sides to open the snap in the middle. This makes it easy to remove the net hung from your back by reaching around to unsnap it. Carrying the net on the back center of your vest also reduces the possibility of the net catching on tree limbs and brush.

81 CHEST PACKS

Chest packs are a substitute for fishing vests. They have the advantage of holding the accessories higher on the chest and back. They hold less equipment, but are ideal when you want to wade deep or fish with only a few items, such as in saltwater and tropical fishing. Many sizes and styles are available, some simple fore and aft bags, and others are complex with special tool pockets and other features.

82 LIGHTWEIGHT TRAVEL WADERS

Lightweight travel waders are best for all fishing. The alternative if you fish a lot of different places is to have two pairs of waders—one heavy neoprene for cold weather and a second lightweight pair for warm-weather fishing. Lightweight travel waders are fine for fishing in warm weather, and in cold weather you can insulate them by donning flannel pajama bottoms or insulated wear under your regular fishing pants.

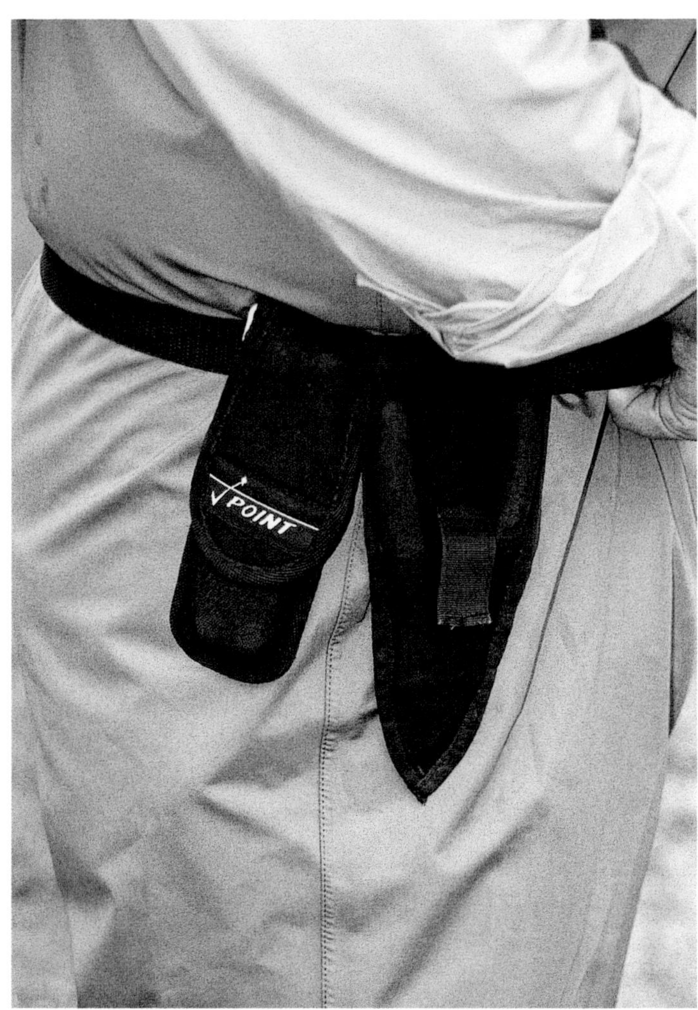

83 BELT YOUR WADERS

Many waders today include a belt that fits around your waist outside of the waders. This is for safety, because if you fall in, the belt limits the amount of water that seeps into your waders. If your waders do not have this, buy a nylon belt or make one from nylon strapping and some snaps or Swedish buckles that allow for instant on/off of the belt. Buy 3 feet (0.9 m) or more (check your waist size with the waders on) of 1-inch (2.5-cm) nylon strapping and mating plastic snaps. Sew one end of the strapping to one snap and thread the other end through the two openings on the other snap. Tighten the belt around your waist anytime you wear waders.

84 BUYING NEW WADERS OR BOOTS

When buying new waders, hip boots, or other wading or heavy boots, do so at the end of the day. That is when your feet swell, making an accurate measurement easier. Also, wear the socks that you would normally wear for fishing. Some anglers wear two pairs of regular socks, some a single pair of very heavy wool socks, and some a pair of medium wool socks over lightweight cotton socks.

This is important, even if buying boots online or by mail order. In that case, put on the appropriate socks at the end of the day, stand on paper on a hard floor, and have someone else trace around your foot. Send this tracing to the mail-order company or use its instructions to convert this information to the correct size. Often the best fit is a half or full size larger in a boot than you wear in a dress shoe.

85 ANKLE SUPPORT

Boot-foot waders are easier to put on and take off and are easier to travel with than separate wading shoes and stocking-foot waders. But for the best ankle support, the high top, heavy-leather wading shoes teamed with stocking-foot waders are best. If you have weak ankles, have broken or badly strained/sprained an ankle, or are fishing over a very rough bottom, strongly consider these separate wader and wading shoe combinations.

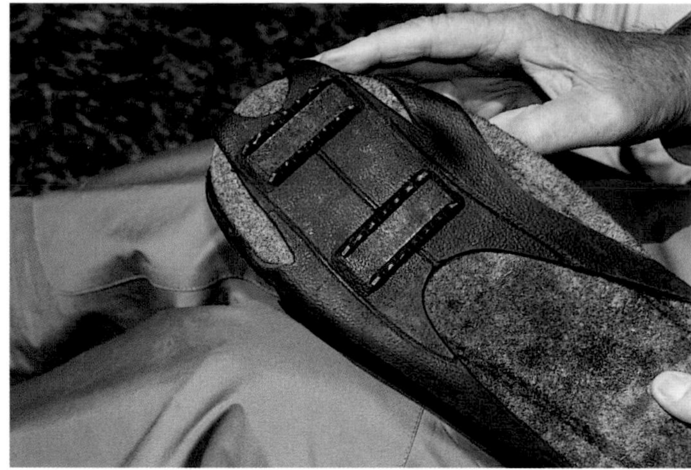

86 SLIP-ON WADER GRIPPERS

Chain or stud types of slip-on rubber grippers are available to fit over waders or hip boots. These are elastic to fit the boot bottom, but with metal studs or cleats to grip the algae-covered rocks. You can use them for both boot-foot and separate wading-boot waders. These are highly recommended for really slippery bottoms, since the studs or chains cut through the scum and algae on rocks and gravel.

87 HIP BOOT STRAPS

Master fly rod guru Lefty Kreh related a tip long ago about the problems of fishing with hip boots. As manufactured, the adjustable buckle on the outside of the hip boot strap often catches fly lines and ruins the cast. To avoid this, remove the adjustable strap from the buckle, reverse the direction of the strap going through the buckle so that the strap and buckle are on the inside (next to your pant leg) and not able to catch the fly line. It will be a little harder to change the strap adjustment, but does cause fewer tangles when casting.

88 KNEE PADS

The best trout fishermen on small streams wear out the knees of their waders before they wear out the soles. Anglers kneel to prevent the small stream trout from seeing them, and are thus able to present the fly more carefully and precisely. If you do a lot of this type of fishing, there are ways to prevent wader knee wear. Get comfortable knee pads from a home supply or hardware store. The most comfortable kind fit on with hook-and-loop fastener straps. Keep them in your fishing vest or with your gear to wear when needed.

89 BACK BRACES

If you do a lot of wading and are over the age of 25, consider wearing a back brace while wade fishing, suggests expert Chuck Edghill. These large braces fit tightly around the back and waist. Hook-and-loop fasteners (or suspenders) keep the braces in place. Wear the brace over your shirt, but under your fishing vest. You can loosen the brace when taking a break. The suspenders may help reduce muscle strain when wading for long periods of time and allow you to fish comfortably longer.

90 EYEGLASSES

As we get older, many of us have trouble tying small flies to thin tippets, particularly with non-prescription sunglasses or when fishing at dawn or dusk. To solve this, buy some of the clip-on close-up lenses. Gudebrod, for example, makes Fold Away Reading Glasses in eight magnifications from +1.50 to +3.25 for any vision needed. They clip onto any visor or billed cap for easy use in the field, and flip out of the way when not needed.

91 SUNSCREEN AND INSECT REPELLENT

Fish can smell sunscreen and insect repellent, so you must keep it off your fishing gear. However, you frequently have to apply and reapply lotions during the day to protect your skin from sunburn and bites. To do this without getting it on your tackle or flies, spread the lotion on the back of one hand and then spread it over your opposite arm, face, ears, back of the neck, front of the neck, and anywhere else needed.

Spread some on the back of your other hand to repeat on spots that you cannot reach with your first hand. The result is total protection without ever getting the lotion on the palms of your hands with which you handle tackle and flies.

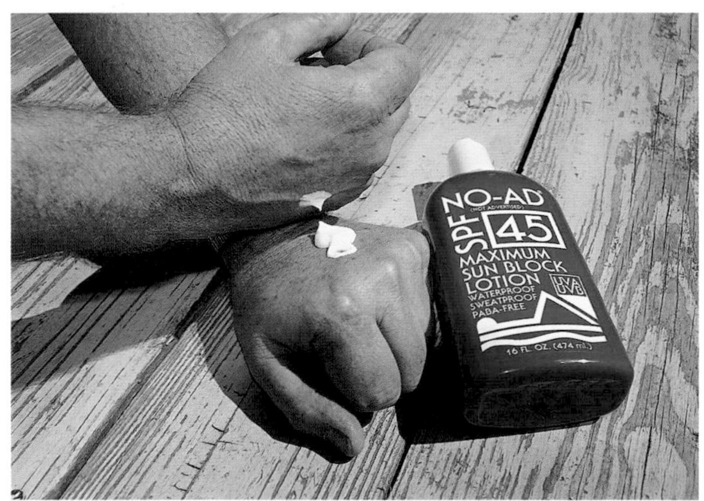

92 SUN SAFETY

If you are out in the hot sun for long periods, are tropical fishing, or have very sensitive light skin, consider "Lawrence of Arabia" headgear for your fly fishing. Several companies make caps or hats with an attached, roll-out neck protector, just as you see in films of Lawrence of Arabia and the French Foreign Legion. While sunscreen is essential, these neck shields provide extra protection for the back of the neck and ears during a long day outdoors.

If you don't want to buy this specialized head gear, you can accomplish the same thing with a standard fishing cap and handkerchief. Use several small safety pins to attach one edge of the handkerchief to the back rim of the cap. For emergency use when you don't have pins, place the handkerchief on the back of your head and carefully place the cap over it to hold it in place. Just don't take your cap off while fishing—you might lose your handkerchief.

93 KEEPING COOL

In the hot sun, one way to keep cool is to wet your hat so that the evaporation cools your head as you fish. Some cap brims are made of stiff cardboard, so wet only the cloth head-covering part. If you are fishing in saltwater, use water from the cooler, since caps dipped in saltwater get sticky, stiff, and uncomfortable. Another way to keep cool is to slip an ice cube or two under your cap.

95 HAT UNDERBRIM

A hat or cap with a light underbrim bounces sunlight reflected from the water surface back into your eyes. A dark brim absorbs the light, which prevents eyestrain. If necessary, you can coat a favorite hat underbrim with black shoe polish or permanent black felt-tip marker.

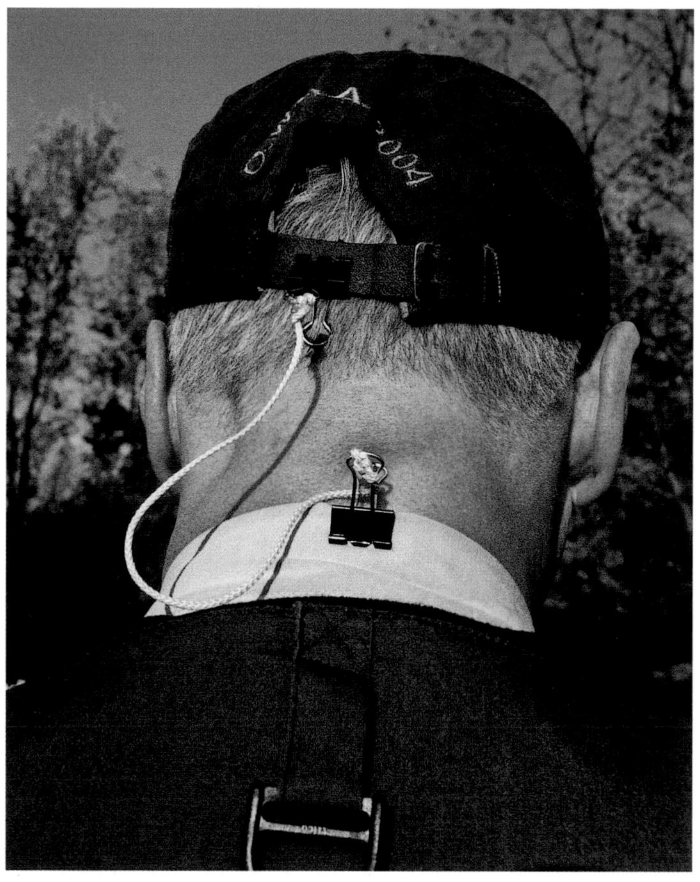

94 HAT CLIPS

Windy situations can cause you to lose a hat or cap in a hurry, and sometimes it will sink before you can get it or can turn the boat around to retrieve it. To prevent this, use a lanyard clip that fastens the back of your hat to the back of your fishing shirt or jacket. If you do not have one or cannot find one, get two spring clips (banker's clips or bulldog clips, available at office supply stores) and tie them to the ends of a shoelace or foot-long (30-cm) cord. Then, when the wind increases, pull the clip out of your fishing vest pocket, and clip to your hat and shirt to prevent loss.

> "The most indispensable item in any fisherman's equipment is his hat. This ancient relic, with its battered crown and well-frayed band, preserves not only the memory of every trout he caught, but also the smell."
>
> —*Corey Ford, "Tomorrow's the Day" (1952)*

96 FINGERLESS GLOVES

Gloves of wool or heavy yarn synthetics provide best warmth when cold-weather fly fishing. The best of these have exposed fingers (fingerless gloves) so that you can handle flies, tie knots, prepare leaders, etc., while fishing without removing your gloves. Alternatives are mittens that have a covered palm opening to allow extending your fingers for tying knots and working with flies.

97 SUN GLOVES

With more and more concern about skin cancer from the sun, anglers should consider wearing sun gloves while fishing. These thin gloves with exposed fingertips (for tying knots and handling flies) protect the backs of your hands from the damaging UV rays of the sun.

98 POLARIZING SUNGLASSES

Polarizing sunglasses allow you to see through the surface and minimize eye glare to make fishing easier and more pleasant. By allowing you to see underwater, they allow you to spot fish and structure and detect currents.

If possible, bring different types of polarizing sunglasses for different fishing and lighting situations. Glasses with gray, copper, or brown lenses provide maximum sun protection and minimum light transmission and are best for bright sun or when fishing sandy flats. They have a light transmission of about 12 to 17 percent.

For dim light situations, use yellow or orange glasses, which provide good contrast and are best for spotting fish. These have a transmission of about 25 to 32 percent.

Blue-gray is often best for offshore and open-water fishing.

The effectiveness of polarizing glasses is dependent upon the angle at which the sun or sun reflection off the water hits your glasses. Sometimes you can improve this by tilting your head slightly to one side or the other to change the sun angle.

99 RAIN PARKA

It can rain at any time, so always carry a raincoat while fishing. When wading, you have to carry it in the large pocket in the back of your fishing vest or chest pack where it can be heavy, bulky, and hot. A simpler method is to carry one of the disposable clear plastic rain parkas that covers completely when wearing chest-high waders and is long enough when wearing hip boots.

Disposable raincoats are inexpensive and available from fly shops, tackle shops, general sporting goods stores, camping supply stores, and many discount stores. They take no more space than a pack of cigarettes, with care can be used a couple of times, and are convenient.

100 SPARE PLASTIC GARBAGE BAGS

Bring spare plastic garbage bags with you on any fishing trip and keep one or two in a back pocket of your fishing vest. In a pinch, you can punch three holes in them for your head and arms to make an emergency rain jacket. They are also ideal to have on hand when you get back to the car to hold any wet or muddy waders, boots, socks, and other clothing, keeping them separate from the rest of your tackle and the clean vehicle.

101 KEEP THE SUN AT YOUR BACK

It is not always possible, but if you can keep the sun at your back while fishing, you gain lots of advantages. For one, it is easier to spot fish and water structure than when looking into the sun and trying to see through the glare on the water. In addition, if fish are facing you, they will be facing into the sun, which minimizes and hides any view of you. Third, it minimizes the chance of fish being spooked by the fly line in the air or on the water.

102 LIGHT LEVELS

If you have a choice, it is best to fish in the very early morning or very late in the day. You can get in some excellent fly fishing in only a few hours by picking the time of day. If you are an early-morning person, plan on getting to the water before dawn, and fish until 10 a.m. or whenever the fishing slacks off. If you are an evening person, get on the water about four hours before dusk and fish until you can't see your fly or fly line anymore.

103 NIGHT FISHING

Fly fishing at night has its own set of thrills and advantages and can sometimes bring the biggest fish. But it also has some difficulties. If you are fishing under a bright moon and your eyes have adjusted to the dark, you can often see your casts. If fishing on a black night, pick out the fly that you will be using before dark, and do not use tandem fly rigs (too dangerous). Use a heavier leader tippet than you needed during daylight (the fish won't see as well either and the heavier tippet won't be spotted). Be sure you thoroughly know the water you are going to fish, and make short, controlled casts in situations where the backcast will not hang up; stay away from fishing surface structure.

Have fun, keep it simple, and don't get into areas or situations where you feel uncomfortable. For additional safety, always fish with a buddy.

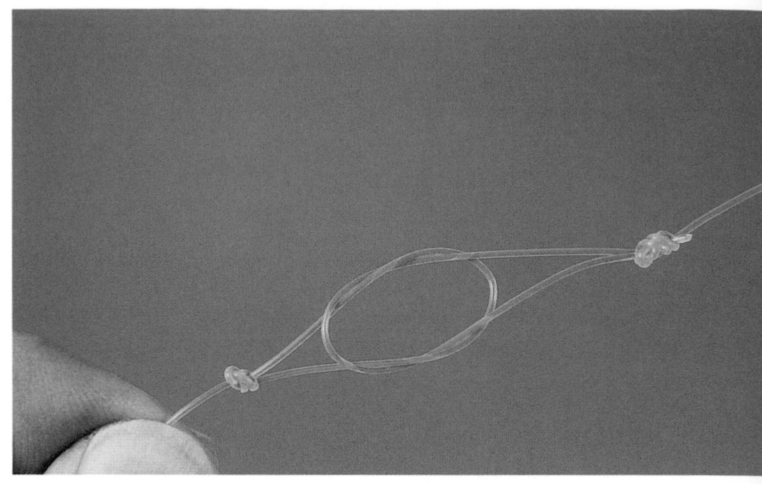

104 CHANGING FLIES IN LOW LIGHT ▲

Fishing at night or even dusk is tough when you have to change flies on fine tippets. One way to avoid this is to pre-tie tippets to flies that you might use during low-light situations. Then tie a loop knot (perfection loop, surgeon's loop, or figure-eight loop) in the end of each tippet and tie a similar loop in the leader where it attaches to each tippet. Make this loop larger than normal, about 2 inches (5 cm) in size, for easy adding or removal from the loop end leader. Then when it is too dark to see to tie on flies, it is simple to disconnect the loops and add a new fly by interconnecting the loops without tying.

105 LIGHTS FOR NIGHT FISHING

For safety, as well as for checking tackle, bring a flashlight for fishing at dawn, dusk, or night. For complete safety, carry two flashlights. One should be a regular hand-held flashlight for use at the end of the day to find your way back to the dock if boat fishing, or to pick your way out of the stream if wading. The other should be a minimum-power light for checking tackle and/or tying on flies while fishing. For this, the best lights are those with a colored head or filter that casts a blue, green, or red light instead of bright white. There are also specialty lights that can be attached to your hat or cap, worn over your head or cap, pinned to your fishing vest, or stuck in a chest pocket with a gooseneck to angle the light downward. In using any of these lights while fishing, try to minimize casting light on the water, since this might scare fish and affect your fishing success.

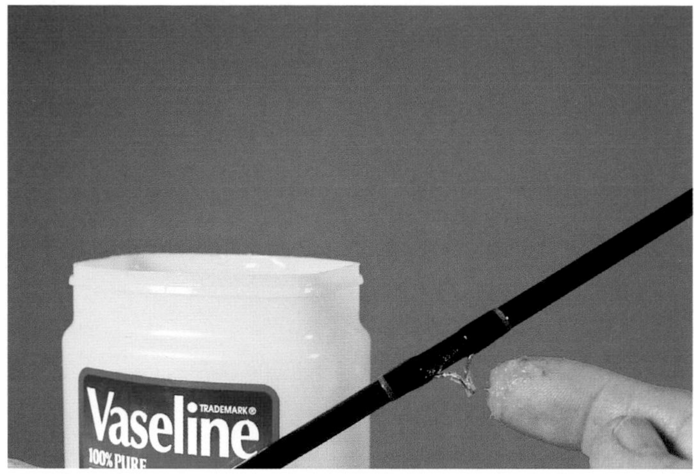

106 PREVENTING ICE IN THE GUIDES

When winter fly fishing, you can do several things to clear ice that forms in the guides. The time-honored solution is to dip your rod under the water and swish it around a little to dissolve the ice. This allows you to make a few more casts before the ice clogs the guides again.

Silicone sprays and homemade anti-freeze sprays help. Loon Outdoors Stanley's Ice Off Paste will last longer than any spray, and you can coat the guides with the paste. The paste prevents water from clinging to the guides, thus no ice.

If you can't obtain Stanley's Ice Off, other products are available that do about the same thing and won't damage lines. These include standard Vaseline and pure silicone pastes and lubricants, which are available from industrial supply, hardware, and some home products supply companies. All keep water from forming on the guides. You can wipe these products off after use, or they will wear off in time when you are no longer fishing in freezing temperatures. If you are using petroleum-based products, some of which may affect fly lines, be sure to clean and dress your line after each use.

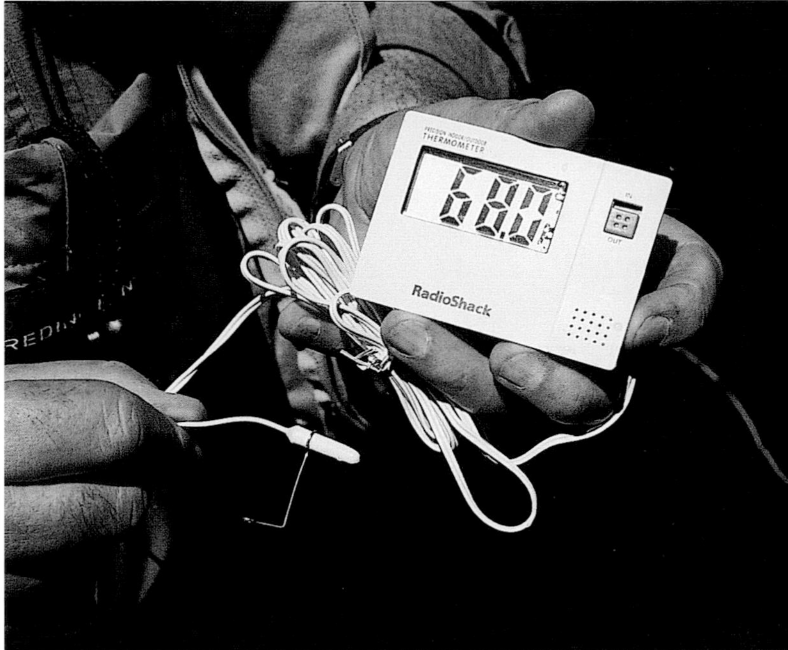

107 ELECTRIC TEMPERATURE GAUGE

Capt. Norm Bartlett, an expert and experienced captain on the Chesapeake Bay and also an avid freshwater fly fisherman, came up with the idea of using a simple digital indoor/outdoor thermometer to check both water and ambient temperature while fishing. The length of thin cable for the outside measurement makes it possible to allow the thermocouple to drag in the water while you are wading, or to hang over the side while boat fishing. The length of the cable allows both deep and surface temperature readings. To get deep readings, carry a 1-ounce (28-g) sinker on a snap that you can fasten to the cord at the thermocouple to sink the probe. Regardless of how used, it can give instant temperature readings. A slide switch makes it possible to instantly check both air and water temperature, and most of them even allow switching between Fahrenheit and centigrade readings.

108 WALKIE-TALKIES

Some small and inexpensive walkie-talkies have a range of up to 5 miles (8 km) and allow easy communication between separated parties. They are ideal for fly anglers fishing different parts of the same stream, or in different boats. They allow checking on the fishing, trading information on best flies, types of water, retrieve methods, and even water conditions.

They do have to be turned on the entire time to be able to signal, but there are ways around that also. One method is to keep the radio off to conserve battery power, but to turn it on "on the hour" to check with one or more buddies. They take little space and work in out-of-the-way areas where the also easy-to-use cell phones do not have service.

109 CAMERAS

More and more anglers are releasing fish and using photos to preserve the memories of their days on the water. For this, small digital point-and-shoot cameras, or camera-equipped smartphones, are ideal, and they easily fit in a pocket. With one memory card, you can take dozens of pictures to record a day's fishing success and outing.

The best way to protect your camera is to carry it in a zipper-seal sandwich bag. Carry the bagged camera in a top pocket of your fishing vest and only get it out when you are in no danger of falling in or getting wet. Secure the pocket shut so that the camera does not fall out when you are leaning over to release a fish or check stream-bottom insects.

Having a camera at all times makes it easy to get "hero" shots of your buddy with a fish, or for him or her to take shots of you with your catch.

110 PHOTOGRAPHING FISH

Lots of bass fishermen hold up their catch for a photo by holding the lower jaw of the fish and twisting to force the fish into an angled or horizontal position. This emulates the poses often seen with bass professionals who fish the tournament circuits. Do not do this, however, particularly if you are into catch-and-release bass fishing! Holding the fish in this way often strains or breaks the lower jaw of a bass, making it difficult for them to survive when released. Instead, hold or support the rear of the fish as you hold it horizontally, or hold it up straight (vertical) by the lower jaw. If the fish is very large (over 5 pounds/2.3 kg), you should support the body of the fish, since this weight hanging from the lower jaw of the fish can injure it.

111 FISHING DIFFERENT

It is a mistake to fish the same fly in the same size and color as your fly fishing partner, because this does not give the fish a choice in "food" selection. By fishing a different fly pattern, size, or color of fly, or fishing at a different depth or with a different retrieve, you give the fish more options. Once you find that the fish are keying on a certain fly, size, or color, or that fishing a certain way helps, then both of you can capitalize on this knowledge.

> "It is the constant—or inconstant—change, the infinite variety in fly-fishing that binds us fast. It is impossible to grow weary of a sport that is never the same on any two days of the year."
>
> —*Theodore Gordon (1914)*

112 GETTING THE MOST FROM A FISHING GUIDE

Guides are well worth the cost for a range of fishing situations. In general, they know where to go and how to fish in any situation, eliminating wasted time and effort. With a guide, all you have to do is follow his or her suggestions and relax as the guide takes care of the other details.

Even for experienced anglers, guides can be helpful when fishing a new area or for a new species of fish. Among the many benefits of working with a guide are:

- Guides are often knowledgeable about the area and can provide commentary on the wildlife, history, and geology of the area you are fishing.
- Guides will be familiar with safe wading areas and safe boating areas, thus providing an additional margin of security when fishing new waters.
- Guides can offer tips on the best flies and which retrieves to use, and they can provide the right kind of tackle for the fishing at hand.
- When boat fishing, guides can provide the right type of boat, complete with casting platforms and other amenities.

To make the most of the experience of working with a guide, be sure to speak with him or her extensively before the fishing trip.

- Find out what you are supposed to bring and what the guide will provide, from equipment to meals.
- Show up ready to fish with your gear already assembled. Leave rod tubes and reel cases at home.
- Determine ahead of time if the guide or captain will fish. Sometimes, at your request, having the captain or guide fish will help you learn the best casting techniques, targets, and retrieve methods.
- Be honest. If you are unsure of your casting skills, knot-tying ability, or fish-fighting ability, ask the guide or captain for help.
- Exchange cell phone numbers with your guide in case of an emergency while on your way to meeting the captain for the fishing day.

113 PRACTICE FLY CASTING REGULARLY

All the best athletes do it—practice, that is. Golfers, gymnasts, and baseball players all practice daily. So should fly anglers. Set up an outfit with a leader and small hank of yarn tied to the leader as a substitute for the fly. Practice all types of casts, including those with high backcasts, wind from various directions, accuracy casts, distance casts, sidearm casts, etc. If possible, practice on water where you can also try the roll cast. If you cast on the lawn, use an old line, since grass is hard on the finish of fly lines. The only cast that you cannot practice on the lawn is a roll cast, basically because there is no water surface tension to hold the line as you make the cast. For this reason, and to get a feel for casting over water, cast on a stream or pond when possible.

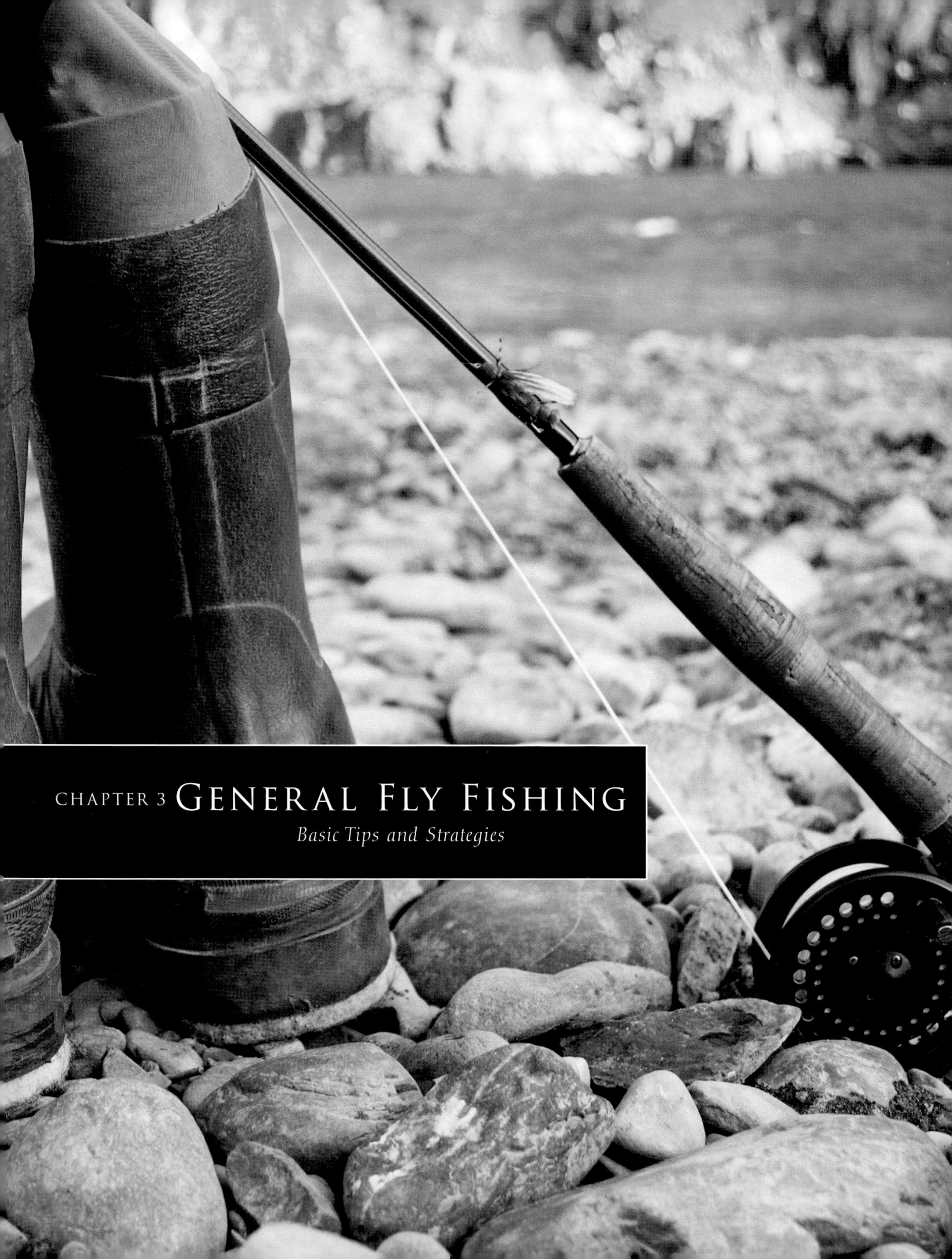

CHAPTER 3 GENERAL FLY FISHING

Basic Tips and Strategies

114 LEADER CAUGHT IN REEL

Leader ends can often get caught in a reel under the line or other leader coils. To find the end of the leader (the leader tippet), use a hook (a large fly works well) to catch one leader coil. Then hold the fly with the leader coil and turn the reel handle as you would if retrieving line. The leader tippet will come free after a few turns.

115 WEIGHTED FLIES

For some fishing, weighted flies are a must. This includes steelhead fishing, fishing for Pacific salmon, and some warm-water fishing such as that for largemouth, smallmouth, and pike. Where possible, avoid tying or fishing with heavily weighted flies. The heavy weight does have the advantage of getting the fly down to the fish, but has the disadvantage of deadening the action and movement of any fly. The heavy dumbbell eye weights in a fly can also cause the hook to ride point up, an advantage in preventing snags when fishing the bottom.

As an alternative, tie flies without weight or with very little weight, and use other weighting methods to get the fly deep. Possibilities for this include using several split shot on a leader, using a sinking or sinking-tip line, or using a "mini lead head" of several feet of lead-core line in the middle of the leader or between the line and a short leader. You can buy these mini lead heads (Gudebrod, Orvis, and Cortland) or make your own from 2-foot (0.6-m) lengths of lead-core line with loops spliced and wrapped into each end for loop-to-loop connections with the leader/line. If so inclined or required in your fishing area, you can also use non-lead weighted line.

116 WEIGHTED FLIES AND LEADER

Another situation that requires a change in casting tactics when surface fishing with a floating line occurs when you are casting heavily weighted flies. Common in steelhead and some trout fishing, this is often called a "chuck 'n duck" method, because of the heavy weight in the fly or leader tippet.

To help prevent problems, cast with a wide loop to keep the fly higher than normal and less of a hazard to the caster. The necessity of these techniques varies with the weight in the fly or on the leader and also the size of the outfit and weight of the line.

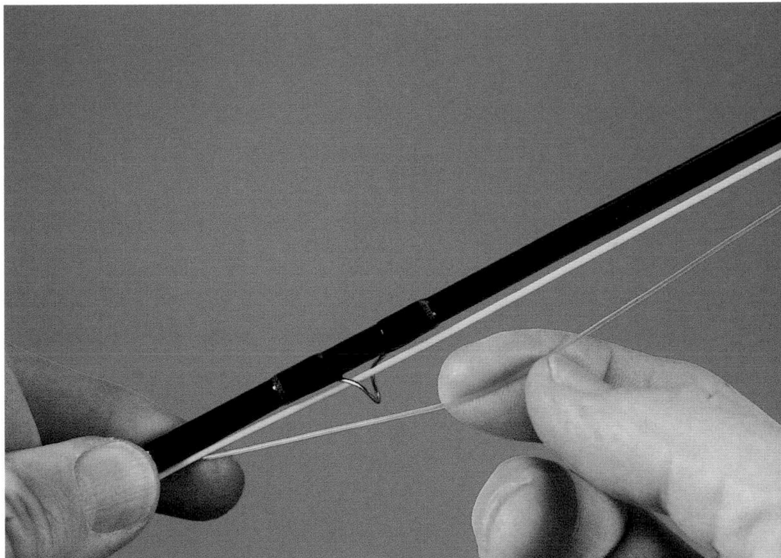

117 PREVENTING LINE TANGLES

Even after securing a fly to the hook keeper or to the guide, you still have a long length of line or leader from the tip-top to the reel seat. To prevent this from tangling with other rods or other tackle when storing gear, hold the line or leader in the middle and flip it around the rod, and over the nearest guide. This holds the line/leader out of the way, prevents it from hanging down, and keeps tangles to a minimum. Just remember that you did this so that you unhook the middle of the line/leader when getting the outfit ready to cast.

118 LOOP CONTROL

Over the years, anglers have suggested several ways to hold coils of line to prevent the current from catching it when wade fishing, or to keep boat fittings from catching the line. One of the best ways is to hold each coil of line on a separate finger of your line hand as you strip in the line. This allows you to carry four large coils of line in your hand without any possibility of them tangling, as might occur if looping coils together in the palm of your hand. This also makes it easy to release the line without tangling when making the next cast or shooting line.

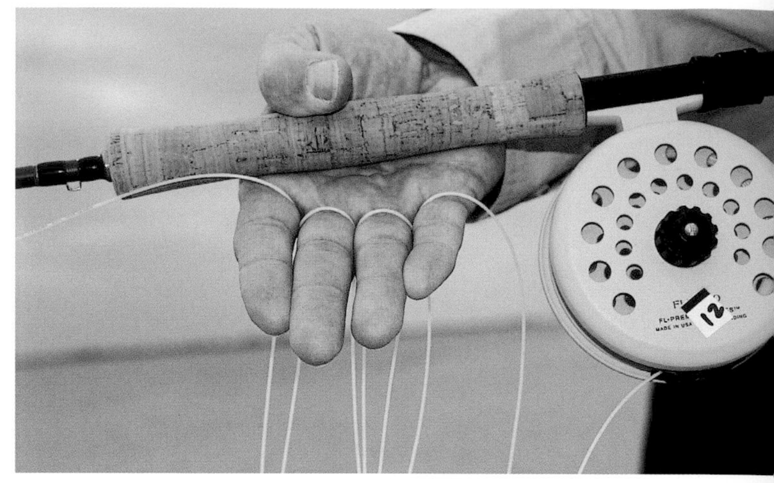

119 LOOPING LONG LEADER

Most anglers fly fish with a long leader—longer than the length of the fly rod. If you slip the fly into the hook keeper and reel the leader through the rod tip, it creates a sharp bend or kink in the butt section of the leader. To prevent this, and keep the line and leader secured, keep the end of the fly line several inches out of the rod tip, hook the fly into one of the upper guides, and loop the extra leader around the circumference of the reel. This allows using the rod instantly, since you do not catch the leader/line connection in the tip-top.

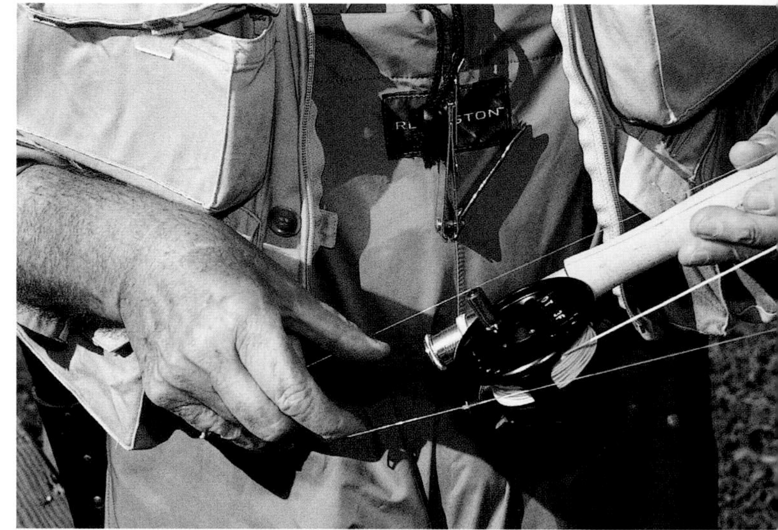

120 FLY FISHING DEEP

The right way to fly fish deep in open water is with a sinking line. While sinking-tip lines are great, the floating portion tends to plane up the sinking-tip end and raise the fly in the water column. To get down and stay down, use a full-sinking line, add a "mini lead head" between the line and the leader, use a short leader, and keep the rod tip low throughout the retrieve. This keeps your fly in the deep strike zone from the moment the fly sinks after making the cast until you pull the line out of the water for the next cast.

121 LEADER LENGTH FOR SINKING LINES

Most leaders come in lengths from about 7½ to 12 feet (2.3 to 3.7 m). However, if fishing deep with sinking or sinking-tip lines, these are entirely too long. Too long a leader bellies up in the water if you have a sinking line and a sinking fly, or causes a non-sinking fly to suspend high in the water column without ever getting deep.

To solve this, make your leader for a sinking line no more than 3 feet (0.9 m) long. Consider a 1-foot (0.3-m) length of heavy butt section and a 2-foot (0.6-m) length of the required tippet size. The butt section might have to be of lower test strength than normally used to be able to easily tie knots to connect the two leader lengths.

122 SINKING LEADERS WITH MUD

If your leaders are not sinking, and creating refraction on the surface to scare trout, use mud to sink the monofilament. Smear the mud along the entire length of the leader to help it soak up water (it will absorb water in time anyway) and sink on the next cast.

123 ANOTHER WAY TO SINK LEADERS

Another way to sink leaders is to take a tip from the past when fly anglers used to carry their silk gut leaders in aluminum cases between layers of wet felt to keep them moist and ready for casting. Manufacturers designed this to help the silk leaders straighten out easily. Store your leaders in a zipper-seal sandwich bag with a few drops of water that the leader will absorb. This allows the leader to sink quickly when fishing and prevents the leader from floating and scaring fish. It also makes it easier to straighten the leader.

124 TIPPET CHECK

After every catch, check your tippet for abrasion or roughness. Lightly run the leader tippet through your fingers, run it over your tongue, or hold it up to the light to spot any rough areas. Check particularly close to the fly. If you find a rough area, cut back the leader tippet if the roughness is close to the fly or replace the entire tippet to retie the fly.

125 IMPROVING WEED GUARDS

If you have a weed guard that is still catching weeds, you can improve it and strengthen it for better weed protection. For the single mono-strand loops that are standard on most weedless flies and bugs, slip the weed guard around and in front of the hook bend. This effectively makes it stiffer. It repels weeds better and still collapses when a fish hits it.

126 FIGHTING BIG FISH

Since you strip fly line out to cast, you can fight fish in two ways: stripping them in or fighting them from the reel. It's best to leave this decision—strip or reel—to the fish. If a fish is small and you can strip it in, do so without reeling in line at the same time. Often anglers trying to reel in line while stripping in a fish at the same time end up losing the fish. If the fish is strong and makes a run, allow the line to run controlled (through your fingers) out of the guides until all the slack line is gone. At this point, drop the rod tip a little and push the rod toward the fish to lessen the shock of the fish pulling line from the reel and against the drag. Then fight the fish from the reel—reeling it in by pumping when the fish tires, and allowing the fish to run when it desires.

127 CONTROLLING FISH

If you pressure a hooked fish with a high rod, it tends to come to the surface, thrash around, and possibly become unbuttoned. A better solution is to use side pressure with the rod held close to parallel with the water. This tends to keep the fish in the water rather than struggling on top, and allows you to turn the head of the fish to lead it to you.

"Nothing grows faster than a fish between the moment it bites and the moment it gets away."

—*Anonymous*

128 LANDING PIKE

Pike have teeth and you can't lip them as you can largemouth bass. An old way to land pike was to put your thumb and forefinger into their pronounced eye sockets and lift them into the boat. Don't do it! In these days of catch-and-release fishing, such mistreatment can damage or possibly blind the fish, dooming it to a slow death. Instead, use a cradle (square net) to land pike.

To make a cradle, buy a rectangle of mesh netting, about 3 feet by 4 feet (0.9 m by 1.2 m). (You can make it smaller or larger depending upon the fish you plan to catch.) Then staple or stitch the long side of the net to 1½-inch (38-mm) dowels, 5 feet (1.5 m) long, to the dowel. It will look almost like a World War II stretcher or a camp cot. To help sink the netting, add a few small pinch-on sinkers along the net. To land the pike, suspend the cradle in the water to sink the netting. Have the angler lead the pike into the cradle. Then lift both sides of the cradle to lift the pike straight up to remove the fly and release the fish.

129 LIP LANDING LARGE FISH

Lip landing large fish, such as stripers, steelhead, and salmon, can be difficult. The fish are strong, with tremendous power to twist out of your grip and break tackle. Many fish, such as big largemouth, trout, steelhead, and salmon, also have small but abrasive teeth that can make you sore. One good tip for these situations is to use a rag or small towel. Wet it and hold it between your fingers, then lip-grab the fish by the towel held in your hand. This creates a better grip, is easier on the fish, and won't abrade your thumb. You can also use a cotton gardening or work glove for the same purpose.

130 NETTING FISH

Nets are the traditional way to land fly-caught fish. Both short-handled wading and long-handled boat nets are available, in a variety of bag diameters and depths. First make sure that the fish is tired and ready to land. Lower the net into the water, and lead the fish head first into the net. Never land a fish tail first.

If the fish is moving head first into the net and strikes the net, it will dive farther into the net. If netted tail first and striking the net, it will leap out of the net. Once the fish is in the net, rapidly raise the net. If the fish tries to jump out of the net, and if you have a deep enough bag, turn the net frame sideways to close the net opening and secure the fish.

131 RELEASING FISH

Once you have caught a fish, taken a couple of quick photos, and unhooked it, you have to release it the right way if not keeping it. Don't just throw the fish into the water. Gently place the fish in the water. If it lacks teeth (trout, bass, stripers, carp, etc.), hold it by the lower jaw and work the fish back and forth to force water through the gills to help it recover. Usually, the fish will dart out of your hand when it is ready to go.

If the catch has teeth, hold it in back of the head—just behind the gills—and by the tail. Work the fish back and forth to help it recover. With all fish, avoid dangerous parts of the fish (gills, pectoral spines, etc.) and wait for the fish to recover enough to dart out of your hand.

132 REMOVING FLIES

The easiest and best way to release fish is to never take them out of the water, but remove the fly while they are tired but resting. To do this, tire the fish enough so that you can control it without touching it. Hold the leader close to the fly and work the fly out of the fish's mouth. Push the fly sharply back to disengage it. If it is a large fly, hold the body of the fly and partly lift the fish up to cause the fly to pull out. Lacking that, use pliers or hemostats to hold the fly and twist it out of the fish. Tools made exclusively for fly removal include the Ketchum Release by Waterworks, which features a small slit-sided collar on a handle. To use this, fit the slit-sided collar over the line and slide it down over the fly to push the fly back and out of the fish. Several sizes are available for freshwater and saltwater fish.

133 SEAMS AND EDGES

Seams and edges are places where two currents touch, where two different flows of water meet, or where a fast current slides past a quiet eddy. Places like this in both freshwater and saltwater are ideal spots to throw a fly. They offer quiet water where game fish can rest while staying close to fast water that can wash a meal past their nose. For this reason, try fishing in the fast or faster current right next to the seam to get fish that are resting but ambush feeding. To produce the most strikes, cast the fly upcurrent and then allow it to swing downstream or downcurrent on a snug line.

134 PUMPING THE ROD

Non-anglers often wonder how an angler can land a heavy fish using a light tippet. The answer is in both the drag and the ability to pump, which is how to fight fish properly. First, the drag must be set much lighter than the pound-test of the leader. To fight fish properly with the fly rod (or any rod), bring the fish toward you by lifting the rod from the horizontal to about a 45-degree angle. Then lower the rod as you reel or strip in your fly line. Continue to do this until you land the fish or until it makes a run and you have to repeat the process. This also allows dropping the rod and allowing the line to run off of the fly reel, should the fish make a run while you are pumping it in. Note that it is also possible to work the rod with side pressure by working the rod back when held parallel to the water, then retrieving line with your hand or reel as you point the rod toward the fish each time.

> "There don't have to be a thousand fish in a river; let me locate a good one and I'll get a thousand dreams out of him before I catch him—and, if I catch him, I'll turn him loose."
>
> *—Jim Deren, proprietor, the Angler's Roost*

135 MAKING WAVES WHEN YOU WADE

Fish react to sound waves. All fish have pores in their scales along a lateral line so that underlying nerve endings can detect water impulses. This means that you must always wade carefully and never create waves that might signal to fish that a predator (you!) is in the area. For best results, always wade slowly and carefully, planting one foot firmly before moving your other foot. Moving sideways to the current creates less water pressure against you and thus generates less disturbance in the water.

136 WADING ON A SANDY BOTTOM

When standing on a sandy bottom, any fast-moving current or tide washes sand out from under your feet. This can occur on a tidal flat, fly fishing the surf, fishing sandy-bottom rivers and streams, and on sandy beaches or flats. To prevent currents from digging you into a hole, or sinking you deeper into the water when you are up to your armpits in your waders, move occasionally before the sand completely erodes your position.

> "Nick did not like to fish with other men on the river. Unless they were of your party, they spoiled it."
>
> —*Ernest Hemingway, "Big Two-Hearted River" (1925)*

137 FISH WITH A BUDDY WHEN WADING

It's always best to wade with a buddy, whether wet wading, in hip boots, or in chest-high waders. You and your friend should be within sight and earshot of each other. This is particularly true on big water.

It is good to have a friend around for help in netting a fish or taking a photo of a trophy catch, but also for safety. Wading can wrench ankles, get you wet, cause you to fall in, or cause other problems.

If you have trouble getting across a certain stretch of river, two anglers can lock arms, take baby steps, and get across by supporting each other and providing additional resistance to the current. This is true whether or not you use a wading staff. It is even better if you both have wading staffs. For the safest wading, each angler should alternate steps so that one provides a solid "anchor" for the other as he or she moves.

138 FALLING IN

No one wants to fall in while fishing. But it can—and does—eventually happen to everyone. What you do next can make the difference in how wet you get. In extreme situations, it can save your life. First, expand your chest or pull on your wader belt immediately to reduce the amount of water getting into your waders. Sometimes you can reduce this to a small trickle. If you can regain your feet, do so immediately. Use your wading staff to help.

If you are in deep water and can't regain your footing, position yourself so that your feet are downstream to fend off any rocks as you float down the river. Hang onto your rod and tackle if possible and try to get to shallow water or a quiet eddy where you can get out. If you take on a lot of water, you might not be able to stand up in shallow water with the weight of water in your waders. In this case, lower your waders and carefully wade to shore. Sit on the bank and raise your legs to pour the water out of each wader leg. Only then stand up, and get back to your camp or vehicle to change clothes.

If you are wet wading (pants, but no waders or hip boots), try to regain your footing, position your feet downstream if floating in deep water, and get out as soon as possible.

In all the above scenarios, a personal floatation device (PFD) such as worn by boaters or a CO2- or mouth-inflatable yoke air vest is a recommended safety device.

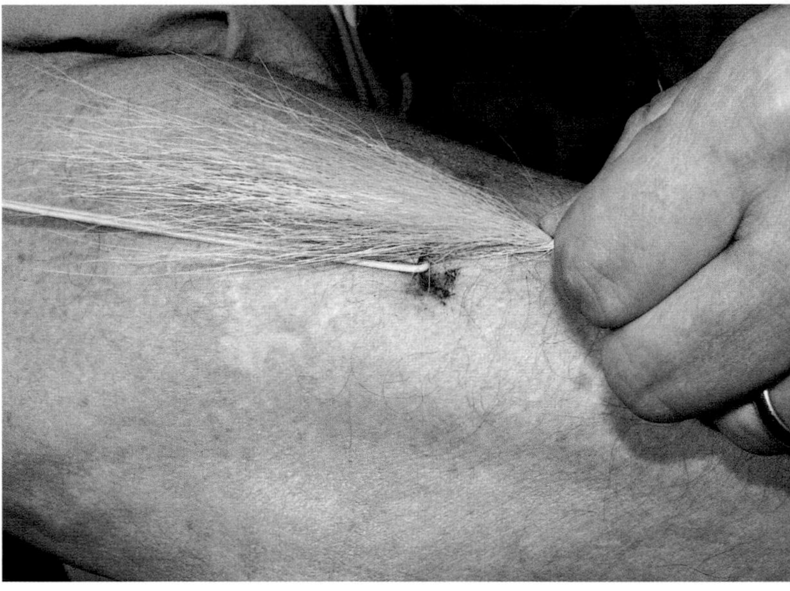

139 REMOVING HOOKS FROM YOU OR FRIENDS

If you fish long enough, you might get hooked or be in a fishing group where someone gets hooked. If this happens with a barbed hook that penetrates past the barb, you can't back the hook out of the flesh. After some barbaric methods of the past (push the hook out through the skin, cut off the barb and then back the hook out!) the best current method recommends pulling the hook out backward using a loop of string.

For this, first cut the fly from the tippet. Then use cord or a heavy fly line looped around the hook bend of the fly. Push down on the eye of the fly hook and then jerk the fly out backward with the loop of cord by pulling on the bend of the hook. If you have antiseptic, add it to the puncture, and cover the spot with a bandage. This is easiest (and sometimes only possible) if someone other than the "hookee" does it. This works well for all areas of the body, but avoid doing this around the neck, face, back of hands, or anywhere that you might have surface arteries, veins, nerves, or tendons.

140 BREAKING TIPPET

If you hook a snag or tree with your fly and the fly wraps around the branches or tangles in the leaves, it is easier to snap the fly tippet, remove the fly, and pull the leader free. This is easier than holding the snag or tree while trying to thread the fly through the tangle. Once you have the fly and the rest of the tippet free, then you can check the leader for abrasion, make any necessary replacements, and retie the fly for fishing.

Another tip is to break off the twig or branch and then at your leisure, unwrap the leader and tippet from the foliage. This is also best to do if you are working from a boat that can drift around, making it difficult to hold position and get the fly free.

141 CARRYING YOUR ROD

When walking through the woods or high grasslands with a fly rod tip first, you can easily poke the tip into a twig or brush and snap it before you realize it. To prevent this, pull the line and leader tight against the rod and carry the rod butt forward with the rod trailing behind you. In most cases, the rod will clear all of the brush and foliage, but if the rod does catch, it is easy to untangle without damage.

142 CLEANING FISHING AREAS

One way to help control angler litter is to carry a plastic trash bag with you and use it to pick up litter around boat ramps, shore fishing areas, and along streams. Since most anglers walk in one direction along a stream to fish it and then walk back to return to the car, use the bag on the return trip to pick up any litter you have encountered. Carry the trash home to dispose of it properly.

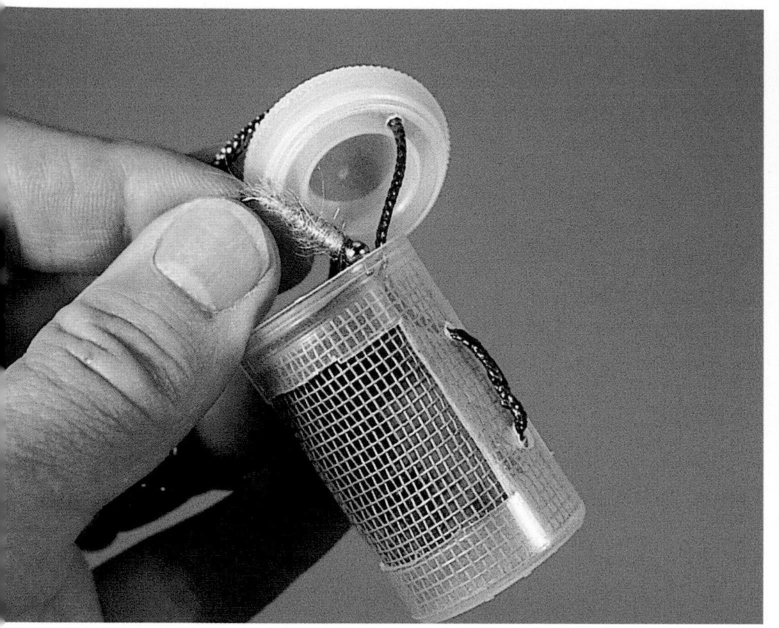

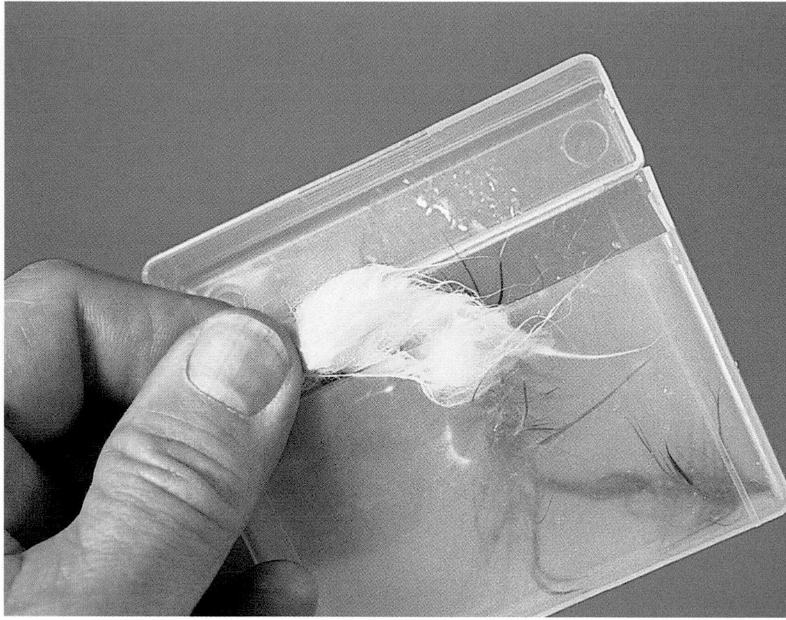

143 DRYING FLIES

It is important to dry flies after use before placing them in a closed fly box. A simple way to do this is to make a fly-drying box for small flies. I first learned of this when fishing in Pennsylvania and a thoughtful fly angler gave me one.

This fly-drying box is nothing more than a plastic film can, with two large "windows" cut into the sides. The liner of the can is a small piece of plastic screening (available at any hardware store as a "patch" piece), coiled, and cut to fit inside the can to prevent fly loss. A cord loop through a hole punched in the side of the can, then through the lid, back through the lid, and into the other side allows the can to hang from your vest while preventing loss of the cap. The screening allows flies to dry as you fish.

For larger flies or different fishing situations, place all used flies in a bag or box for later drying. If fishing in saltwater, rinse the flies in fresh water at home, dry thoroughly, and replace them in their boxes. A simple container can be anything, including a zipper-seal plastic bag, plastic zippered pencil case (such as what can be used for storage of large flies), or any of a number of small plastic boxes (such as Tupperware or pencil case boxes).

CHAPTER 4 CASTING

From Line Control to Mending to Retrieving

144 CASTING EASE

There are fishing situations for both short rods and long rods, but as a general rule, long rods are better. With a long rod, you have more leverage to make longer casts. Long rods also require less effort and muscle strain. They are better shock absorbers, since the longer the flexible lever (the rod), the less likely it is that the fish can snap the leader tippet.

Long rods are also good for "dapping," a technique of fishing with the tip of the rod dropping the line straight down to allow the fly to float on the water surface or, when nymphing, deep in the current. You do this without casting and without the line floating on the surface. You can poke long rods through the brush of a mountain trout stream to present a fly easily without casting. A light, short rod, however, might work better on some small meadow streams when throwing small terrestrials and tiny midge patterns.

145 CASTING ABOVE THE WATER SURFACE

Cast as if the water is 3 feet (0.9 m) higher than it really is to make a delicate presentation of a fly when trout fishing. That way, the line and leader straighten out and the fly will drift to the water surface gently, rather than slamming down hard as it might if casting to the water surface. The result can often make the difference between a trout that takes and a trout that ignores your offerings.

146 TANDEM RIGS

At one time "casts" of three flies on a leader were standard—one on the "point" (the end of the leader) and two dropper flies above. Tandem rigs of two flies are still a good idea, since they give fish a choice of two offerings, and can greatly increase your chances of hooking up. Possibilities include two dries, two wets or nymphs, two streamers, or a combination, such as a nymph and a streamer or a subdued nymph and a bright wet fly.

147 CONTROLLING LINE LOOP

Loop control of your line is a must if you are to fly fish effectively. In most instances, you will want a tight or small loop for pushing out a line for both distance and accuracy. In some cases, you need a wide loop, as when casting sinking lines or large, heavily weighted flies.

To control the loop size, control the angle of your rod on both the forward and backcast. To make a narrow loop, stop the rod power in a high position, following through only after you make that stop and to finish the cast. To cast a wide loop, continue through more of the cast than above to allow the loop to open more on the cast, and prevent tangles of weighted flies and sinking lines. Practice this often, first with a floating line and then with a sinking line until you understand the physics involved, the need for different types of casts, and the technique required to make them consistently.

> "Fishermen are born honest, but they get over it."
>
> —*Ed Zern,* To Hell with Fishing *(1945)*

148 COUNT DOWN FISHING

A great way to fly fish for deep fish is to use the "count down" method. This involves using a sinking fly and sinking or sinking-tip fly line, and counting down with each successive cast. By counting, you are essentially "timing" the sink rate of your fly. Counting "one thousand one, one thousand two," and so on, makes for a reasonable count in seconds. By making such a count after each cast and before a retrieve, and increasing the count by one or two with each successive cast, you can determine the correct count to strike fish at a certain depth. Once you hook a fish, use the count to get to the same level in the water column to take fish during subsequent casts.

149 CASTING SINKING FLY LINES

The best way to cast a sinking fly line after retrieving the line all the way back is to make an aerial roll cast. Since the line is deep, it is impossible to pick the line up off the water as you can with a floating line. Instead, wait until you have only about 15 feet (4.6 m) of line out. Then bring the rod back and roll the sinking line out of the water and into the air. Make this a high, aerial roll cast to prevent casting the line out on the water again. Once the line straightens out in the air, bring the line back in a backcast and make the few necessary false casts to get the line out again.

150 CASTING SINKING SHOOTING HEADS

You must cast sinking shooting heads, such as the Teeny lines, those by other manufacturers, or those that you make yourself, differently than regular fly lines. First, shooting heads or lines are usually about 30 feet (9 m) long, and typically attached to a running line with a loop-to-loop system. Loops are typically included on commercial lines, or you can make your own by whipping a folded-over loop in the end of the line (see page 31). The running line looped to the shooting head is typically a thin, level fly line or a special braided shooting line, such as Gudebrod 25- or 35-pound-test (11.3- or 15.9-kg) Shooting Line, that is a bright-orange braided mono.

To cast a shooting line, work the shooting head outside of the tip of the fly rod so that as you double-haul, you are working the end of the shooting line back and forth. You do not want to pull the connecting loops back and forth through the tip-top. Double-haul as you keep the line in the air, and make wide loops with your rod angle control. Once you have made a few false casts, double-haul, and shoot the line to the target, allowing the stiff shooting line to flow up out of the stripping basket or off the boat deck. Since the shooting line flows through the guides faster and easier than any fly line, you achieve a far longer cast than one possible with a standard weight-forward fly line.

151 BACKCASTING

If you rip the line off of the water for a backcast, you spook fish throughout the area. To prevent this, keep the rod tip low, strip in line until you are ready to cast, and then lift the rod until only the leader or part of the leader is on the water surface. Then (and only then) lever the rod back to make the backcast and raise the rest of the leader and the bug or fly off of the water. The result is a smooth, clean pick-up with minimal disturbance of the water surface for an easy backcast to get the fly or bug back out to waiting fish.

152 AERIAL ROLL CAST

If you fish long enough and in enough different places, weeds ultimately catch on your fly. One way to remove weeds without physically handling the fly is to strip the line in, and with the fly a dozen feet (3.7 m) from you, bring the rod back to make a roll cast. Then make a rapid aerial roll cast, throwing the line into the air prior to making a backcast. Make the backcast as soon as the line straightens out from the roll cast. Done right, this will often strip the weeds from the fly as you rip the fly out of the water or as the fly changes direction on the backcast. As you cast, check the fly in the air to make sure that it is clean and free of weeds.

153 SIDE ROLL CAST

Use roll casts where there is no room for a traditional backcast. Traditionally, anglers make roll casts straight overhead, like hammering a nail. A better way to make them is with a side cast, bringing the rod back, pausing, and then casting forward parallel with the water to roll the line out to the quarry. This works better, is easier, and allows for a longer cast than a traditional roll cast.

154 HIGH BACKCAST

"Backcast" is probably a poor word to use for the technique of flipping the line back in preparation for the forward cast and retrieving the fly. Often, beginning fly anglers bring the rod back too far and at too much of an angle so that the line hits the water. This reduces the power of loading the rod for the forward cast and also often makes for a high, jerky forward cast.

To make a good cast, make a high backcast, with enough power to keep a straight line, then come forward to power the forward cast. This ensures that the line will stay high and make a good casting technique. Another problem with a low or angled backcast on small streams is that you can hit and break off your fly on rocks in back of you.

155 WEAK BACKCAST

If you can't get weeds off of your fly by a rapid roll cast, or if you see a knot in your leader, the only way to correct this is to handle the line/leader and remove the weeds or untie and retie the knot. One way to rapidly do this is to pick up the line and make a very weak backcast over your left shoulder (assuming that you are a right-handed caster). Do this so that you can catch the leader as the line collapses just as it gets to you with this very weak backcast. Then with the leader in hand, untie or retie any knots, and clear the fly for the next cast.

156 CASTING WITH THE WIND

For right-handed fly casters, a wind coming from the right is the most difficult to deal with. To minimize the impact of the wind, turn 180 degrees and cast so that your rod arm is on the far side of the wind. For this, your final cast has to be a backcast after several false casts.

An alternative is to keep the wind to your right, but cast with the rod angled over your left shoulder to keep the line and fly from blowing back in your face. You might also have to compensate by casting slightly to the windward side so that the line blowing back will place the fly in the target area. If you are left-handed, simply follow the directions for casting with the wind from the left.

If the wind is coming from the left, it will not bother right-handed casters, other than requiring you to compensate for the wind in where you direct the cast. If you are left-handed and the wind is coming from the left, you should follow one of the two methods suggested for right-handed casters with the wind from the right.

For casting into the wind, all casts should be low and to the side and parallel to the water. This will lessen the force of the wind on the line and cast direction. Alternatively, you can make a high overhead backcast, then a strong, forceful, and low forward cast to drive the line and fly into the wind using a narrow loop.

When casting with the wind direction, you can use the wind to get a longer cast. First throw a low, forceful side cast to the rear. It should be as low as possible to the water and will not be as long as a regular backcast. At the end of the backcast, swing the rod to a vertical position to make a high forward cast with a wide loop. The wind will catch the line and the wide loop and carry the line and fly as far as you wish.

Casting with the wind

Casting into the wind

157 MENDING LINE

One way to get more drift to a fly is to "mend" the line. Mending the line is a method of flipping the line upstream to prevent it from dragging downstream by the current and developing a belly to race the fly through the water where it will be unattractive to fish. To mend line after the cast, tighten the line slightly, hold the line and rod, point the rod tip toward the line direction, and flip the rod in an upward arc to cause the line belly to flip upstream and give the fly more natural drift time.

158 DOUBLE-HAUL

The double-haul is a little like learning to pat your tummy while rubbing your head—or is it the other way around? The double-haul is a way to accelerate and speed up your line to make good casts and to get more distance when required.

To make the double-haul, first pick up the line for the backcast by pulling on the line while raising the rod to make the backcast. Then, as the backcast forms, hold the line but allow a short length of it to slide through the guides. Allow the backcast to straighten out. Then pull forward on the line to accelerate it while pushing the rod forward to make the forward cast. This combination of pulling on the line while pushing the rod forward accelerates the line to make long casts possible and easier.

159 CASTING FROM SHORE

If you can cast effectively from shore, don't wade. Wading is important but also can create bottom noise, make ripples and pressure waves that spook fish, and create the potential of falling or slipping. If you can cast from the bank and get to the fish, do it. For this, use a standard overhead cast if you are in field or meadow situations, or use a standard or side roll cast if you are on a tree-lined bank.

160 SWINGING THE FLY

One of the most effective retrieve systems for running water is to make a cast across the current or stream, and then allow the fly to swing in an arc through the current until it is straight downstream. This is a classic cast and retrieve system for Atlantic salmon, Pacific salmon, shad, stripers, trout, river smallmouth, and other game fish.

To completely cover the water in a long pool, make one or two such casts, and then make a large side step downstream and repeat. This allows the fly to swing through a new section of water a foot or two (30 to 60 cm) below the first cast. By repeating this regularly, you can easily cover an entire pool.

161 RETRIEVING LINE

There are several good ways to retrieve fly line when stripping in flies. Each retrieve type has an advantage. By folding the line over repeatedly in your hand, you can keep the line snug with a drifting or slow retrieve. This is ideal for fishing nymphs. For faster stripping of streamer flies, retrieve the line so that you can hold coils in your hand. If fishing from a boat, you can strip the line onto the casting deck, but do not step on the line when making the next cast or when a hooked fish makes a run.

162 LINE CONTROL ON RETRIEVES ▲

When retrieving a fly, make sure that you never completely let go of the line. Hold the rod in your rod hand and run the line over your index finger. Then make the twitches, jerks, pauses, strips, and other retrieve moves with your line hand, pulling the line through the index finger of your rod hand. That way, when you drop the line with your line hand to reposition it for the next strip, you still have control of the line through your opposite index finger. This also allows you to strike a fish, should one hit during this transition moment. Do this by tightening the index finger of your rod hand, then picking up the line with your line hand to fight the fish.

163 RETRIEVE AS SOON AS FLY HITS WATER

Some fish do not react well if a fly lands but does not move immediately. This applies to barracuda, among others. For fish like this, cast, but begin your retrieve just as soon as the fly hits the water to attract any fish in the area. Barracuda usually lose interest in the fly if cast and not moved immediately.

164 FISHING FLIES DOWNSTREAM

Some trout are so easily spooked that they shy away from any fly where they can see the leader, regardless of how fine the tippet is. One way to fool these fish is to cast from an upstream location, and allow the fly to drift straight downstream to them in their feeding lane. By doing this, the trout see the fly before seeing any leader and often take after a short follow. The one problem with this is that you must allow some extra time for the fish to take the fly so that you do not pull the fly straight upstream and out of the fish's mouth after it strikes.

165 DOWNSTREAM SWING

You can easily take some migrating fish by using the downstream swing. These fish include shad, steelhead, and salmon (Atlantic and Pacific), which are anadromous and ascend streams to spawn. They often run through a riffle to rest at the tail end of a pool before moving on. To catch such fish, an ideal retrieve is to position yourself so that the fly line drifting straight downstream swings in the current where the fish are holding.

You can also benefit by causing the fly to swing back and forth. To do this, swing your rod to one side so that the current catches the belly of the line, and ultimately causes the fly to swing to one side. Then throw the rod to the other side where the current will catch the line belly again and cause the fly to swing back. This back-and-forth movement across the current at the tail of a pool often triggers fish to strike.

166 FALSE CASTING

Shallow-water fish are particularly susceptible to being spooked when a fly line is cast over them. This is particularly true of trout and saltwater flats species, such as bonefish and permit. To prevent this when false casting, cast to the side of the fish to get the right distance and then only on the final cast make the cast toward the target. This lessens the possibility of the line scaring the fish.

167 TIMING THE STRIKE

Timing is everything, particularly when it comes to striking fish. The best advice is to wait until you feel the fish to set the hook. This is true even if you see the pick-up of a bonefish when sight-fishing, or the boil of a bass when popping a surface bug. If you react to what you see, rather than what you feel, you can pull the fly out of the fish's mouth before it completely takes it. With a surface strike, allow the fish to turn with the bug or fly in its mouth before striking. On underwater pick-ups when sight-fishing, wait until the fish moves away or turns and you feel the weight of the fish.

168 THE LAST CAST

Whenever you reel in line to move to a new fishing location or at the end of the day, hold the rod tip in the water or against something solid such as a bush, a mossy bank, or boat deck. Without this support, the line can sometimes tangle around the rod tip, requiring time to untangle or even breaking the end of the rod. With the rod tip in the water, sometimes you can even get a strike on that last cast.

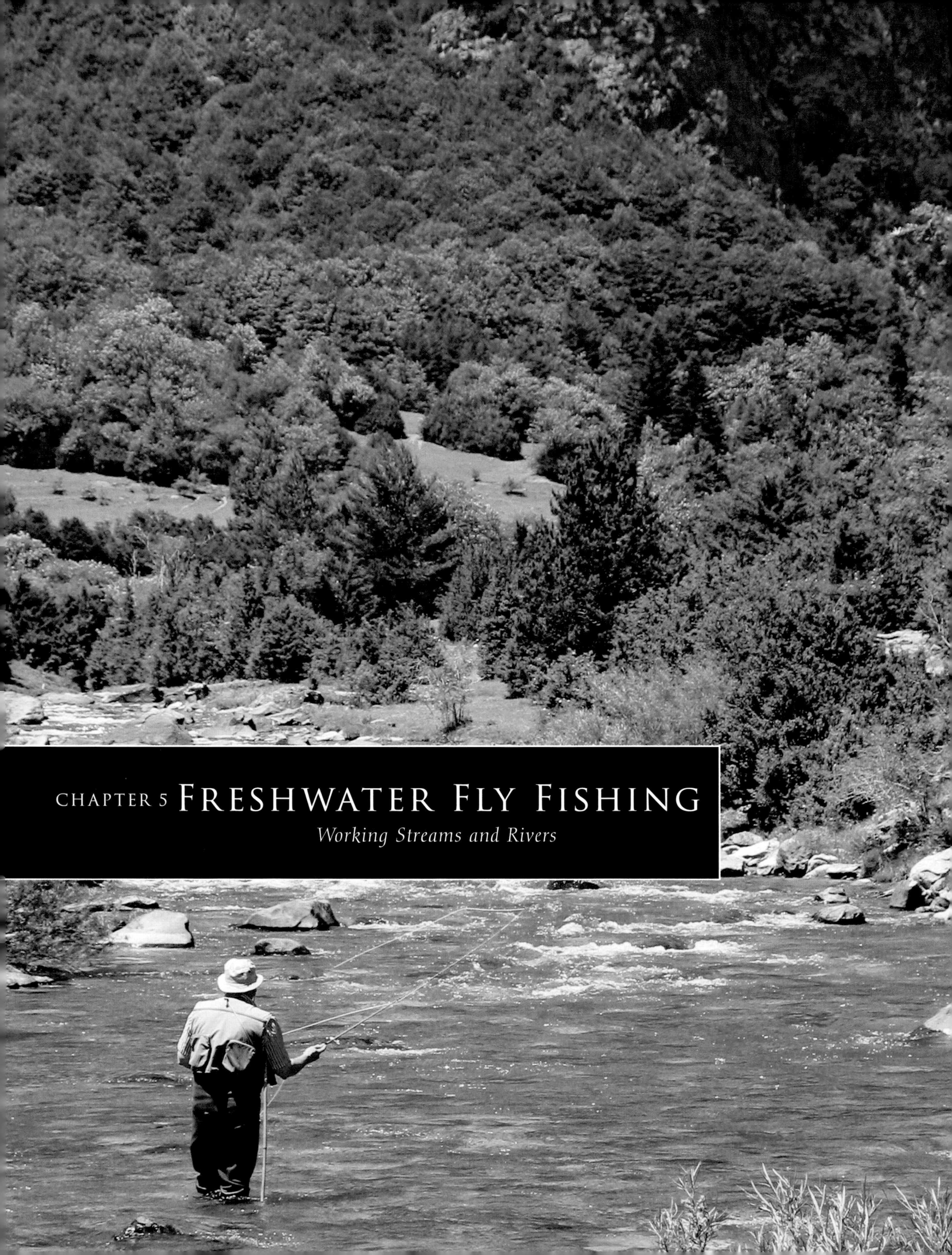

CHAPTER 5 FRESHWATER FLY FISHING

Working Streams and Rivers

169 FRESHWATER FISH DANGERS

Catfish spines are very sharp and carry a toxic substance that can cause a painful, festering wound. To land a catfish up to about 5 pounds (2.3 kg), reach carefully around the sharp spines on the dorsal fin and pectoral fins. Grab the fish from the top by holding it with your hand immediately in back of the dorsal fin and the index and middle finger bracketing one pectoral fin.

Pike, pickerel, and muskie have big teeth. The best way to land pike to avoid hurting yourself or the pike is with a cradle—essentially a long, rectangular net. To land pike or muskie without a net, lift the fish by the area just in front of the tail and just in back of the pectoral fins. You can handle smaller pickerel the same way.

Big trout and bass have tiny teeth that can hurt. But they will not do much damage unless you handle them excessively. You can use the same landing method as with pike, but with trout and bass, it is a good idea to hold the lower lip at the same time you support the back of the fish just in front of the tail.

170 SPOTTING FRESHWATER FISH

There are different ways to spot different freshwater fish. Trout reveal themselves by rising to the surface to take insects. But you can also spot their flashes on the bottom as their bellies show when turning to search for nymphs. You can find carp and smallmouth in shallow waters rooting around rocks in search of crayfish. They often travel together, each taking advantage of the other's food gathering methods.

Panfish, such as bluegills, often take bugs off the surface. In the springtime you'll find their round, light-colored beds along the banks in shallow water. You'll find largemouth beds along the shore also, but they are larger and often found in very shallow water. Smallmouth have similar beds, but usually in deeper water.

Nervous water or any water during which you see baitfish moving or nervous can signal smallmouth, largemouth, or one of the pike or muskie families.

171 READING THE WATER FOR LARGEMOUTH BASS

Studies have shown that largemouth bass like structure, particularly wood. Thus, the place to cast a fly or bug for largemouth bass is around any wood structure. Logjams, stumps, standing timber, wood piers or docks, brush piles, boathouses, duck blinds, and similar wood structure are ideal for shallow-water bass. If wood is not available in largemouth territory, then fish rocks or any other available structure.

The exceptions to the above occur in mid-summer and mid-winter when bass are deep along break lines, and in the summer and fall when they are cruising the shallows for food each morning and evening.

172 READING THE WATER FOR SMALLMOUTH BASS

While smallmouth bass seem similar to largemouth, smallmouth like structure of gravel or rock far better than the wood favored by largemouth. Thus, cast bugs and flies around boulders, rocks, ledges, shelves, gravel beds, and such on smallmouth rivers. Since they are often taking nymphs and hellgrammites from the bottom, another spot to try with large, black, weighted nymphs is to fish the bottom of sandy or gravel areas through deep, long pools. If rock is not available on smallmouth rivers, then fish wood or other available structure, since smallmouth adapt to any situation.

> "I consider him, inch for inch and pound for pound, the gamest fish that swims."
>
> —*James Henshall,* Book of the Black Bass *(1881)*

173 READING THE WATER FOR TROUT

Trout are river and stream fish, and you have to know how to read the water to know where to cast your fly. Fish are just like people—only wetter. They like comfort and food. Trout get both by staying close to the bottom or to rocks and boulders in the stream. These spots have far less current than open mid-stream water, so they can rest comfortably. These spots also have food wash by continuously, so that a trout can swing out to grab a bite to eat and then return to the comfort and safety of its holding spot.

As a result, fish deep with weighted flies; fish in the white water of plunge pools where waterfalls enter a pool; fish the tails of pools; and fish in front of, in back of, and beside any rocks, ledges, or boulders in the stream. The exception to this occurs when trout are taking dry flies or on big constant-flow waters where trout hang around waterweeds for shade and comfort.

174 CHUMMING ON A TROUT STREAM

In the 1950s and '60s, the books and research of Charlie Fox and Vince Marinaro noted the importance of "chumming" in trout streams to locate trout and trout lies. They developed and fished with terrestrial patterns to imitate the inchworms, grasshoppers, leafhoppers, crickets, beetles, termites, and ants that live along a stream. Often these natural insects fall into a stream where the trout gobble them up. You can chum the same way with land insects, throwing them into the water to locate trout, finding the best feeding lane in which to throw a fly, and conditioning trout to feed. Just make sure that this practice is legal in your fishing area before trying it.

175 CASTING UPSTREAM TO TROUT RISES

When trout rise to take an insect off the surface, they create a ring that quickly sweeps downstream. In addition, trout often drift downstream to examine a floating insect before taking it. Both of these often create false impressions as to where a trout will take a fly or first sees a fly. Make sure that you cast well upstream of where you see a trout taking insects, but make sure that the fly follows the exact insect feeding lane of the trout.

176 YO-YO LIFT

Natural nymphal forms of insects, such as caddis, mayflies, and stoneflies, live on the bottom of a stream. At the end of their life cycle, they rise to the surface, emerge from the water, and develop into winged insects. With different species, this occurs all the time, almost all year round.

To capitalize on this, fish nymphs deep on trout streams and use your rod to lift the nymph up; then allow it to fall to the bottom again as it drifts downstream.

This method of nymph fishing, popularized by Jim Leisenring some 65 years ago, is an effective way to fish since it closely simulates the movement of nymphs swimming to the surface. For best results, use a weighted nymph or some split shot on the leader tippet to keep the nymph deep.

177 DAPPING FOR TROUT

An easy way to take trout in a small stream is to dap for them. This is a method of dropping a fly directly from the rod tip to the water, rather than casting the fly to the fish. To do this, use a long rod, 9 feet (2.7 m) or longer. For best fishing, try small streams where you can poke the rod out from the brush and drop a fly to a feeding trout. The advantage of dapping is that you can present a fly without any drag problems associated with casting since only the fly should touch the water surface.

178 DRIFTING A FLY TO AN UNDERCUT BANK

One trick to get trout to hit when they are hiding under overhanging brush or an undercut bank is to drift a fly to them. Often this is impossible if snags are in the area, but there is one method that makes this easy. The trick is to pick a tree leaf from along the bank and hook your fly to the outer edge of the leaf. Use a dead, dry leaf so that it will float. Position yourself above the trout lie and pay out leader and line to drift the leaf with the current to the position of the fish. Once you are in the right area, make a quick, sharp jerk to pull the hook free of the floating leaf and allow the fly to drop into the water in front of the trout.

179 "LAZY S" CAST

Water in the middle of a stream runs faster than water along the sides, creating a current that pulls on the fly line to create a belly in the line and drag the fly unnaturally. To prevent this and get a longer natural drift, make a "lazy S" cast.

To do this, make a normal cast, but use a longer length of line than necessary. On the final forward cast, wiggle the rod sideways to create S's in the line as it lands. These S's take longer to wash out in the fast center current, creating more time for the fly to drift naturally.

180 CONTROLLING THE "LAZY S" CAST

Once you get comfortable with it, there are ways to control the "lazy S" cast so that you can place the S's where you want in the line, to be washed out by the current and give you a longer drift. To make "S's" throughout the length of the cast, shake the rod through the entire final forward cast. To make S's at the end of the fly line and close to the fly, shake the rod at the beginning of the forward cast and then stop. You will get these curves in the line only on the front half of the line.

To make S's in the rear of the line, wait until the final cast is starting to straighten out and then make the side-to-side shakes to create slack in the line. Note that you can also control just how much slack you want by making either slight shakes for minimal curves, or hard side-to-side shakes for lots of curves across a fast current or for a longer drift.

181 SNAGS FROM DOWNSTREAM FISHING

To get unsnagged when you are hooked downstream, have a little patience. Allow slack and pay line out through the rod guides until you get a large belly in the line. This belly must extend downstream of the snag for this method to work. In many cases, the water resistance and pressure on the line belly is enough to pull the fly free.

If this does not happen automatically, wait until you get a large belly of line, stop paying out the line, hold it, and then jerk the rod strongly to the side. The result will pull on the line belly, which in turn creates downstream pressure on the fly to pull it free. It does not work all the time (nothing does) but it is a quick, easy fix for many snag situations.

182 SHAKING THE ROD TO FREE SNAGS

There are several ways to get flies off of snags. One is to shake the rod lightly and very rapidly. To do this, hold the rod high so that you have a direct line from the rod tip to the fly, with no line on the water. Then shake the rod rapidly, but not hard. You don't want to break the tippet or risk the rod. What you do want is to set up a series of rapid movements of the tippet connected to the fly to jerk the fly free.

183 SNAGS FROM SURFACE STRUCTURE

To get free when snagged on a surface rock or log, use a modified roll cast. Keep the line loose, since you do not want to drive the hook deeper into the snag. Then raise the rod or hold it at your side for a standard roll cast or side-armed roll cast. Usually, the side-armed roll cast is easier to make and more effective. Make the roll cast loosely and the rolling line will usually pull the fly backward and off the snag. If it does not come free, try again with a more forceful roll cast.

184 LEAF-HOOKED FLIES

If a fly catches on a tree leaf, you can often use your fly rod to retrieve it. For this, raise your fly rod and catch the fly by the hook with the tip-top of the rod. Then carefully pull the fly free, pulling straight on the fly rod to dislodge the fly from the leaf. Note: This can be dangerous to the rod if done incorrectly, or if you have to pull too hard. If you have a very expensive fly rod or if the fly catches on a twig instead of a leaf, you will be better off sacrificing the fly than risking the rod.

185 FISHING A FARM POND

If you are a right-handed fly caster, and fishing a farm pond from shore, work around the pond clockwise. If you are a left-handed caster, work counterclockwise. The reason is that you can keep the line closer and parallel to the bank, and hold your false casts up over the water rather than over brush or grass. You can work your flies or bug easier this way, since your rod hand will be closest to the water.

186 STRIKE INDICATOR

One way to use tandem rigs very effectively is to use a nymph on the end of the leader with a bushy dry fly about 18 inches (45.7 cm) up the leader. This dry fly can be on a dropper extension of the leader or tied to the end of the leader with an 18-inch length of tippet material connecting the nymph to the hook bend of the dry fly. This allows a fish to take either on top or down deep, and also allows the dry fly to serve as a strike indicator for the nymph.

Fly Fishing Only

CHAPTER 6 SALTWATER FLY FISHING

Reading Water, Locating Fish, Choosing Flies

187 SALTWATER FISH DANGERS

Many saltwater fish are more dangerous than freshwater fish. Dangers include teeth (barracuda, bluefish, and sharks), sharp gill plates (snook), crushers (drum, redfish, grouper), and spines (white perch, dolphin, cobia). Unless you know the species that you are catching, and know how to handle it, be especially careful of the teeth, crushers in the back of the throat, and sharp spines on any fish.

188 BIG-GAME FLY FISHING

Big-game fly fishermen after billfish use very heavy outfits to throw very large flies. Often these flies include a large foam head to keep the fly on the surface where the billfish expect it after being teased to the boat transom with a large billfish teaser. However, hard foam heads often cause the fly to slide right out of the fish's mouth without hooking it. Many anglers are now using soft foam heads made from foam similar to that used for upholstery.

This foam absorbs water and sinks in time, but the big advantage is that it collapses when hit, thus allowing the fly to slide into the corner of the fish's mouth for a positive hook-up. Also, you are only throwing these foam-head flies when you have a fish behind the boat, and not blind casting all day where the floatability of the fly and head might be of concern.

189 BOTTOM-FEEDING FISH

Bonefish, redfish, and other shallow-water bottom feeders leave puffs of mud as they scrounge along the bottom. These puffs of mud, or marl, are keys to fish being in the area. Just realize that they are often indicators of where the fish were, not always where they are now. Also, highly dispersed puffs indicate areas where fish have left, since the dispersion of silt can only occur over a period of time. If you see puffs of marl progressing in a given direction, cast your fly ahead of the most recent puff to intercept the fish, or look for other signs (tailing, flashes of their sides, nervous water, etc.) that indicate fish in the area.

190 SPOTTING SALTWATER FISH

Anglers sight-fish fly rod quarries. You can spot some fish, such as bonefish, redfish, and permit, by their tails above water as they root along the bottom in shallow water. Tarpon roll on the surface, completely different from the typical moving dorsal fin of cruising sharks. You can find stripers and bluefish breaking on the surface taking bait, while you can sometimes see reef fish while they work around coral and flash in the water.

191 SPOTTING BIRDS THAT SIGNAL FISH

Gulls, pelicans, and terns are often great "bird dogs" to find fish. Use binoculars to spot them and check what they are doing. Experts consider 8X50 binoculars as the best for this. Birds signal fish activity as follows: Randomly flying birds or birds sitting on the water mean no fish. Hovering birds in a given area, yet not diving, are usually signaling deep fish or bait—neither bird nor fly can reach it. Birds actively diving are seeking bait that game fish (such as stripers, bluefish, sea trout, and similar inshore species) drove to the surface.

192 FLY FISHING UNDER DIVING BIRDS

To fish effectively under diving birds in saltwater situations, modify your casting slightly. First, make short casts that get to the fish without casting through a flock of birds. Second, with due care for others on the boat, make side casts that keep the line, leader, and fly close to the water surface to minimize high casts that might catch birds. Once you cast, lower the rod tip so that the line falls rapidly to avoid bird contact. If a bird follows your fly, allow it to sink or jerk it rapidly to keep from hooking the bird.

193 TIDES

Most saltwater fish move and feed more on a moving tide. A falling tide concentrates game fish at creek mouths and inlets where bait tumbles off of a flat or out of a marsh. Incoming tides concentrate fish around buoys, jetties, and other structure where they can ambush bait at high tide. Few fish move or eat on still water when the tide is dead high or low.

194 POPPING AND SWAPPING

One way to catch wide-roaming fish when fly fishing from a boat is a "popping and swapping" method that is ideal for stripers, bluefish, and many tropical reef fishes. To do this, carry a large spinning outfit rigged with a chugger from which you have removed the hooks. Then one angler in the boat (or the guide) can cast and work the lure to attract fish and pull them within fly casting distance.

With the fish within casting distance, the fly caster (already rigged and prepared, of course) casts a similarly large popper to land on top of, or close to, the spinning chugger. By immediately working the fly rod popper and allowing the spinning chugger to rest, the fish will switch to the moving popper for a quick hook-up. Use this same technique when fishing from shore to bring fish to within fly casting range.

195 CHUMMING IN SALTWATER

One of the best ways to catch saltwater fish on a fly is by chumming. To do this, anchor a boat and then release a chum slick of ground baitfish and fish oil. Another alternative is to drift over a reef and suspend a chum bag off the bottom to attract fish to your deep-fished fly. There are lots of different chums available, including any ground-up mix of baitfish, clams, shrimp, and the like; cat food, prepared bagged or frozen chum, chum fish oil, etc. Often you can combine these to make a long-lasting chum. Just make sure that you grind any homemade chum fine, since the purpose of chum is to attract fish with scent, not to feed them.

196 WADING IN SALTWATER

Stingrays often hide in the sand, where they remain camouflaged. On tropical flats when you are wading for bonefish or permit, this can be a real danger if you step on one. To guard against this, slide your feet along the bottom rather than taking steps to lift your foot from the bottom. Sliding your foot will cause any stingray to scurry away without stabbing you.

CHAPTER 7 FLY FISHING FROM BOATS

Tactics for Anchors, Drifting, Line Tangles

197 CASTING FROM A BOAT

In a lot of fly fishing situations, there is an angler at each end of the boat, often with a guide on a poling platform at one end. A line drawn through those two or three people is usually on the boat axis. For this reason, never cast along the axis of the boat for fear of hooking your partner or the boat guide.

Except for unexpected fish that appear off the bow or stern, guides will position the boat so that the fish or casting targets are to the side where both anglers can get a shot at them. The exception to the above occurs when you have to position the boat in the direction of the cast, because of tide or currents. For these situations, check with your buddy or the guide first, make sure that they duck or are out of the way, and only then make your cast. Each time you do this, check first and warn others in the boat of your intentions.

198 CASTING DISTANCE

If you are boat fishing with a buddy who is new to fly fishing and who can't cast more than about 40 feet (12.2 m), it does no good to position the boat 60 feet (18.3 m) away when it is his or her turn to cast. He can't reach the fish and his attempts will only result in poor casts and frustration. If necessary for shallow-water fish, stay as low as possible with both of you crouching to reduce visibility to the fish. In most cases, it is best to stay as far as possible from a casting target, shoreline, points, structure, or feeding fish, provided that you can comfortably reach the fish and get a fly to them accurately.

199 DUMMY CASTS

When boat sight-fishing, strip off all the line you need and then make a cast before you start searching for fish. Then strip the line back in. If you don't take this step, the line that you cast will be underneath the line just stripped from the reel and may cause a tangle or delay when you are ready to make a critical cast to a fish.

200 PUSH TO BREAKING FISH

If you run your boat right up to a school of breaking stripers in coastal waters, the engine noise might put them down. To prevent this, consider the tide and/or wind. Stop the engine a little more than a cast length away from the school. Then let the wind or tide push your boat into the fish so that you can cast to them easily and effectively. Fished this way, the fish will not be aware of your boat or presence as they would if you were to motor into the school of fish.

201 DRAG ANCHORS

When fly fishing a shallow river in a small boat, it is best to drift downstream, casting to each likely fishing spot. To slow the drift and control the boat, use a drag anchor that will not stop the boat, but which will slow the drift.

To do this, use a length of rope and 3 feet (0.9 m) of heavy chain to make a total length just short of the length of your boat. Connect the chain to the rope with a thimble and rope clamps. Use the same method at the other end of the rope to add a snap link that you can attach (when desired) to the boat bow eye or front handle.

The boat will drift stern first, and two fly casters can fish—one to each side of the boat and at right angles to the boat axis.

With this system, you can put out all or enough of the rope to slow the drift for effective fishing, while preventing the boat from turning like a top in the current. Also, if you use an outboard engine, you can leave the drag anchor out when running the boat. The short rope will never allow the prop to catch the chain.

Do not do this if you have a lot of shelf rock or other obstructions in the river. Shelf rock, or any rock or structure that can catch a chain link, makes for an unsafe boating situation.

202 HOOKED FISH UNDER THE BOAT

If the water is deep enough, hooked fish often dive under the boat or swim under the boat to the opposite side. This can happen with any fish, but is particularly common with saltwater species. Stick the rod straight down into the water far enough for the line to clear the rough bottom and to prevent rod breakage. On a large charter boat, this might mean extending the rod into the water up to the grip. Take special care in shallow water that you do not stab the rod into the bottom and break it.

If you can't coax the fish back to your side of the boat, keep the rod tip under the water and work around to the opposite side of the boat to where you can lift the rod and resume fighting the fish. Walk the rod around the bow or stern in doing this, whichever end is easiest, and with less possibility of tangling line. If anchored from the bow, you will have to take the rod around the stern and work the line under the engine prop.

203 FIGURE-EIGHT BOAT RETRIEVE

One trick that pike and muskie anglers use to attract strikes from a following fish is to work the lure (often a big spoon) in several large figure-eight patterns next to the boat. This technique often infuriates pike or muskie into striking. You can do the same thing with a fly, working it in a figure-eight pattern close to the boat before you pick up the line for the next cast.

This requires several things, only applicable to pike and muskie fishing. One is that you retrieve the fly all the way to the boat to catch the followers that often occur with these species. The second is that you use a short leader—about 4 feet (1.2 m)—so that you have the end of the fly line outside of the tip-top when making these figure-eight patterns with your rod. This prevents tangles and breaks when a fish hits, which might occur if the line/leader connection were in the guides. The third is to use a 9-foot (2.7-meter) or longer fly rod to give you the leverage to work the fly in these "infinity" patterns. The fourth is that you have the line in a stripping basket or neatly coiled to prevent any tangles that can cause a break-off when the pike makes a run after striking.

204 LINE-STRIPPING BASKETS, TIP ONE

Capt. Norm Bartlett has come up with an easy-to-make and easy-to-use boat line stripper, similar to the high-priced stripping baskets sold for the purpose. Norm buys a tall, perforated laundry basket from a discount store, adds a few bricks to the bottom for weight, and covers the bricks with indoor/outdoor carpeting to protect the fly line. These are easy to store (you might want two for two fly casters on a typical flats or center-console boat) and work well to keep line from blowing around the boat deck. Place them in the boat where needed and strip line into the tall, open-weave basket. Since these have a slight taper to them, you can store them by slipping one into the other.

205 LINE-STRIPPING BASKETS, TIP TWO

Another easy-to-use and inexpensive boat line stripper is the fold-up spring-style leaf buckets sold in home and garden supply stores. These fold flat for storage and open instantly for use. Most are 18 inches (45.7 cm) in diameter and 24 inches (61 cm) high when in use. Manufacturers also sell these as foldable laundry baskets, so you can find them in household supplies or domestics in a general or department store.

206 FISHING BAREFOOT

A big problem when boat fishing without a stripping basket is that you can step on the line on the casting deck, ruining a cast or breaking off a running fish. To prevent this, some anglers fish barefoot so that they can feel the line underfoot and clear the line before or during a cast, and when a hooked fish starts to make a run. If you do fish barefoot, just make sure to use a good sunscreen on your feet to prevent a painful burn.

207 CLOTHING

If fishing from a boat, wear only shirts with button-down collars. The reason is that in shirts without button-down collars, the collars can flap and abrade your face on a long run to the fishing grounds, or during high winds on any fishing trip.

Also remember to remove all items from your shirt or jacket top pockets and place them in storage on the boat or in a gear bag for safekeeping. When fishing on a boat, you might have to lean over the gunwale to land or release a fish taken on a light tippet. Or you might want to rinse your hands after catching a fish and before handling a camera to take a photo. In any of these tasks, you can easily lose the contents of a shirt pocket—pens, pencils, notepads, pocket cameras, cell phones. Just as bad, even if you do not lose them, you can break these items as you lean your chest against the inside of a gunwale to unhook a fish or help release it.

208 PREVENTING LINE TANGLES

To prevent line tangles when fishing from a cluttered boat, follow these tips. Carry a 6- to 8-foot square (1.8- to 2.4-meter) net with about a one- to two-inch mesh. Add pinch-on sinkers to the corners and center the rim of the net, then throw this net over any tackle where you are standing to fish. You can stand on the net and strip out line and the line will not get caught on tackle box handles, reel handles, lures, or other equipment. You can still see and use the covered tackle, but the net protects the line and leader from tangles.

Even on cleared decks, line can get tangled with shoe laces. One way to prevent this is to use slip-on water shoes that lack laces. Just be sure to wear socks to prevent your feet and ankles from getting sun burned. If wading a saltwater flat, these shoes might even provide some protection, although they will lack any ankle support.

If wearing boat or wading shoes with laces, use tape to cover the laces to prevent fly lines from getting caught in them. Duct tape works well and peels off cleanly at the end of the day.

Fly rod guru Lefty Kreh suggests replacing laces in wading and boat shoes with elastic cord, such as is available from sewing supply stores. Run the cord through the lace holes, knot at the top, and tie off with a square knot. Seal the knot with flexible glue. This makes it easy to open the shoe to put it on, keeps the shoe in place, and does not have any tied knots or laces to tangle fly lines.

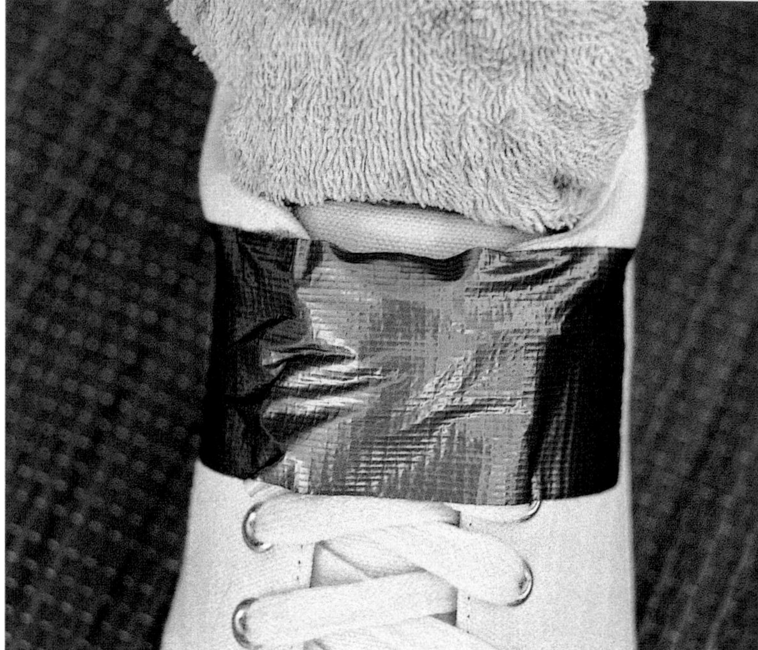

209 COVERING CLEATS

When fly fishing from boats for warm-water and saltwater species, cleats often catch fly lines. While some newer boats have retractable cleats to prevent this, most boats do not. To prevent cleats from catching fly lines, cover them completely with duct tape. This will prevent line tangles, but you can also easily remove the tape once the fishing day is over.

210 ELECTRIC MOTOR CONTROLS

Electric motors are used more and more on all boats—not just bass boats where their use originated. Saltwater flats and center-console fly fishing boats use long-shaft styles. To prevent fly lines from tangling up in the foot controls, throw a large towel over the controls. Sometimes it helps to moisten the towel to prevent it from blowing around. You can still use your foot to control speed and direction, but the fly line won't catch in the control mechanisms.

211 BOAT LEADER BOX

While you want a leader wallet for wading, a leader box is best for a boat. These are available commercially, but a small inexpensive one can be made from a Spirit River All Around Dispenser that has six separate compartments, each with a spool and each compartment with a slot for the leader. These are designed for fly-tying materials, but in years of tests, they work equally well for leader material. Use two rubber bands to further secure the snap lid, and one rubber band around the front to hold the leader ends. I carry two of them—one for leader materials in sizes of 2-, 4-, 6-, 8-, 10-, and 12-pound-test (0.9-, 1.8-, 2.7-, 3.6-, 4.5-, and 5.4-kg); the second for heavier leader material in sizes 15-, 20-, 25-, 40-, and 50-pound-test (6.8-, 9.1-, 11.3-, 18.1-, and 22.7-kg).

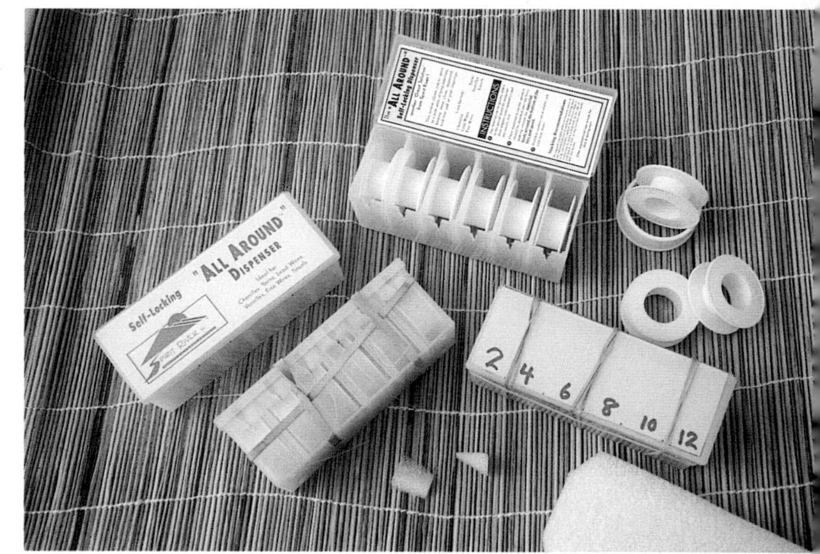

212 PROTECTING RODS, TIP ONE

Capt. Norm Bartlett, inventor that he is, has a simple solution for protecting rods on his center-console boat. He uses closed-cell foam pipe insulation with a large inside diameter. This is usually sold in 4-foot (1.2-meter) lengths, four to a pack. This makes an ideal sleeve or soft case for a rod, ready rigged down to the fly, but broken down into its two sections. You can fold the two sections over with the line or leader, secure the ends with half of a pipe cleaner or twist tie, and slip the two sections into the case to protect the rod down to the handle.

To keep the pipe insulation from coming apart (they are partly split to be separated to fit over pipe), use a soft glue, such as Marine Goop or Pliobond, to seal the longitudinal seam. You can also glue two pieces together, end to end, make longer cases for longer rods, and then cut to length.

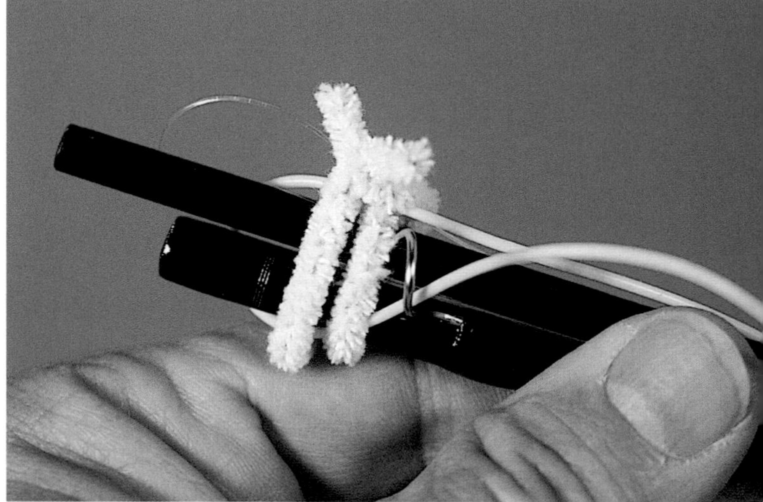

213 PROTECTING RODS, TIP TWO

One way to store a ready-rigged rod in a hard case is to buy a length of 2-inch-diameter (5-cm) PVC pipe. Buy thin-wall PVC pipe, cut to length for your rod, about 56 inches (1.4 m) for a 9-foot (2.7-m) rod. Use a hacksaw to cut a long notch in one end into which the reel can slide. Smooth this notch with sandpaper and drill two small holes on each side at the end. Add a knotted loop of bungee cord through the holes. Rig the rod ready to fish right down to the fly, and then break down the rod into two pieces. Add half a pipe cleaner wrapped around the ferrule end to contain the rod sections, line, and leader, and slide into the case, with the notch providing room for the reel. Use the short loop of bungee cord around the end to keep the rod from sliding out. The rod is completely protected this way, yet ready to use in seconds by removing from the case, pulling off the pipe cleaner, ferruling the rod, and casting.

214 PVC FLY ROD HOLDERS

Fly rods are difficult to store in most small boats. One way to make simple protective holders for them is with lengths of thin-wall 2-inch (5-cm) PVC pipe, secured alongside the gunwale of the boat, with a flat support of aluminum strapping or wood to support the grip. Add bungee cord to the handle support to hold the rod grip in place while running the boat. Several of these added to any boat allow you to store rods in the same way that a sword is held in a sheath. To flare the ends of the PVC to keep from damaging guides, heat the end of the PVC pipe with a torch (do not burn it) and taper it by flaring it on a tapered glass soda bottle. Allow the pipe to cool while on the bottle so that the plastic memory does not return it to a straight pipe.

215 PROTECTING REELS

One quick and simple way to protect a reel in a boat is to use an old sock. The neoprene or cloth case that usually comes with better reels is ideal, but if you don't want to risk damage to the case, the sock protects the reel, keeps the metal from damaging the gel coat on the boat, and also lessens any fish-scaring noise of the reel hitting the boat. Thick socks are best for this.

216 FLY BOXES AND BAGS

Large flies, such as those used for bass, pike, and saltwater fishing, will not fit into standard fly boxes. There are several good options for these when boat fishing. One is to use the clear-front, nylon-zippered pencil cases that have grommets for fitting into a three-ring school notebook. You can easily see the case contents, and even color-code these bags if you like, since a half dozen colors are available. To store them, get a sturdy, zippered, three-ring notebook, or store them in a ringed spinnerbait case, such as made by Tackle Logic, Shimano, and others. These include thin zipper-lock envelopes (although they are very lightweight) and can easily hold a dozen or more of the nylon pencil cases.

Another alternative is to use one of the large cases that have smaller, clear-vinyl front-zippered compartments designed to hold hardware lures (jigs, spinnerbaits, buzzbaits, and the like).

CHAPTER 8 CARE AND CLEANUP

Keeping Equipment in Prime Condition

217 GUIDE DAMAGE

An easy way to check for a rough guide is to run a woman's stocking through the guide to see if the stocking will catch on any rough areas. Other products that also work include a length of fine floss or a cotton ball. On both of these, strands of fibers will come off on rough or frayed edges. These methods work for both snake guides and stripping guides.

Once you find a damaged guide, replace it with a new guide or take it to your fly shop to have it repaired. If it is not replaced, repeated fly casting can quickly ruin your expensive fly line.

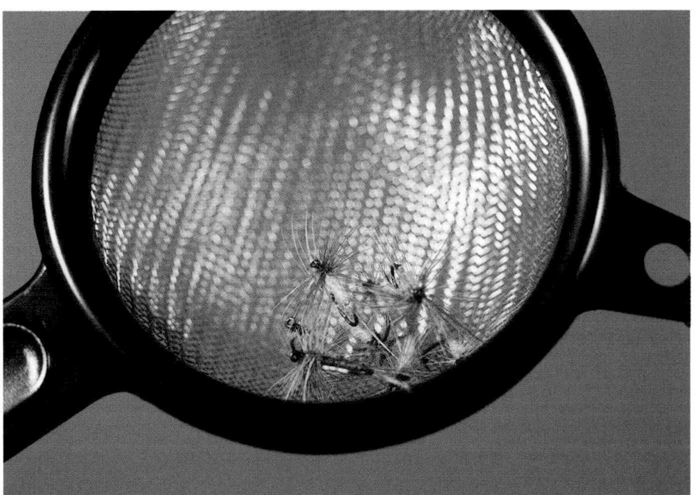

218 STEAMED FLIES

By the end of your fishing season, trout flies can become pretty ratty-looking and bedraggled from catching fish. The same thing can happen with any flies. To spruce them up for the next season, steam them with a teakettle. This is an old trick, often suggesting steaming flies one at a time, holding them with tweezers. To make this a simple and quick operation, put a number of flies in a tea strainer and steam them together. Just make sure that you allow all of the flies to dry thoroughly before returning them to their boxes.

219 STORING FLY RODS

If storing fly rods in their cases, you must make sure that the rod and the inside of the case are completely dry before casing the rod and capping the case. If unsure, case the rod and leave the cap off for moisture to dissipate. Failure to do this may result in a cased wet rod developing bubbles or the finish peeling when removed for fishing the following season. Another way to store a lot of rods is to make a wall rack where you can store them horizontally on shelves, or on overhead racks where they are out of the way and protected, yet easily available.

For a ceiling rack, make a series of looped cords on a board or lathing strip, stapling a 6-inch (15.2-cm) length of cord every 2 inches (5 cm) to make a series of loops. On a second lathing board, add a series of 1-inch (2.5-cm) cup hooks, again every 2 inches (5 cm). Then nail the boards up in the rafters. Place the two boards parallel and far enough apart so that the handle of the rod and the butt end of the tip section rest in the loop and the cup hook holds the rod ends about two-thirds up the length. Break down the rod to support all sections this way. If you have rods of different lengths (or two-, three-, and four-piece rods), adjust the two boards at an angle to each other so that they are close together at one end for short rod sections, and farther apart at the other end for longer rods and rod sections.

> "There is no use in your walking five miles to fish when you can depend on being just as unsuccessful near home."
>
> —*Mark Twain (1835–1910)*

220 CLEANING FLY REELS

Care of your tackle requires washing that tackle after each trip, particularly when fishing in scummy or algae-filled water or around saltwater. You also have to lubricate the reel to keep it running smoothly. To keep the reel corrosion-free, remove the line annually, clean the reel thoroughly, and spray the reel with a demoisturizer, such as WD-40. This will protect the reel on future trips.

To clean your fly reel, disassemble it according to the manufacturer's instructions. In most cases, this involves nothing more than springing a lever on the axle shaft to remove the spool. If the reel is a simple click-and-pawl type, add a little grease to each tooth of the gearing. If the reel has other mechanical parts, oil or grease them according to the manufacturer's instructions. If you are unsure of how to do any of this, contact the manufacturer (write, call, or e-mail) or take the reel to a reliable fly shop for service.

You can store fly reels in their cases, provided that the cases are dry and clean and do not have any salt residue on or in them from saltwater trips. Be particularly careful when storing saltwater reels in leather cases, as the leather absorbs and holds corrosive salt. Another method of storing reels is to hang the reels from hooks in perforated boards, separating the reels by line size for easy selection when you go fishing.

221 WASHING REELS AND LINE

To wash fly reels, fill a sink with warm water, add a little dish detergent, and allow the reels to soak for a short time. Use an old soft-bristle toothbrush to scrub around the handles, portholes in the side plates and spool, and around the reel foot. Once the reel is clean, rinse it thoroughly and place on a towel to dry. Turn the reel over periodically to allow all water to drain. Store the reel for the next trip once it's completely dry.

Most fly lines come with a little pad of fly line cleaner and instructions for cleaning your fly line. If you have lost this, you can use any fly line cleaner, or get a small packet of line cleaner from your local fly shop. First stretch the line between two points, almost like a clothesline, wrapping (not tying) the two ends so as to not damage the line. Then use the cleaner on a pad or clean rag to rub the line and remove any dirt or grime. Do this several times if necessary, to remove all dirt.

Once the line is clean, "dress" it with a line conditioner to keep it slick and easy to cast. More and more companies are now making both the cleaner and dressing in one substance, so that you can accomplish cleaning and dressing with one or two wipes of the line. Once you clean and dress the line, make sure that you buff it with a dry, clean rag to remove any excess dressing and cleaner. In all cases, make sure that you do not allow other materials (demoisturizers, insect repellents, sunscreen, etc.) to come in contact with the line, as they might harm it.

222 WASHING FLY RODS

The easiest way to wash fly rods is to take them in the shower with you at the end of a fishing trip. Otherwise, wash them with a garden hose, using a sudsy wash cloth or rag to remove all grime and salt (if fished in saltwater), and use a discarded toothbrush to clean around the reel seat hoods, guide feet, and cork grip. Rinse thoroughly and allow the rod to dry. Complete, thorough drying is a must if you are going to store the rod in a closed rod tube.

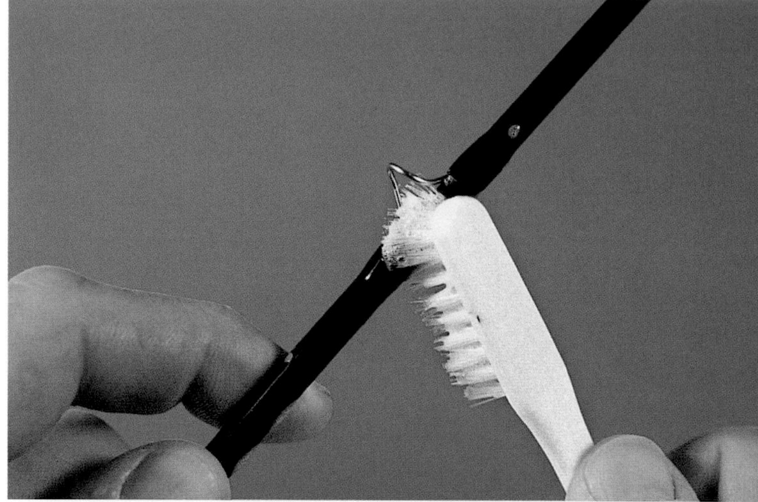

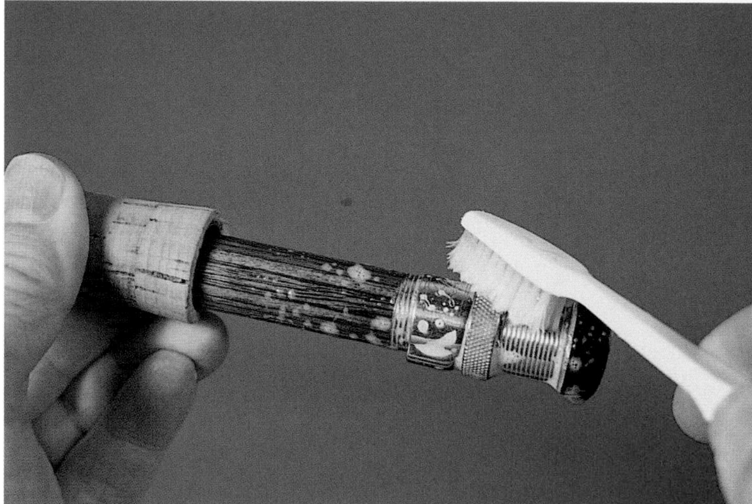

223 LUBRICATING FERRULES

Candle wax is ideal for lubricating and sealing ferrules on graphite-to-graphite ferrules found on virtually all current rods. Periodically, coat the male end of the ferrule with a candle stub to protect the ferrule. This will make it easy to seat and hold firmly. It also makes it easier to dismantle each time. Do not do this if you are using a metal-ferruled split-bamboo fly rod.

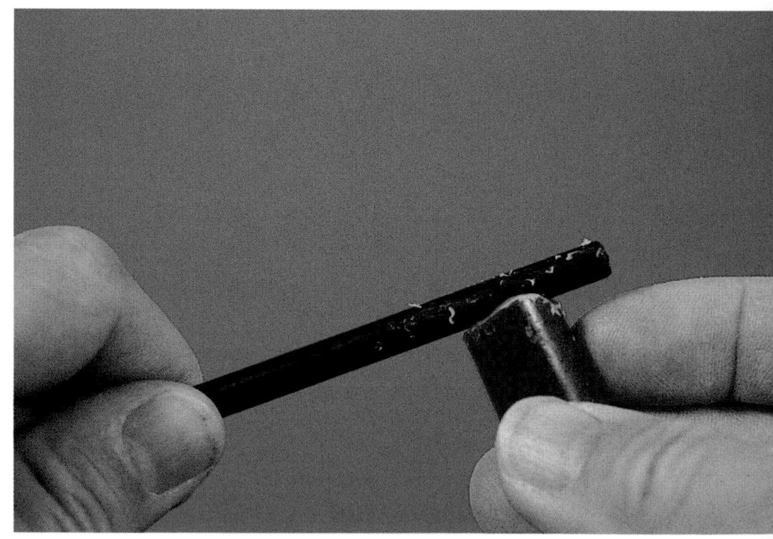

224 LUBRICATING METAL FERRULES

If you have a split-bamboo fly rod that has metal ferrules, you should still lubricate the ferrule to make joining and separating easy. The easiest way to do this is to rub the male ferrule lightly against the corner between your nose and your cheek. This area around your nose always has a little oil, which is just enough to lubricate the ferrule without making it so oily that it gets stuck. Never add anything such as 3-in-One oil or any other general oil to the male ferrule—you might not be able to get the rod sections apart with the suction created after joining the two ends.

> "Just as in cooking there's no such thing as a little garlic, in fishing there's no such thing as a little drag."
>
> —*H. G. Tapply,* The Sportsman's Notebook *(1964)*

225 BACKING OFF THE DRAG

Most drags designed to slow the run of fish consist of one or more hard and soft washers, similar to the brake pads and rotors on your vehicle brakes. These "soft" washers may be graphite, cork, plastic synthetics, or similar materials or combinations. To keep these washers from becoming compressed and failing the next time, back off the drag at the end of each fishing day.

226 DRYING HIP BOOTS AND WADERS

It is important to dry out your hip boots or waders after each trip. Sweat buildup can, in time, rot out the inner lining. Dry them by hanging them up and inserting a vacuum hose on "blow" into each leg until the boots dry. You can also use a hair dryer, but make sure that the hair dryer is on the "cool" or "blow only" setting, not forcing heat into the boot.

You can also fold the boots open to air-dry them. To keep the boot leg open to dry, use an insert, such as the soft-foam swimming floats that are sold each summer. Do not use things such as a "tube" of wire hardware cloth, a roll of sheet metal, or a cut length of PVC tubing, since any of these might have a wire end or ragged edge that could cut the boot.

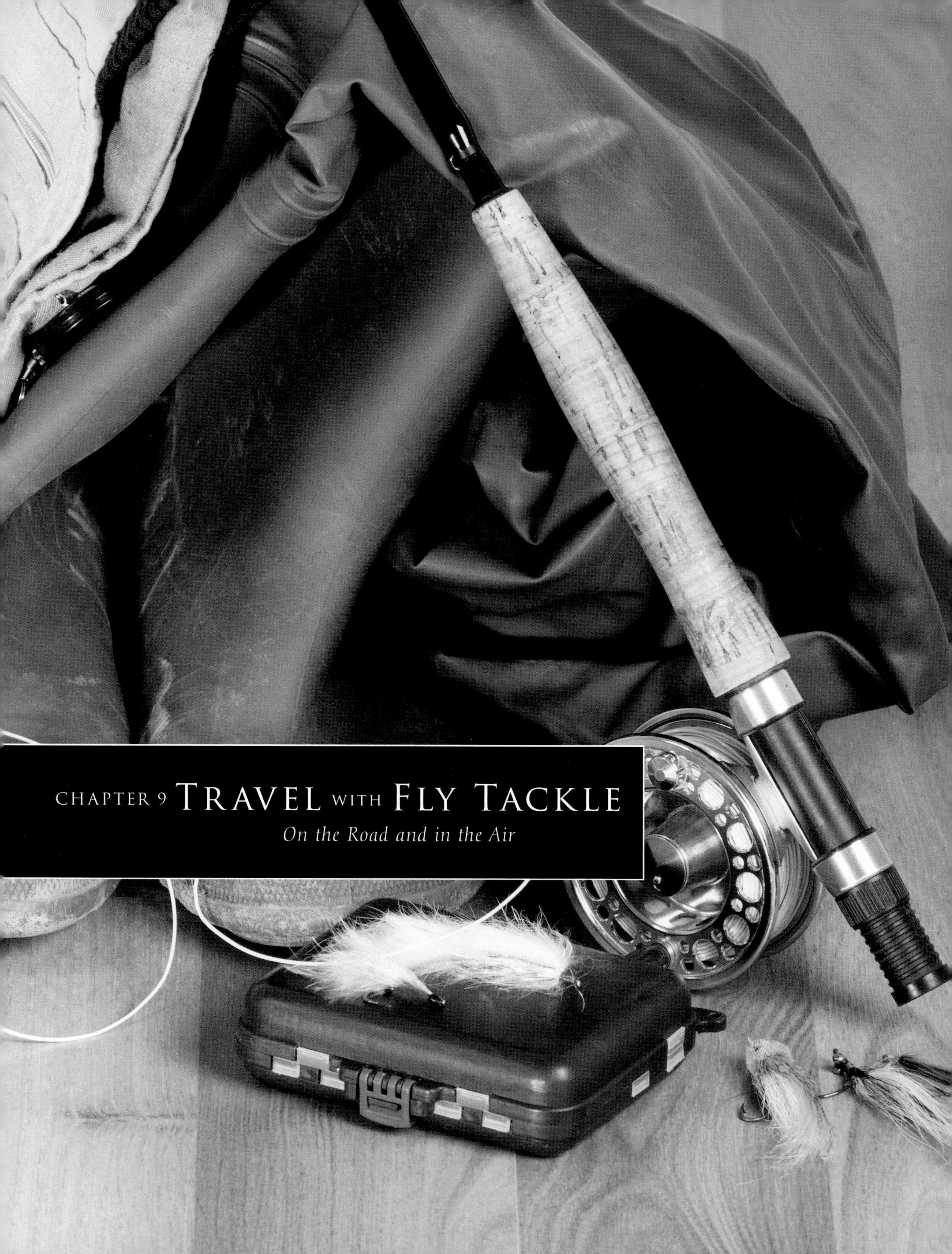

CHAPTER 9 TRAVEL WITH FLY TACKLE

On the Road and in the Air

227 TRAVEL BOOT-FOOT WADERS

Air travel is becoming increasingly difficult and increasingly confining in the amount of luggage allowed as baggage. For any travel, consider lightweight, travel-style boot-foot waders. They are lighter to carry, less cumbersome to use than the separate stocking-foot and brogue waders, and easier to pack. If fishing in a cold climate, you can insulate them by adding flannel pajama bottoms, long johns, or sweatpants under your pants.

228 ROLLING DUFFLE BAGS

Today manufacturers make many duffle bags long enough to carry travel rods. They have stiff bottoms and rollers so that you can drag them around without damage. These are ideal for travel, since you can pack your travel rods in the case and lessen the possibility of a separate rod case going astray. Just make sure that you have a long enough duffle and that the zipper opening allows you to pack the rods. For 9-foot (2.7-m) four-piece rods, you need an opening to take 29- to 30-inch (73.7- to 76.2-cm) rod cases, and for three-piece rods, you need an opening to take 39- to 40-inch (99.1- to 101.6-cm) rod cases.

> "I fish all the time when I'm at home; so when I get a chance to go on vacation, I make sure I get in plenty of fishing."
>
> —*Thomas McGuane, "Fishing the Big Hole,"* An Outside Chance *(1990)*

229 DUFFLE BAG HANDLES

Duffle bags are ideal for carrying a lot of fishing gear on trips. Most of them have two strap handles, both of which you have to hold to carry the duffle. Unfortunately, many baggage handlers for airlines, rail, and bus lines (or even your friends unloading a vehicle) might grab just one handle and tear the handle from the heavy bag. To prevent this, buy one or two screw-type chain links, called "quick links" in hardware stores. Use these to attach the two handles. That way, even if a baggage handler grabs only one strap, the two straps can't separate to tear the bag. These links also make it easy for TSA personnel to remove and open the bag for inspection.

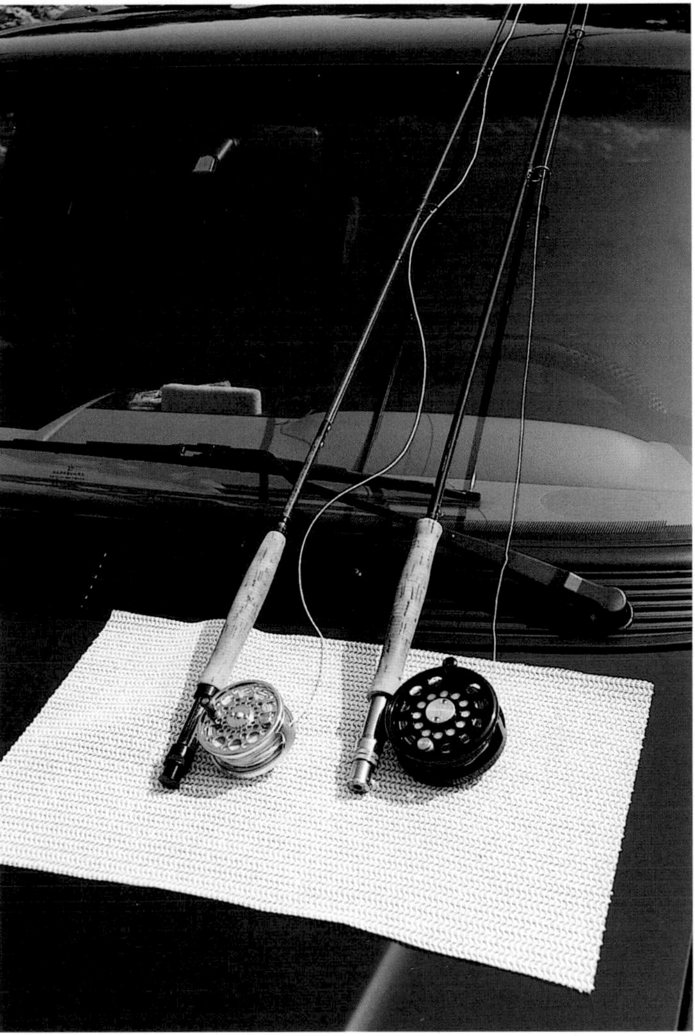

230 FLY TACKLE AND CARS

Many anglers, returning to the car after a day of fishing, place their fly rods on top of the car for safe keeping while loading other gear or removing boots or waders. Don't do it—too often anglers drive off with the rods still on the roof, with obvious disastrous results.

The right way to do this and protect the rods is to lay the rods on top of the car, reel forward, with a long loop of line hanging over the driver's side of the windshield. That way the rod is protected and you will easily notice the loop of line if you forget to put the rods away. This works with all colors of fly lines, in any background situation.

An alternative method of protecting rods is to carry with you a small square (12 by 12 inches or larger) of rubberized sheeting, such as is used in kitchen cabinets. Place this on the hood of the car, on the driver's side, and place your assembled rod reel forward, on the mat. Allow the rod to extend over the roof of the car in front of the driver's side. The rubberized sheet protects both the car hood and the reel finish from damage and also protects against any slipping. The mat sheet rolls up easily and can be stored in a glove compartment of the car.

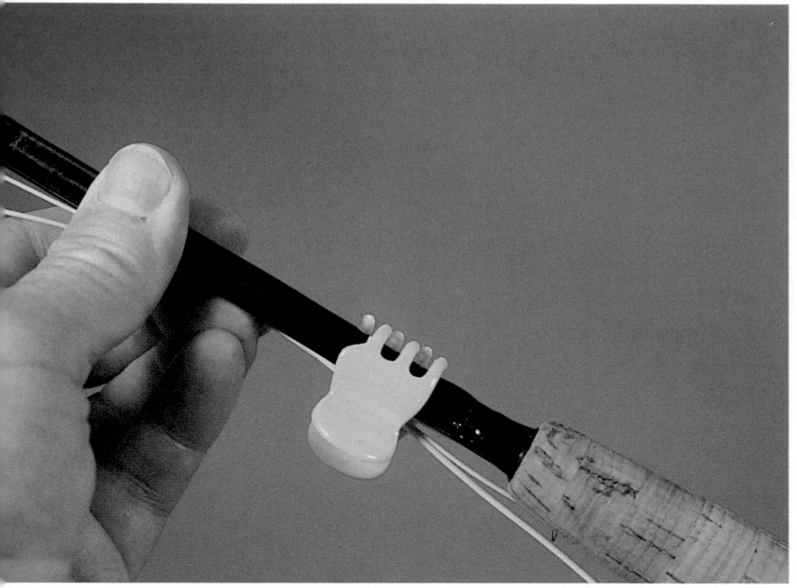

231 ROD STORAGE IN VEHICLES

The best way to travel with rods in a car is to keep them in their rod tubes, storing them carefully in the trunk or on the back seat. If you do not use, or do not have, rod tubes, bundle the rods together and store them on top of other gear so that they are not broken.

If moving while fishing, reel in excess line, break down the rods into two sections, and lay carefully on top of other gear. Many anglers break down rigged two-piece rods into two sections for travel in cars and to carry in boats. Usually these rods are completely rigged down to the fly and ready to cast once reassembled.

Capt. Norm Bartlett came up with a neat way to keep the two sections together to reduce tangles and possible damage. He uses the small spring-type hair clips to hold the rod parts together. He uses two of these, one on each end of the rod (but above the grip). These go on and come off instantly and are easy to use. They are also available in a variety of sizes to fit your individual needs. Get a bright color so they won't get lost.

Other possibilities are to use a rubber band, plastic bag twist ties, or pipe cleaner to hold the sections and the line together to make it easy to assemble once at a new fishing spot. Another alternative is to use one of the car-top rack systems that are available now.

232 TRAVEL RODS

Even though they are a little more expensive and less readily available than standard two-piece rods, more and more fly anglers are buying their rods in three- or four-piece travel styles. This makes packing and storing rods easier, particularly when traveling by plane to distant fishing locations. If you travel a lot to fish, consider this, or consider adding a stock of travel rods to your tackle inventory.

233 TRAVEL NIGHT LIGHT

Often traveling fly anglers find themselves in a variety of different motels or fishing lodges. And sometimes you have to get up at night to go to the bathroom. Carry a small night light in your toiletry kit and plug it into a bathroom socket. To keep from leaving it on the last morning of your trip, write out the word "LIGHT" on a business card and place it on the sink counter. You are sure to see it and grab the light before you leave in the morning.

234 FIELD KITS

If going on a long trip or international fishing expedition, consider carrying a field emergency kit. You will need only one for your party. You can customize such a kit for your needs. My kit fits into a six-compartment lure box and contains the following:

- small screwdriver kit;
- small-handled socket wrench set;
- cigarette lighter;
- spare scissors;
- small pocket flashlight with fresh batteries;
- rubber bands;
- candle stub (for lubricating rod ferrules, to use as a light, or to start an emergency fire);
- small wire cutters;
- small pocket folding tool kit;
- extension butts for rods;
- nail clipper;
- spare folding pocketknife;
- spare hook hone/file;
- pipe cleaners (for securing rod sections and cleaning small parts).

Make up your own field kit as desired, based on your needs and fishing tackle, using the above as a guide. If flying, realize that even with checked baggage, you might have to remove some items, such as the cigarette lighter. Check with the airline first.

235 AIRLINE SECURITY AND FISHING TACKLE

With recent terrorist threats and security scares, airport security has gotten much tighter, and it has created challenges for traveling with fly tackle. The simplest solution is to not carry on any fishing tackle. Also, consider the following suggestions:

- Pack all gear in suitcases or duffle bags. Rolling duffle bags are ideal for this, provided that they are the long style that will hold a rod case (or cases) for a 3- or 4-piece 9-foot (2.7-meter) fly rod.
- Pack reels in padded reel bags.
- If you do not have protective reel bags, use a thick sock or layer of underwear.
- Layer fly boxes and other accessories so that they are padded by clothing.
- Fold travel waders, boot-foot-style or stocking-style (your choice), and place them at one end of the duffle bag for extra padding and protection.
- Empty your fishing vest to make it simpler and less bulky to pack, and store at the other end of the duffle bag.
- Store items such as fishing knives, pliers, hook hones, disgorgers, hemostats, gaffs, thermometers, screwdrivers, wading staffs, etc., in one place or preferably in one bag or container so that inspecting federal Transportation Security Administration (TSA) security agents can find these items.
- Similarly, keep all fly boxes in one area so that agents can find and check the hook contents of the boxes.
- Store all liquids, such as fly floatants, leader sinks, insect lotions and sprays, sunscreen, etc., in two (one inside the other) zipper-seal plastic bags for safekeeping. Use sealed bags to prevent damage to luggage contents should one of the items leak.

236 CUSTOMS SLIPS

If you buy products outside of the country, you may only bring back a certain dollar value before officials charge a tariff. Since many cameras, video cameras, laptops, electronics, and even some fishing tackle is made in other countries, it pays to get Customs slips of all this equipment before leaving the country. Take all your foreign-made equipment to the nearest Customs office and fill out the paperwork for each piece of equipment.

Each slip requires that you supply your name, address, and the name and serial number of each piece of equipment. Usually, you can list up to about six pieces of equipment on each slip, depending upon how large you write. The Customs officers on duty will check the serial numbers on your slip against your equipment, and then mark each slip with an official Customs stamp. The good news is that once you do this, these slips are good for life. Just be sure to take all of them with you on any trip out of the country.

237 PHOTOCOPY YOUR PASSPORT

If traveling to a foreign country, make one or two photocopies of your passport. That way, should your passport get lost or stolen you will at least have a copy of the front page with the passport number and other vital information for getting a new passport or help from embassies, Customs offices, or US consulate offices. Make sure that you keep all such copies safely secured, and in a different location than the location of your passport. Realize that this could change with Homeland Security regulations, so check first, and if not allowed for any reason, at least write down your passport number.

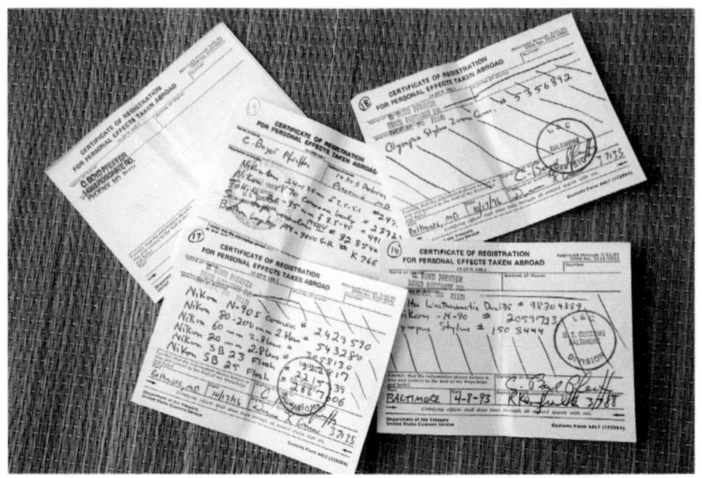

238 PHOTOCOPYING VALUABLES

If you are traveling, consider minimizing the number of credit cards that you carry to prevent problems should they be lost or stolen. Also, make a photocopy of all credit cards that you carry, making sure that the credit card numbers are visible. In addition, write down on this copy the US or international phone numbers for reporting lost or stolen credit cards to the credit card company to prevent fraudulent use. Be sure that you keep this list separate from your wallet, but in a safe place where thieves will not find it. In addition, consider photocopying any other cards that you might need while on your trip. Possibilities include health insurance cards, car registration, voter's registration cards, visas, etc.

239 CONTROLLING TRAVEL EXPENSES

If two or more of you are going on a fly fishing trip together, make it easy by pooling common expenses, such as tolls, gas, tips, shared motel rooms, and even meals if the meals for each are about the same cost. Appoint one person "treasurer" to pay all common expenses. Then each person adds to a kitty a set amount for paying these expenses. When the fund is low, each person adds more money to rebuild it. After the trip is over, redistribute the excess money to all. A nice touch, if traveling by car, is to leave in some extra money for the vehicle owner for an oil change, car wash, etc. Keep all the money and receipts for expenses in a bag. A child's zippered pencil case or similar sturdy bag is ideal for this.

PART 2

FLY TYING TIPS

CHAPTER 10 GETTING STARTED WITH FLY TYING

240 THE RIGHT LIGHT FOR FLY TYING

For good results, use bright light when tying flies. Good choices are fluorescent lights or the small strong halogen lights. These halogen lights can get hot so keep this in mind, especially for summer tying.

You can also use multiple lights to illustrate different parts of a fly for optimal tying results. These are most likely to eliminate shadows or distracting areas that can impair your ability to tie the perfect fly.

Today, you can also buy lights that are balanced for sunlight so that you can see your fly as you tie it in the exact same illumination as it will appear outdoors and to the fish.

241 PREVENTING EYE STRAIN WHILE TYING FLIES

There are several ways to prevent eye strain when tying flies. One way is to buy a background plate or easel from an art or office supply store. Most of these are clear plastic. Use a clip (banker's clip) to hold to it plain colored poster board or matte finish blotter boards. Change these as desired, and use colors that contrast with the fly you are tying for maximum visibility and ease of eye strain.

You can also do the same thing just by using colors that contrast with your fly. If tying dark flies, try a light background. When tying light colored flies, use a dark background. For colored flies, a medium blue background is often good.

An easy way to do all this is to cover your fly tying bench with a matte finish blotter board as for a desk and change colors as required for different flies. Non-glare matte finish blotter boards do not reflect light and are usually best for these applications.

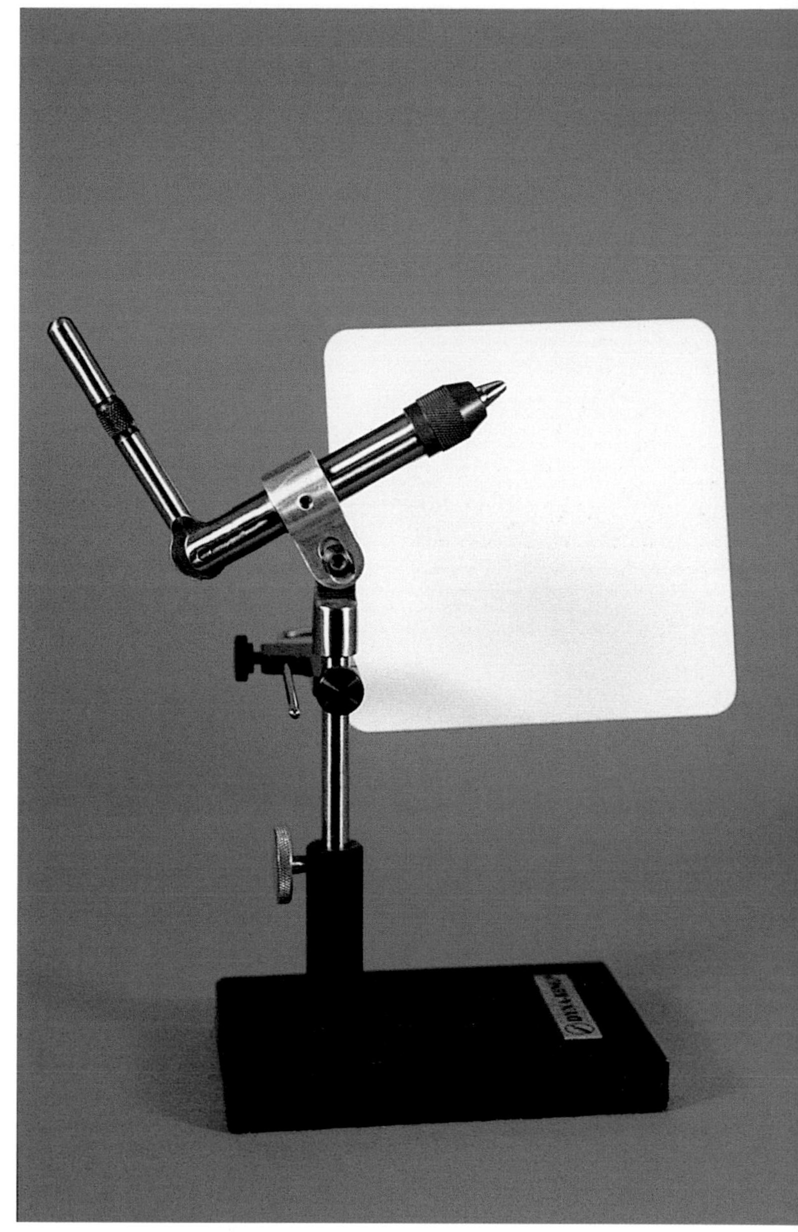

242 STACKER PROTECTION

One way to keep a stacker (hair evener) from harming your fly-tying bench is to glue a patch of rubber gasket material to the base. Cut out the rubber gasket material to the shape of the stacker base and glue it to the bottom. Gasket material is available anywhere auto supplies are sold.

Alternatives to the gasket material are the thin foams available in craft and art stores, and inner tube patches. Use any flexible glue such as Pliobond, Ultra Flex, or contact cement. You can also use a square of gasket material on your tying bench as a pounding surface on which to hit the stacker to even hair and fur.

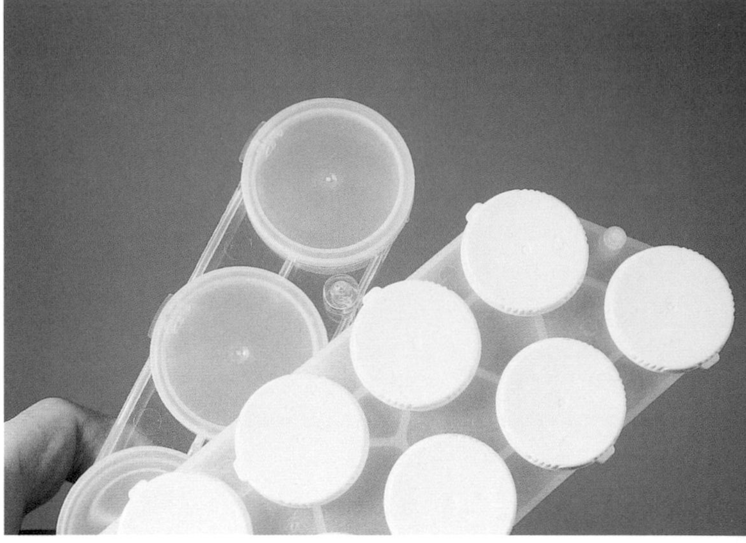

243 STORAGE

If you have trouble storing beads, check out the bins and containers at craft and art stores for this purpose. You can get racks of bins in several sizes, both as to the individual bin size and also the number of compartments that are in each rack. Most sell for only a few dollars and also allow stacking of the racks for those using a lot of beads in their tying.

244 BUYING YARN

If you tie lots of flies of one type and color, good body materials are available at any sewing, knitting, or craft shop. For the quantity that you get, the materials are far cheaper than similar materials from any fly shop. These shops carry yarn and other stranded materials in many sizes, materials, colors, and textures.

The one problem with these is that they are usually available only in large spools or skeins that would be more material than any flytier would ever use. One solution is to purchase materials with your fly-tying buddies, or a fly fishing/fly tying club, then divide the materials into manageable lengths and split the cost with those involved. You can all get a lot of material for a little cash this way.

245 FLY-TYING COMFORT

Physical therapists may tell you that fly tying is not a good "job" to have, and that it is detrimental to rotator cuff muscles and posture, and can cause back problems. (The same goes for fly casting, but that is a different story.) To prevent injury, have a definite fly-tying work area with a comfortable chair, large work surface, and a vise at a comfortable position. Professionals tell you to place the vise jaws slightly above elbow height and about forearm length or less in front of you. Take lots of breaks when tying flies, and stretch and rotate your arms when possible.

246 PROTECTING NATURAL MATERIALS

To store natural materials and protect them from insects, place them in an airtight container, such as Tupperware. Make sure that there are no insects in the materials and add some moth flakes or mothballs when sealing them for storage.

247 USING MOTHBALLS

Mothballs or moth flakes can adhere to fly-tying materials, making them unusable. To prevent this, keep the moth repellent separate from the fly-tying materials, even when in the same airtight storage box. One way to do this is to keep the moth repellent in an open plastic bag next to the fly-tying materials stored in a box. This way they can't come in contact with each other, but you've protected the fly-tying materials with the fumes. You can also place the mothballs in a small open cardboard box or mailing envelope. If you use an envelope, punch some holes through the envelope to allow the mothball fumes to escape and protect the materials. You could also use a 35mm film canister punched with holes. With mothballs in the closed canister, fumes escape through the holes to protect materials without direct contact.

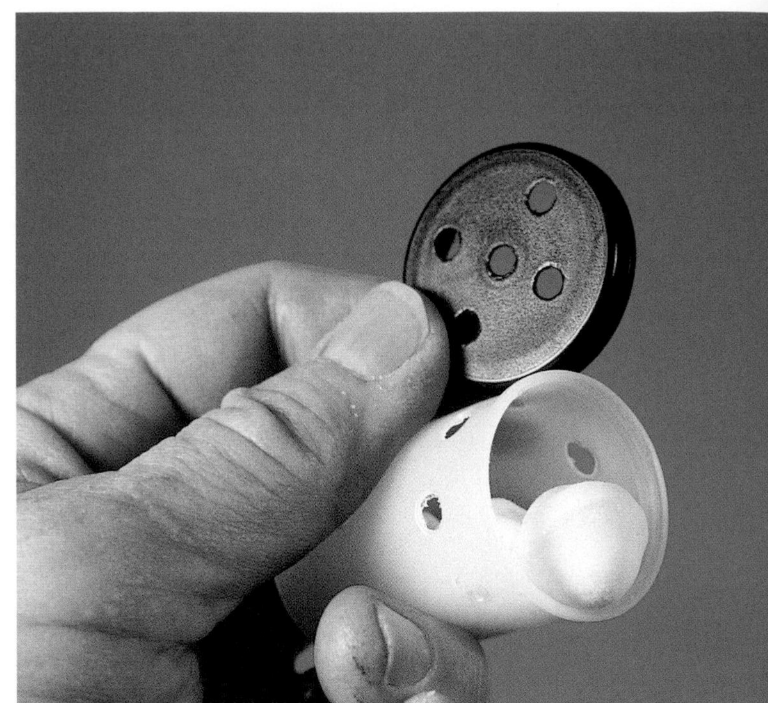

248 BUYING FABRIC

If you plan to buy fabric, make sure that you do not overbuy. Most fabric that you use (vinyl, cloth-backed vinyl, suede, Ultra Suede, fleece, felt, etc.) is sold in bolts that are 36 to 54 inches (91.4 to 137.2 cm) wide. However, you do not need to buy an entire yard of cloth. Most stores will sell you an eighth of a yard (12 cm), reducing the cost of most materials to only a few bucks at most. You still receive 4½ inches (11.4 cm) times the width of the material bolt—a lot of material for tying flies.

249 STORING BULK MATERIALS

If you have a lot of bulk fly-tying materials, an ideal way to store them is in plastic containers such as shoeboxes and sweater boxes. These are readily available from general and discount stores. They are not airtight, so be sure to add mothballs to any boxes containing natural materials. To know what you have in each box, use self-stick labels from an office supply store to label each box with a black felt-tip pen.

250 SAVING SAMPLES

If you like a particular fly-tying material, cut off a short length or piece of it and staple or tape it to a 3- by 5-inch (7.6- by 12.7-cm) index card. Label the card with the important information such as material, brand, color, manufacturer, supplier, price, etc., so that you can order more when you run out. Make sample cards for all materials that are unusual or rare and store the cards with materials in a plastic index card box or file.

251 ORGANIZING STRANDED MATERIALS

Craft stores sell small plastic boxes with cards included for wrapping and storing stranded materials such as yarn, chenille, floss, etc. These are ideal for storing a large number of different colors of these materials. The cards fit into the compartments in the plastic box. You can re-spool any materials from their original packaging onto these cards to make a system with one box containing all the colors of a given material. Label the box to indicate the contents.

252 PREPARING MATERIALS IN ADVANCE

Tying up a bunch of the same fly in the same size? Streamline your operation by first preparing all the materials that you need—selecting the hackles, tail fibers, wings, etc., of the same size, and laying out the other materials—body, ribbing, tinsel, throat, etc.—that you use for that pattern. By having available all the materials for a quantity of flies, you streamline operations and save time selecting hackle, tails, body material, etc., each time for each fly. Commercial flytiers often use this trick when tying large quantities of one fly of one size. You can also use it for as few as a half-dozen flies.

253 COUNTING TAILS OR LEGS

Got a few more tails in your flies than on the natural insect? Got a few more legs than the six that insects are equipped with? Don't worry—fish can't count. What you want is a fair approximation of what their meals look like. When tying a dry fly, you want it to float well in the surface film. This often requires more tails than the natural insect has, and a far thicker hackle than is warranted by the six legs of an insect.

254 SAMPLE FLIES

When you tie a new pattern of fly that you like, tie several and keep one as a sample for future reference. Keep these samples in a small plastic bag, and store with an index card listing the pattern recipe. To protect the fly, you may wish to keep dry flies, some nymphs, and similar structured flies in a container, such as an empty 35-mm film canister or empty hook box.

255 SMALLER FLIES MEAN SMALLER MATERIALS

When tying flies smaller than you normally tie, you will need to shorten, slim, and scale down the materials. This requires smaller hackle, shorter tails, thinner dubbing or body material, and even thinner tinsel ribbing. It also means fewer bucktail or synthetic fibers in a wing, and fewer strands of flash on the side of a fly.

256 EXAMINING FLIES FROM ALL SIDES

Examine each fly that you tie from both sides as you tie it to make sure that it is symmetrical. This is especially important if adding flash to wings, positioning a wing or throat, or similar steps. Mistakes are much easier to correct when the fly is still in the vise and the thread is still on the hook than after finishing and sealing the fly head. One easy way to do this is with a rotating vise that allows you to easily check both sides of the fly.

257 STORING NECKS

You can store fly-tying necks in a file cabinet. Place each neck in a clean plastic bag and then in a manila folder. If you like, you can even label the folder so that you have a filing and identification system. Then place several folders in a hanging Pendaflex folder to keep them flat and straight. Do not use a "box bottom" hanging folder, since this allows the necks to sag and bend, damaging them for fly tying.

258 WASHING NATURAL MATERIALS

If you use materials that you get from hunters or road kills (be careful and check local regulations for this), you should wash the materials and dry them before storage.

To do this, wash necks, furs, and skins in a mild detergent, rinse thoroughly, and then dry. Dry by hanging outside from a clothesline and make sure that they are hanging in the shade to prevent the sun from causing residual fat to liquefy. Once the materials are completely dry, store them flat with mothballs in a suitable container.

259 COMBING OUT UNDERFUR ▲

Use a moustache comb, available from any drug store, to comb out the underfur of deer hair and other natural furs from which you want the underfur removed. The moustache comb is ideal, not only for removing the underfur before tying with the guard hairs (bucktail streamers, deer body fur bass bugs, etc.), but also to collect underfur to use for dubbing. You can use underfur like this by itself for dubbing or mix it with other furs or synthetic materials to make a mixed dubbing.

260 COLLECTING INSECTS

Some anglers and flytiers get heavily involved in aquatic entomology; others do not. In any case, it helps to have on hand a few insects to use as examples when tying flies.

To do this, use a fine-mesh net to dip insects from the water, capture them while they are floating, or net them in the air as they are flying. To get nymph forms of insects, wade the shallows and lift over a few rocks to gather mayflies, caddis cases, and stonefly nymphs from the rocks. Turn the rock back to its normal position when finished so that you don't harm the remaining insects.

You can also use your net to capture emerging insects along with mature insects flying and mating. Place all insects in small bottles with rubbing alcohol for future reference. Label as to time, date, and place captured. Later you can add further information as to type, or genus, and species.

Alcohol (and formaldehyde used by professionals) will fade the colors on the insects, so make separate notes as to color or check with books for suggestions when tying your own patterns.

261 TYING SMALL FLIES

If you have trouble tying small flies, start by tying some of the same pattern, but in larger sizes. After you are comfortable with tying the flies, move to tying them in the next size down until you reach the size you desire. This allows you to develop and perfect your skills gradually. Realize that each time you go to a smaller size, you also reduce the size of the materials incorporated into the fly.

262 PREVENTING EYESTRAIN

To prevent eyestrain, dull the highly polished metal finishes on the vise using fine steel wool or even gun bluing to reduce glare. This usually only works on ferrous metals—it does not work on stainless steel or certain brass fittings. A quick and removable substitute for this is to cover the post of the vise with a dull tape, such as masking tape.

> "Fly tying is the next best thing to fishing; it is the sort of licking of the lips that eases a thirsty man in the desert."
>
> —*Arthur Ransome, "Fly Tying in Winter,"* Rod and Line *(1929)*

Chapter 11 Tools and How to Use Them

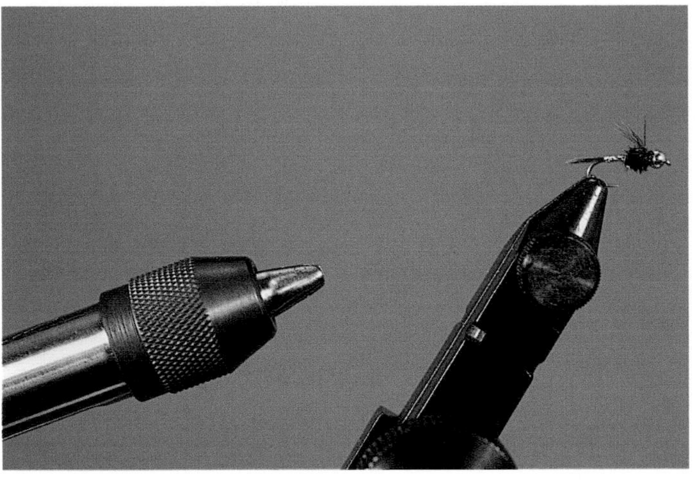

263 VISE ANGLE

If you are tying small flies and need more room for handling materials, try adjusting the angle of the vise (if possible) to a steeper angle. This allows more room for your fingers to handle materials and hold materials in position on the hook for tying.

264 CHECKING FLIES

If you do not have a rotating vise, but still want to check both sides of a fly as you tie it, keep a small-handled cosmetic mirror on your fly-tying bench. This allows you to hold the mirror up to see the far side of the fly without the time-consuming task of taking it out of the vise.

265 CHECKING SMALL FLIES

When tying very small flies, or if you have trouble with your eyes, consider using a magnifier. Fly shops sell magnifiers made exclusively for fly tying, but you can also get the same thing from office supply stores. Some magnifiers also have a built-in circular fluorescent rim light to provide lighting for the fly. The magnifiers that fit on your head are particularly useful. They move with you and do not add another piece of equipment between you and the vise.

266 MAKING THROATS

To make a throat on a streamer fly or wet fly, use a rotary vise. Turn the vise jaws 180 degrees to position the fly hook point up. (If your vise does not rotate, remove the hook and replace it upside down.) This makes it easier to tie in a throat, since you will be using the soft loop method and pulling the thread down on the throat rather than up as if tying it without the hook reversed. This is far easier and makes for a more secure tie, while also allowing you to make sure that you line up the throat with the hook shank.

267 INEXPENSIVE HALF-HITCH TOOL ▲

The front end of an inexpensive empty ballpoint pen makes a fine half-hitch tool. The best types are those with the clicker cap to extend/retract the ink point.

Unscrew the pen and discard all but the tapered plastic or metal end. The tip end fits over the eye of small flies and the taper allows you to easily slide off half hitches after you wrap the thread around the barrel of the pen. If you have several of these, drill out one or two to larger size holes to fit larger hooks.

268 TYING SMALL FLIES

To see flies easily, get reading glasses designed for the distance you work from your fly-tying vise. You might be able to use the inexpensive models available from most stores if you do not have any serious eye problems and if both eyes need about the same correction. Measure the distance from your eyes to the fly-tying vise at home, and then choose glasses that work well at that distance.

269 NATURAL FLOAT FLIES

To make a fly float lower in the surface film, use scissors to trim the bottom hackle. The result is a fly in which the tail, body, and hackle are all floating in the surface film, thus more closely imitating an emerging mayfly. This is basically what Comparadun flies do.

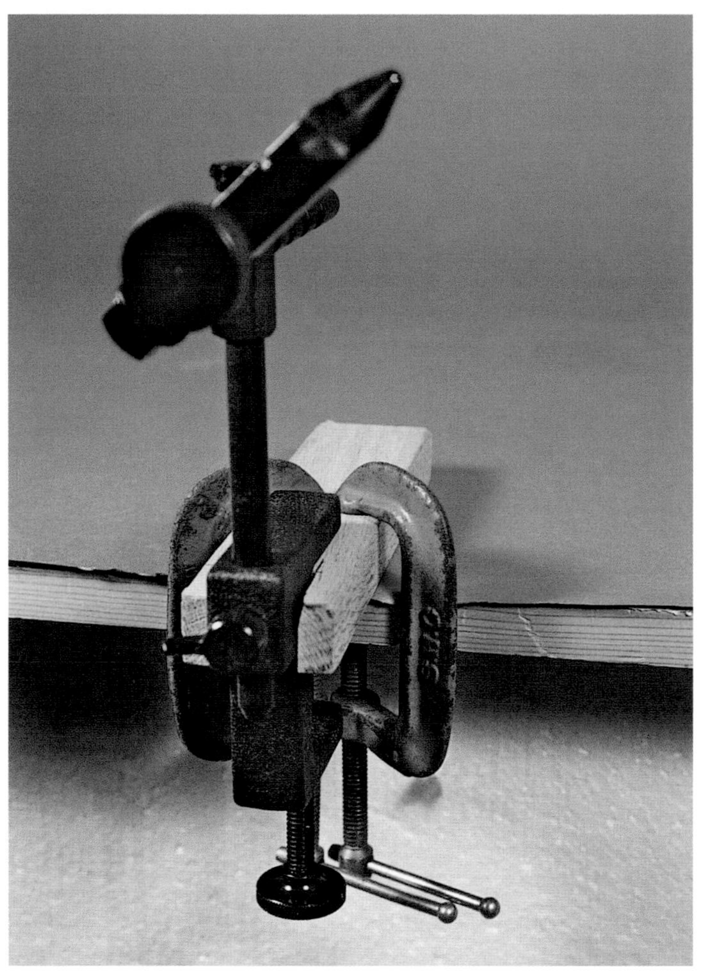

271 ROTARY HACKLE PLIERS

To keep dry fly hackle from twisting while winding it in place on a fly, use one of the new rotary hackle pliers. You'll also find them faster to use, since they don't require rotating the hackle pliers with each turn to prevent hackle twist.

270 CLAMP AND BOARD

If you don't have a pedestal vise, but travel and take your clamp-on vise with you, you must have a way to clamp it to tables that are too thick for the clamp that comes with the vise. An easy way to solve this is to carry with you a small board and one or two larger "C" clamps.

The best board is shelving about 0.75-inch (19-mm) thick measuring about 4 by 6 inches (10 by 15 cm). To use, clamp the board to the table or bench using one or two "C" clamps and leave about 2 inches (5 cm) of the board extending over the edge of the table. Then clamp the "C" clamp vise to this extended part of the board and tie away.

272 PEDESTAL VS. CLAMP VISES

There are pros and cons to the kinds of vises you can choose from. Clamp-on vises are more secure and allow vertical adjustment of the vise. You must clamp them to a table that the clamp will not damage, and one that is not too thick—2 inches (5 cm) is about the maximum.

You can place pedestal vises on any table for use anywhere. You don't even need a special table or work area for tying and you can place them on surfaces other than tables or countertops.

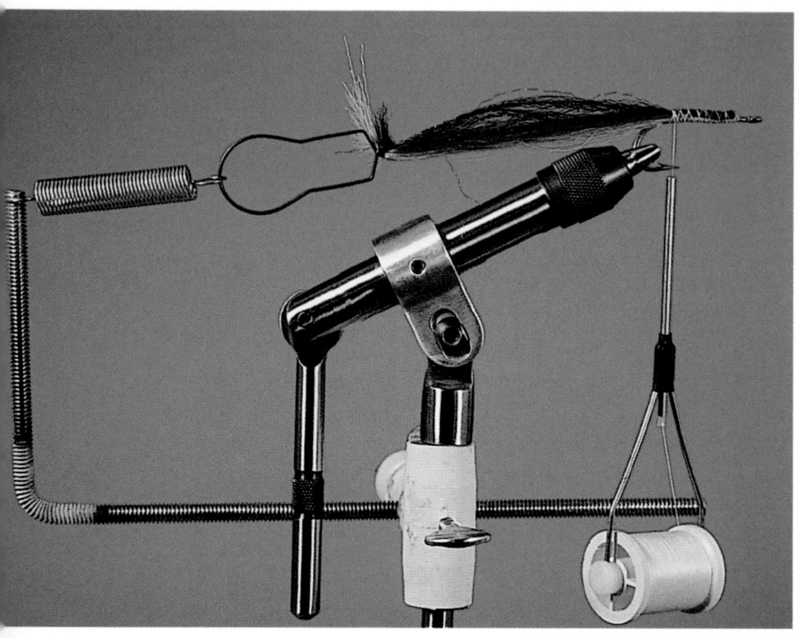

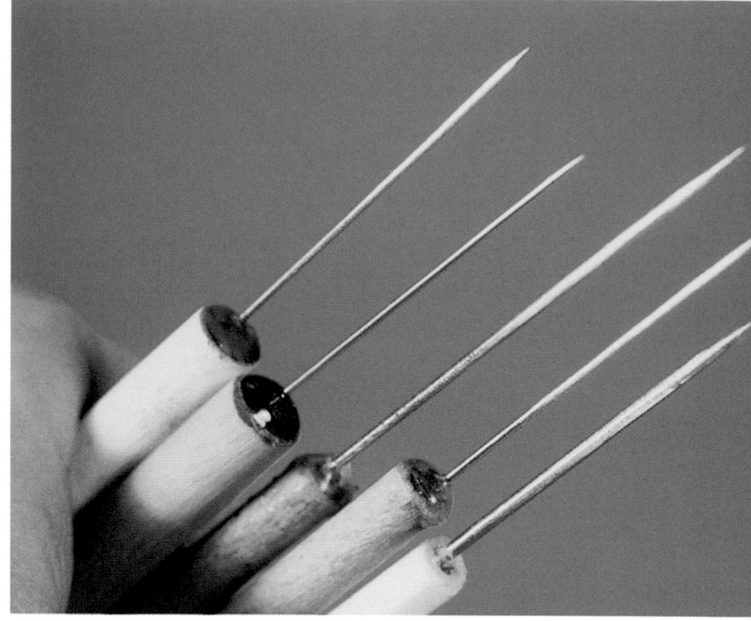

273 HORIZONTAL GALLOWS TOOL

Bead-chain leeches, some 'cuda flies, long pike flies, and tandem-rigged flies require a horizontal gallows tool, or some way to hold the tail of the fly so that it does not interfere with tying the rest of the fly. To do this, set up a clamp to hold a vertical post to the left of your fly-tying vise. Run a tension spring (available from hardware or home supply stores) from the vertical post to a hook or hackle pliers.

274 BEAD-CHAIN LEECHES

One easy way to hold bead-chain body out of the way when making bead-chain leeches is to bend a paper clip into a sharp "J" shape at one end and an eye (like a large hook eye) at the other end. Use the "J" to hook onto the last bead of the bead chain and attach the other end of this hook to the spring of the horizontal gallows tool. This allows holding the bead chain out of the way for tying materials to it to tie a weighted leech.

275 SIMPLE BODKIN

Get a large sewing needle (a darning needle is a good size), drill a tiny hole straight into the end of a 4-inch (10-cm) length of ½-inch-diameter (1.3-cm) dowel, and epoxy the eye end of the needle into the hole. Make a number of bodkins this way, since different sizes are handy for different tasks. Large, coarse bodkins are ideal for making pilot holes in foam bugs for inserting the hook; medium bodkins are best for placing head cement precisely on the head of a small fly; and small bodkins are good for separating fibers in wet fly and dry fly hackle.

276 TOOL RACK

It won't be neat, but you can make a simple rack for your fly-tying tools from a scrap block of shipping foam. Use a pencil to punch holes for bodkins, bobbins, whip finishers, dubbing spinners, scissors, etc. Use a piece of pipe or tubing to cut and make blind holes for stackers, bottles of head cement, and similar items.

277 BEAD-CHAIN FLY HANGING RACKS

To make a rack for hanging flies while head cement cures or while paint on bugs dries, make a wide U-shaped wood bracket for a base and sides, and then string bead chain across the top, stapled to the top of the side supports. The bead chain keeps the flies from sliding together and being ruined, even if there is a little slack in the chain. Several sizes of bead chain are available, depending on the size of the fly that you need to hang. Bead chain is readily available through hardware and home supplies stores.

278 FLY DRYING RACK

Stick pins—headfirst—into a wood board (drill a hole for each pin in a row) to make a rack that allows you to hang flies by the hook eye instead of the bend. This prevents head cement from clogging up the eye of the hook.

The best way to do this is to drill tiny holes in the board, add a drop of glue to each hole, and insert the head of the pin. Bend the pins into a hook shape so that the fly head does not glue to the board holding the pins. Place the board on a stand about 6 inches (15.2 cm) high, so that the flies can hang straight down.

279 HAIR PACKER

A fender washer is a good tool to use as a hair packer for pushing spun deer hair when making deer-hair bass bugs. These are large-diameter washers with small holes. Most external diameters are from about 1 to 1½ inches (2.5 to 3.8 cm). The inside diameter of the holes start around ⅛ inch (3 mm). Get several of the smallest sizes to fit over different-size hook eyes. These are readily available from any good hardware store.

280 ANOTHER HAIR PACKER

Another easy way to make a hair packer is to cut ¾-inch-diameter (1.9-cm) dowels into 4-inch (10.2-cm) lengths, then drill straight into the end of the dowel. Make several, with holes ranging from about 1/16- to ¼-inch (2- to 6-mm) diameter, to fit over the eyes of hooks on which you tie. Drill the hole deep so that you can slide it over any size hook shank. The dowel is easy to hold while pushing it over a hook eye to compact the hair on a bug.

281 BOBBIN REST

Sometimes it helps to have a bobbin rest by which you can extend your thread or bobbin to the side of the vise to complete certain tying operations. You can buy these or you can make your own temporary rest with a length of coat-hanger wire. First untwist and straighten the coat hanger. Then bend one end in a spiral several times around the post of your fly-tying vise.

Remove the coat-hanger wire and bend the end of the last coil into a slightly tighter wrap that "grips" the post. Re-attach the coil to the post, with the long end of the wire at the top. Then bend this out to the side, make a second right-angle vertical bend, and make any small U or V shape bends at the end with pliers to hold the thread or bobbin. Use wire cutters (wear safety glasses) to remove any excess wire.

The result is a simple, flexible rest that swings out to the side to hold your thread and bobbin. You can swing it back out of the way on the vise or remove it at any time. And the price is right.

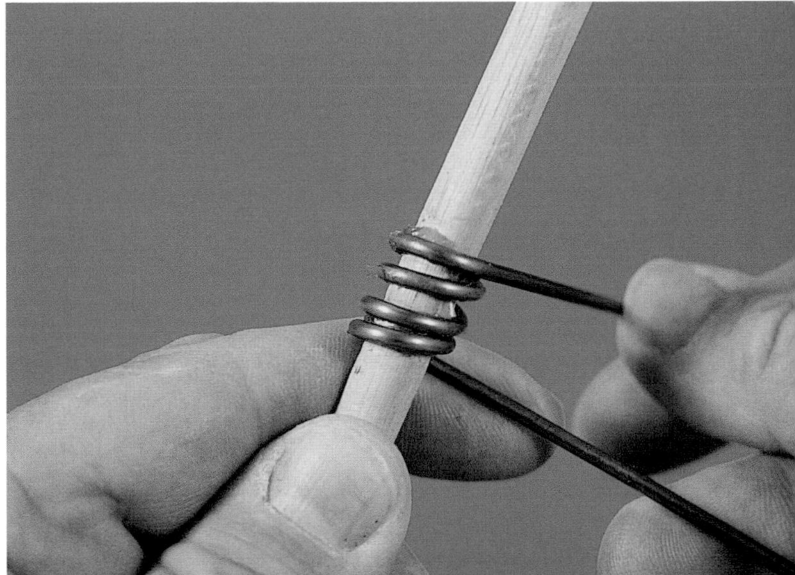

282 PREVENTING HEAD CEMENT AND OTHER CEMENT SPILLS

It is not uncommon to spill head cement or other bottled cements and finishes that can ruin flies and materials and even a workbench surface. To prevent this, use a small block of wood or foam shipping material with a hole cut to hold a bottle. For round bottles such as nail polish, use a spade bit to drill almost through a small block of wood for a hole sized to fit the bottle. You can use a small pipe to cut partly through a piece of shipping foam to accomplish the same thing.

Another way to prevent spills is to place your bottle in the center of a 4x4-inch board or cardboard, and use masking, duct, or shipping tape to secure the bottle to this base. If you plan to remove and replace the bottle, wrap a strip of cardboard around the chosen bottle, tape the strip together, and then tape it to the base.

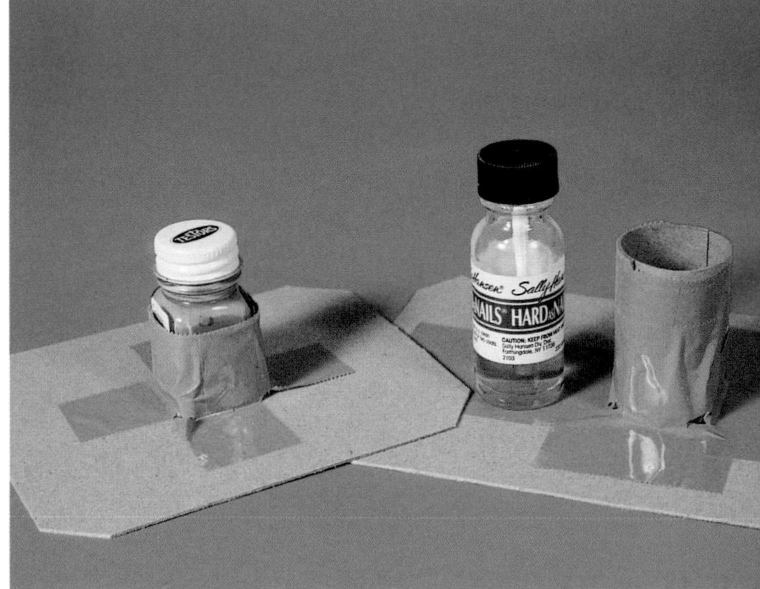

283 MAKING SIMPLE DUBBING TEASERS

Dubbing teasers fluff out dubbing to make any fly look more lifelike. To make simple dubbing teasers, take an old toothbrush and with a razor blade cut the bristles to about ⅛ to ¼ inch long. These shorter, stiffer bristles make it easy to comb out the body or a yarn or dubbing fly.

Another way to make a simple dubbing teaser is to glue a strip of the "hook" side of a hook-and-loop fastener to a popsicle stick. The hooks on this part of the tool make it easy to comb out the fibers or any yarn or dubbing fly.

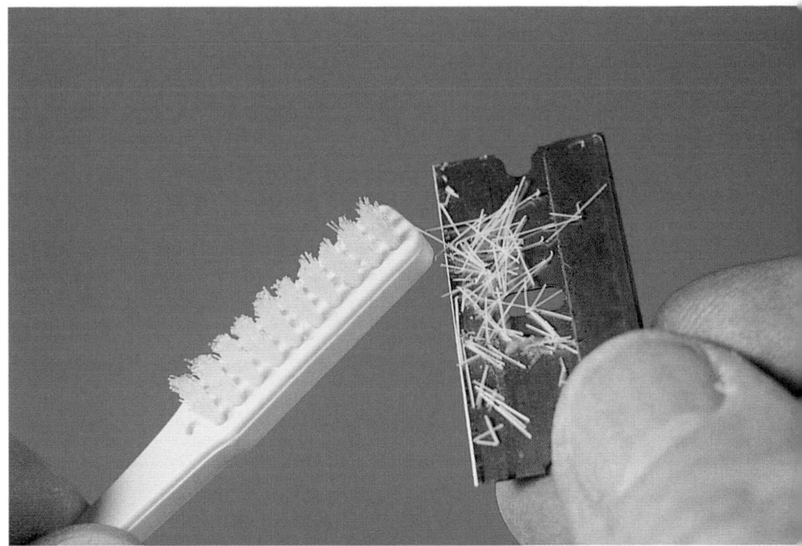

284 MIXING DUBBING

An easy way to mix a large amount of dubbing material is to use two small, fine-tooth dog combs to work the material back and forth to mix different materials. Add a little of the dubbing material at a time and mix the two or more colors and materials back and forth until there seems to be a complete homogenized mix of color and fiber.

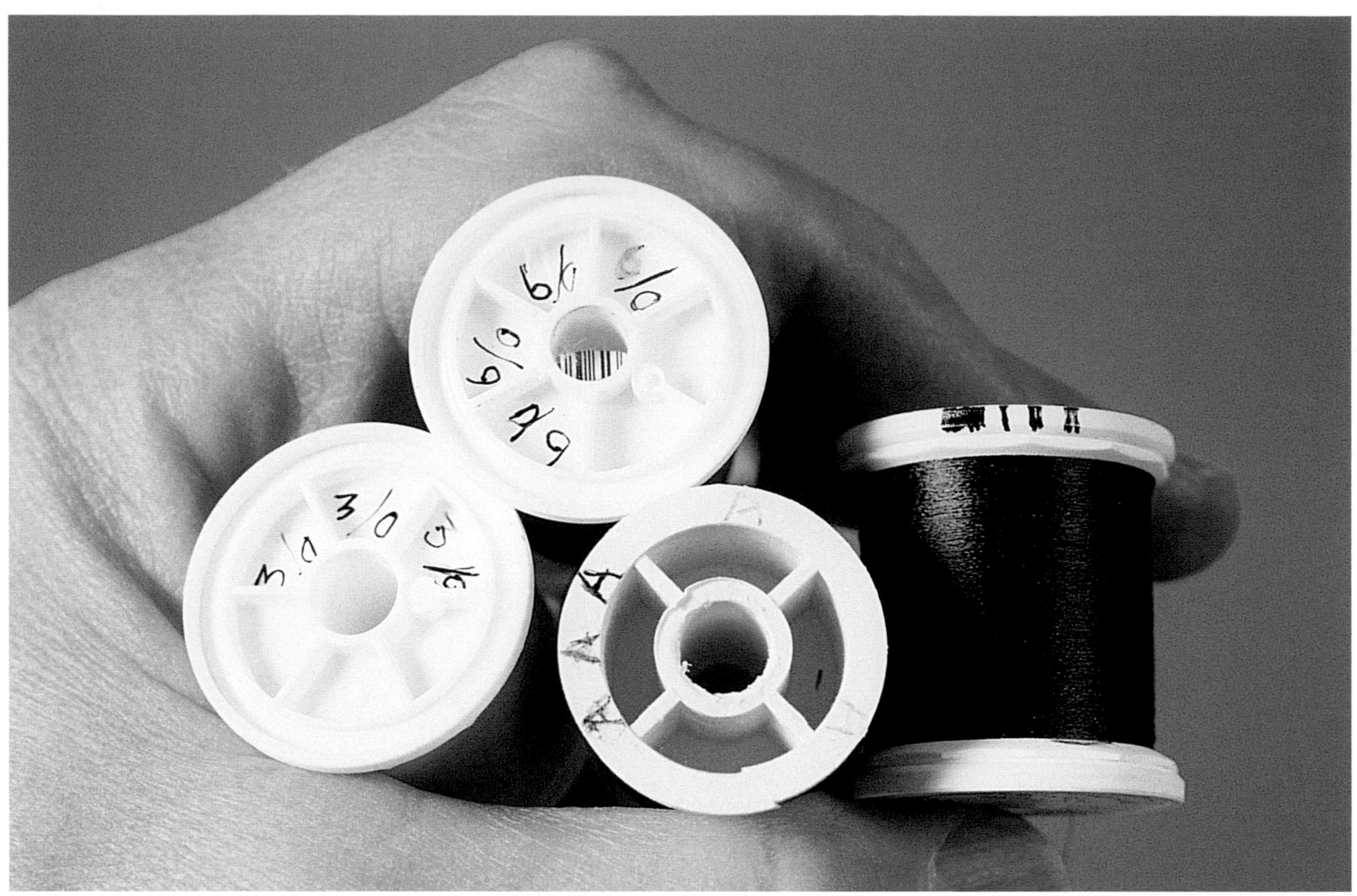

285 LABELING THREAD BOBBINS

There are several ways to mark and keep track of thread bobbins used when tying flies. One method is to use a fine, felt-tip permanent pen to carefully write the thread size on the edge or rim of the spool. If the width of the spool edge is not wide enough to write the size (3/0, 5/0, 4/0, etc.), you can use the fly line designation of using a narrow mark for "1" and a wide mark for "5." Thus, three straight marks or "III" can indicate a 3/0, and so forth.

With a computer, you can set the type to the smallest size and key in the thread sizes or other thread designations, which can be printed, cut out, and glued to the center shaft of the bobbin for that size thread.

Another way to mark thread sizes is to write the thread size on a small self-stick label and attach the label to one arm of the bobbin.

Lastly, you can use a fine felt-tip pen to write the size of the thread on a small plastic washer and slip the washer onto the one arm of the bobbin before adding the thread spool.

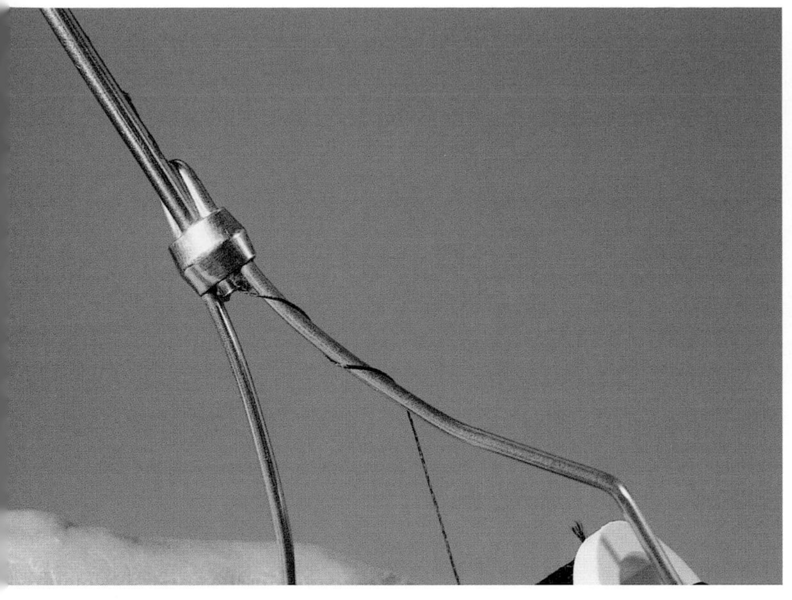

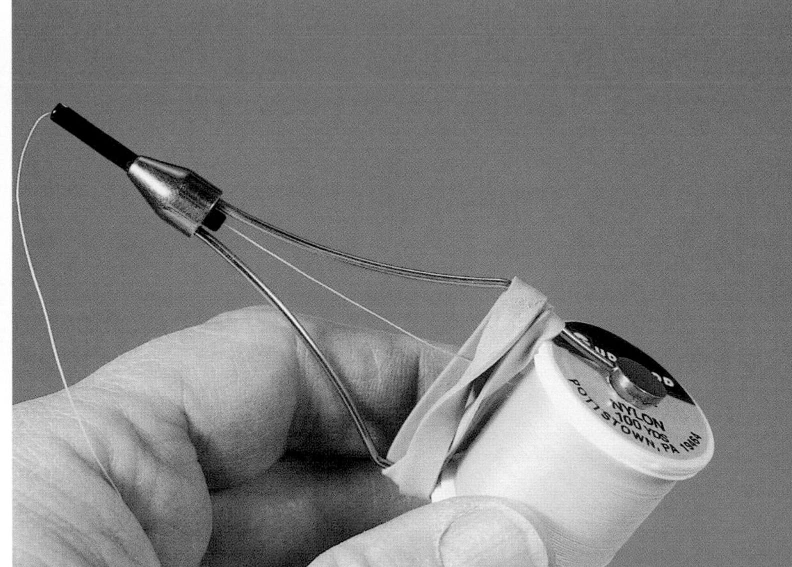

286 BOBBIN ADJUSTMENTS AND OTHER BOBBIN USES

To create more tension to thread coming off of the spool when tying flies, try wrapping the thread once or twice around one arm of the bobbin to create more friction on the thread. This works best on bobbins with long side arms.

Another way to create more thread pressure is to use a bobbin on which you can place several wraps of a rubber band around the legs to press in the legs holding the spool.

Thread bobbins can be used for more purposes than just holding thread. They are also ideal for holding small spools or ribbon, floss, yarn, various types of wire, lead for weighting flies, chenille, etc. Bobbins make it easy to wind these materials onto a fly with no waste of materials.

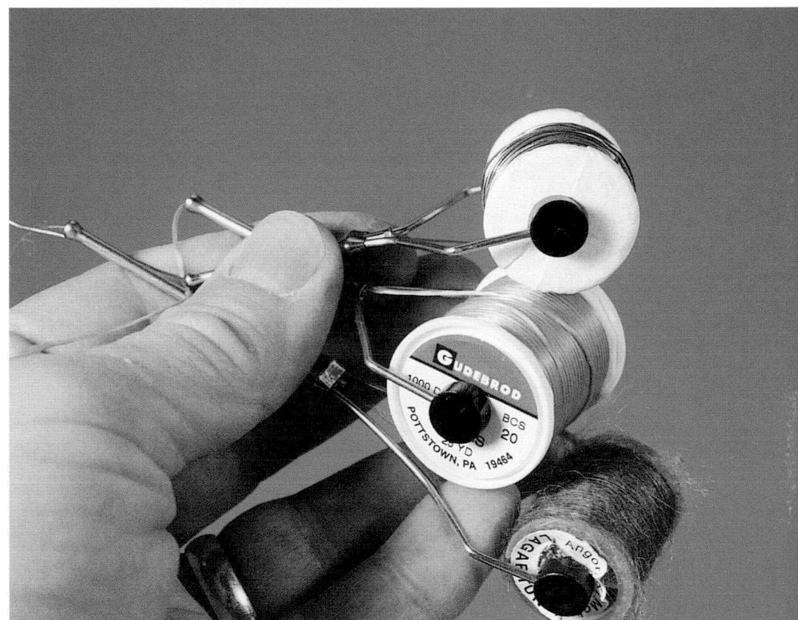

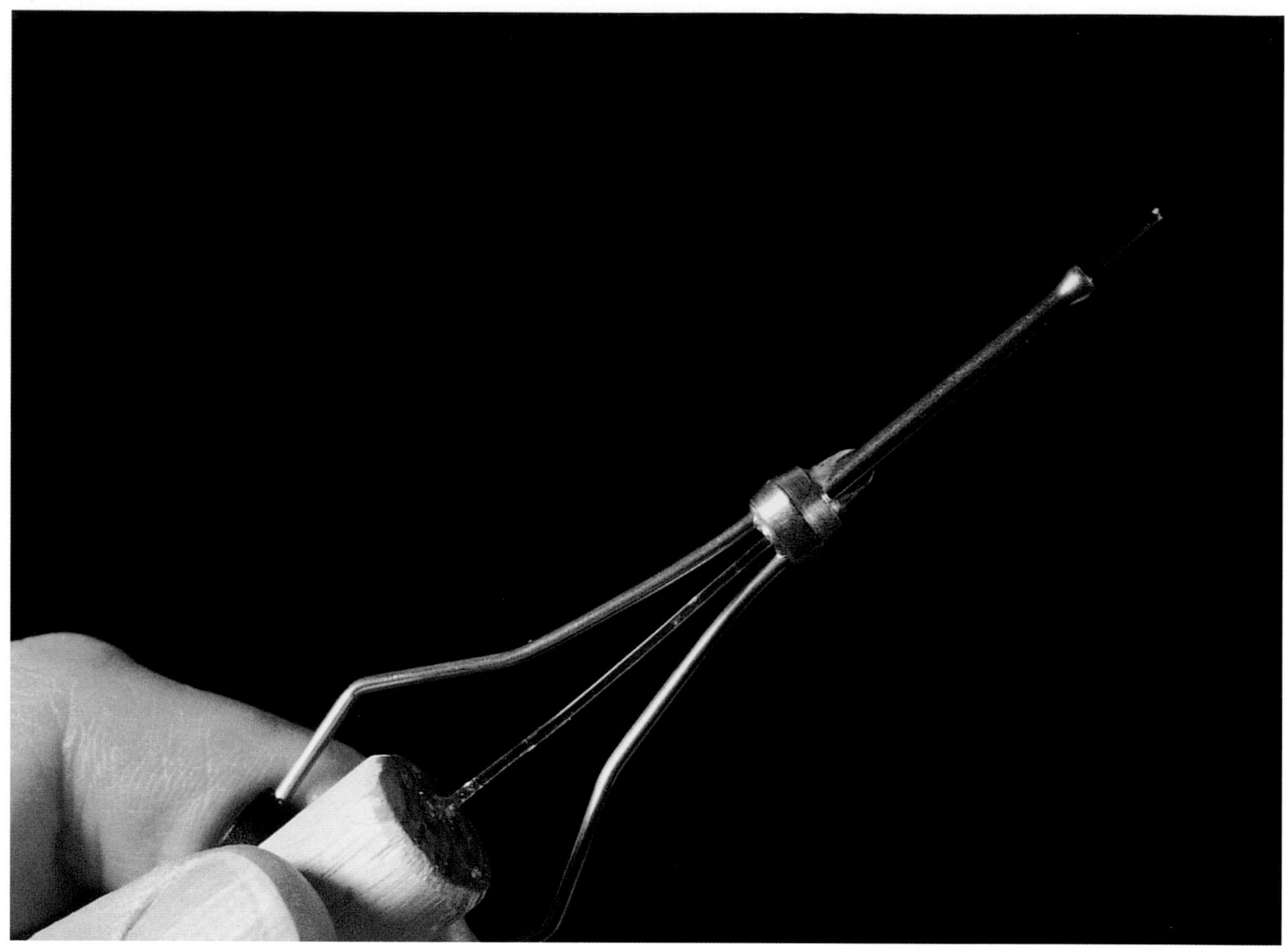

287 CLEANING THREAD BOBBINS

Run heavy mono through the shaft or tube of a bobbin to push out collected wax residue that accumulates when using pre-waxed thread. 50- to 100-pound mono (22.7- to 45.4-kg) works well, as do some of the sizes of the Weed Wacker–style of weed cutters.

Push the mono through, remove the wax from the end, and then remove the mono. To make a permanent tool for this, glue one end of the heavy mono into a tiny hole drilled into the end of a 4-inch (10-cm) length of ½- to ¾-inch (12.7- to 19-mm) dowel. Bright-colored Weed Wacker nylon shows up distinctly on your tying bench.

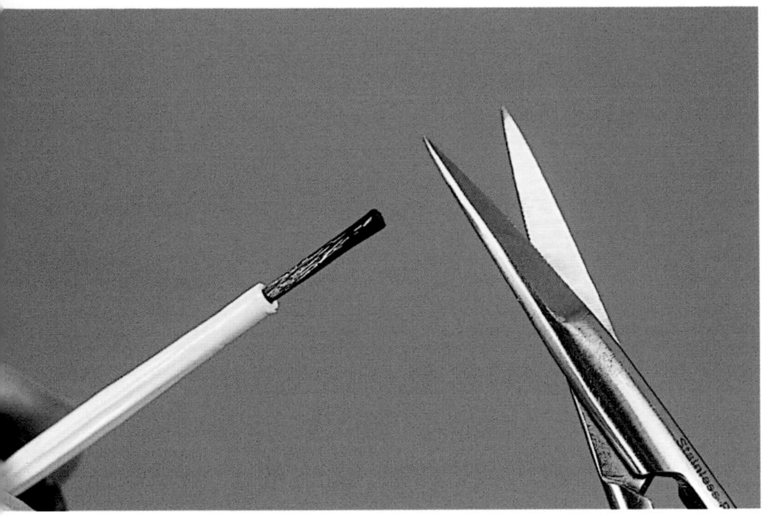

288 BOTTLE BRUSHES

To use nail polish to seal the head or thread wraps on a fly, first trim the brush in the bottle cap. To do this, remove the brush and wipe it clean. Then use scissors to cut upward into the brush at an angle to taper and thin the brush end. Be sure to clean your scissors after doing this trick.

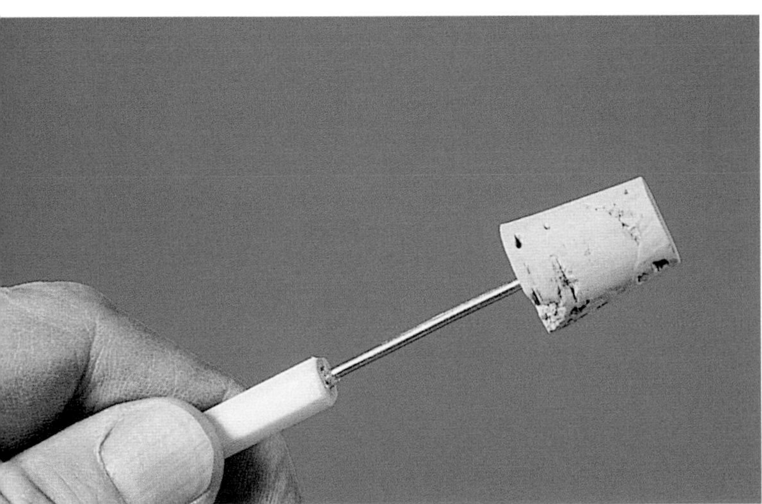

289 BODKIN PROTECTION

To keep a bodkin from stabbing you, stick it in a small bottle cork when not in use or stick it into a foam tool rack. If your tool rack is made of hard wood or plastic, glue or tape a section of foam to one side or the back to store bodkins.

290 TYING SUPPLIES

Various types of racks are available for stacking dispenser boxes of dubbing, stranded materials, etc. These make it easy to have a lot of materials readily available for tying different flies, while taking up little bench space.

One main supplier of these items is Spirit River, whose products are available through fly shops and catalogs. They also make racks to hold a lot of these boxes in a vertical stack or on a rotary file system. You can also make your own racks from scrap wood or lengths of aluminum angle.

291 MIXING DUBBINGS

One way to thoroughly mix various furs and synthetic materials for dubbing is to use a mini-blender, like a coffee grinder. Beware that sometimes the fur floats up in the blender without completely mixing.

To solve this problem, make a "lid" from a plastic food container lid that fits snugly into the blender opening. Cut this plastic to size and then add a handle with a bolt and nut through an empty thread spool and a hole in the lid. Use this to push the material down to get it mixed properly. Take care that you do not overmix, which will cause knots and tangles.

292 HEAD CEMENT

Save those snap-cap lids that come on a lot of condiment bottles and jars, such as ketchup, mustard, mayonnaise, or hot sauce. Also save small bottles, such as the short and squat screw-lid spice bottles. When both are empty, match the snap-cap lids with the small jars or bottles. Clean both and use the bottles for head cement and other liquid products that you use for fly tying.

The snap-cap makes it easy to open by snapping the lid back and inserting a bodkin to remove a small drop of head cement. Don't store a lot of head cement this way, since there is still some evaporation of solvent through these caps. In time, evaporation will cause the head cement to thicken.

293 ALTERNATE DUBBING WAX

If you are short of dubbing wax or want to try something different, use some of the warm-weather (soft) ski wax. Make sure that it is room temperature and add it to the tying thread, loop, or dubbing strand to hold the dubbing material prior to spinning it in place and then wrapping it on the hook shank.

294 MARKING MATERIALS

To create the mottled appearance of nymphs, use a light-colored body of wool, yarn, dubbing, EZ-Dub, or similar body materials, and mark as desired with an appropriate color felt-tip marker. You can get felt-tip markers in various tip sizes from art supply stores. Colors to check out include olive, dark olive, brown, tan, gray, light gray, black, dark gray, wine, and dark green.

Before trying this on a just-completed nymph, try the marker on a piece of scrap material to check how it looks and also the degree of bleeding that occurs. Often some bleeding blurs edges and makes for a more natural-looking nymph.

295 MARKING BAITFISH FLIES

Most baitfish for warm-water and saltwater species have unique markings. Yellow perch and bluegill have vertical bars; mackerel have spots and undulated markings on their backs; pinfish, striped killifish, Atlantic, and chub mackerel have thin vertical bars; sardines have a longitudinal line of dots; juvenile shad have a longitudinal line of large dots; and tomcod, toadfish, and sculpin have mottled sides.

You can easily duplicate these on simple flies by using light-colored soft materials such as Aqua Fiber, Neer Hair, and similar materials. Mark these flies with felt-tip markers to add the necessary lines, dots, stripes, and mottling. Tie these flies in the appropriate background or belly color, and then use permanent felt-tip markers of the right color to add the stripes, spots, dots, and mottled dark areas.

To do this, finish tying the necessary flies, then lay each on a sheet of cardboard or white paper, and mark each by patting the side of the fly with the felt-tip marker. Next, turn the fly over and repeat with similar markings on the opposite side. Make sure that you do not soil the finished side with felt-tip marker ink on the paper that transfers to the fly. Change the paper background often to avoid this problem or work on a clean section of paper each time.

296 QUILL WING DIVIDERS

If tying traditional dry flies or wet flies where you are using barbs from duck-wing quills for the fly wings, there is an easy way to get equal wings.

Use a pair of compass dividers set to the distance for the width of the wing. For this, you want the type of divider that has two points, not one point with the other a pencil or pen nib. The two points allow separating the barbs to get the exact number for each wing.

Realize that you have to use paired quills for this, and select the same width fly wing area from each part of the two quills. Adjust the divider points to separate the quill fibers from the rest of the quill and then cut off the portion desired. If you can't find, or do not want to buy, these compass dividers, you can do the same thing with a paper clip or stiff wire, bent straight and then folded in half to place the two ends at the distance required to measure the wings.

If you change the wing size, you have to slightly re-bend the wire to reflect this change.

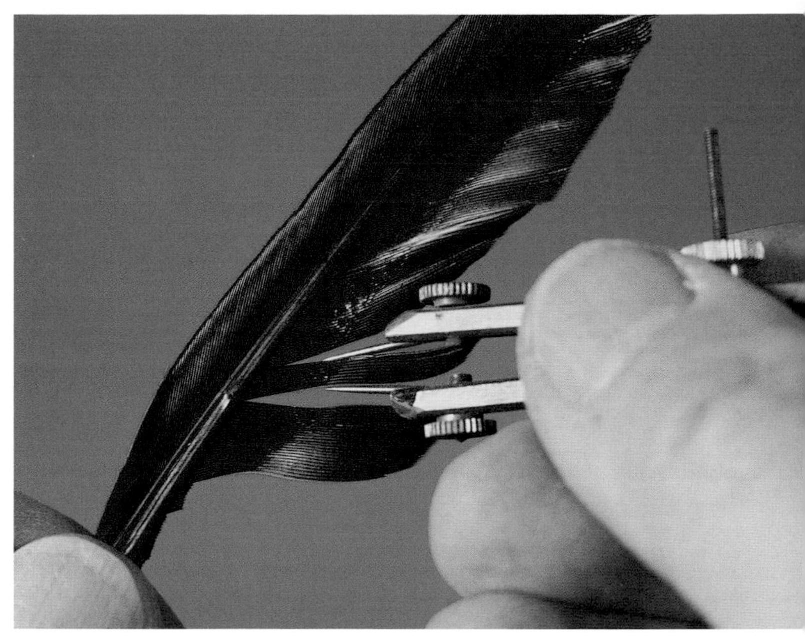

297 BODKIN CLEANER

Bodkins are great tools for all sorts of fly-tying tasks. You can clear the head cement out of a hook eye, pull matted hackle out from a thread wrap, fussy-out a body material, add cement to a fly head, pull up a whip-finish without tangles. The only problem is that cement, glue, and goo can clog bodkins. To avoid this, drill a ¼-inch (6-mm) hole in the top of an empty film canister and fill it with steel wool. Put the cap back on and then poke the bodkin several times through the hole into the steel wool to clean it of cement.

CHAPTER 12

THREAD

Tying On and Tying Off

298 TYING OFF WITH A HALF-HITCH TOOL

A whip finish is far better than a couple of half hitches to finish a fly. But instead of using the regular whip finish with your fingers or a tool for that purpose, try using a half-hitch tool. To complete a whip finish with a half-hitch tool, make a few thread wraps around the tool before seating it against the hook eye and sliding the thread off onto the hook shank. This makes a whip finish, even though it looks like you are just making a more complex half hitch. Because three turns of the thread around the half-hitch tool is about the maximum that you can make, two of these whip-finish variations are often best to secure the head of a fly.

299 SPOTTING DEER HAIR FOR ATTRACTIVE BASS BUGS

One way to make attractive-colored spots in a deer hair bass bug is to use different colors of deer hair.

First stack or spin the deer hair body. Then, in the area where you want a spot, fold a small bundle (cleaned and trimmed) of a contrasting color deer hair around the tying thread, hold the bundle by the two ends, and pull it into position with the tying thread.

Use this technique to make spots, stripes, variegated patterns, and even spots within larger spots. Pulling the spot in place with the thread allows you to position the spot of color exactly where you want it.

"No man is born an artist nor an Angler."

—*Izaak Walton*, The Compleat Angler *(1653)*

300 HANDMADE HALF HITCHES

If you do not have a half-hitch tool, you can make a half hitch on a fly with your fingers. To do this, use your right index finger to maintain tension on the tying thread, then create slack in the tying thread to create a loop that you can place on the far side of the hook and pull tight to make the half hitch.

You can also do this using two fingers, starting the same way you start to make a whip finish. Once you make your loop with your two fingers by rotating your wrist to create a loop, place the loop on the far side of the hook shank, and pull tight.

301 MAKING DURABLE FLIES WITH HALF HITCHES

One way to make very durable flies is to half hitch the thread after each step in the tying process or after adding each material. This secures the material so that it is less likely to slip or come out. It also prevents a fly from coming completely apart when a toothy fish strikes.

302 CHANGING THREADS

One way to make a neat head when tying a large fly is to make the minimal wrap to hold the materials and then tie off the thread with a whip finish. Next, tie on with very fine thread, clip the excess, taper, and complete the head. Tie off carefully with a whip finish. Seal with head cement.

The thinner-diameter thread makes a neater fly head and requires fewer coats of head cement to make for a smooth, polished head.

303 TYING POINT-UP FLIES

If you are tying bonefish flies, Clouser minnows, or other flies that ride point up, be sure to put them in the vise point up for easy tying. This applies to flies that have the wing angled back toward the hook point, often with dumbbell eyes tied to the front of the hook shank for weight and stability. When adding dumbbell eyes, tie them on the top of the hook shank (opposite the point side) first, and then turn the hook over in the vise to add materials as above.

304 THREADING BOBBINS

To get thread through the bobbin shaft, insert the end of the thread into the shaft or tube opening, then suck on the tube (like sucking on a straw) to draw the thread through the bobbin. Make sure that you have enough slack thread when doing this so that you end up with the thread sticking out of the bobbin shaft.

305 WORKING WITH A WHIP FINISH

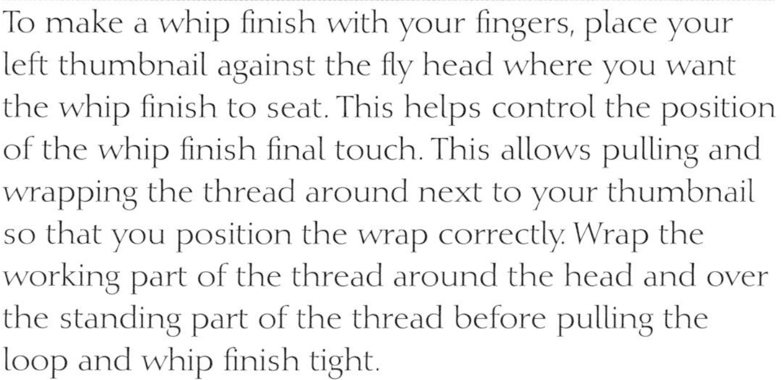

To make a whip finish with your fingers, place your left thumbnail against the fly head where you want the whip finish to seat. This helps control the position of the whip finish final touch. This allows pulling and wrapping the thread around next to your thumbnail so that you position the wrap correctly. Wrap the working part of the thread around the head and over the standing part of the thread before pulling the loop and whip finish tight.

If you make a whip finish with your fingers, pulling it up can cause the loop of thread to twist and knot to tangle with the thread on the fly. To prevent this, make the wraps of the whip finish with your fingers, but then use a bodkin to hold the loop as you pull it tight with your other hand. This controls the loop to prevent tangles and makes it possible to pull the loop tight against the fly head. Remove the needle point of the bodkin as you finish pulling the loop tight.

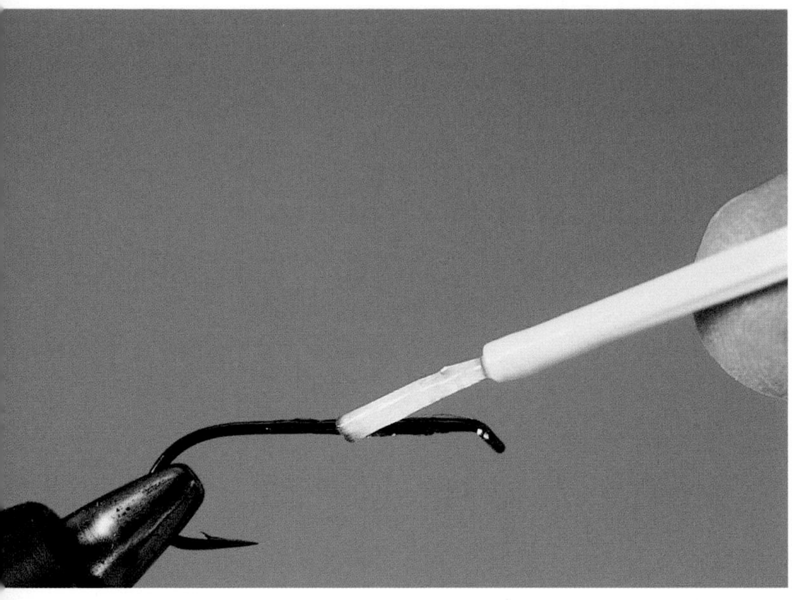

306 PREVENTING THREAD FROM SLIPPING

To make sure that the thread does not slip when tying on, put a tiny drop of head cement or nail polish on the hook where you tie down the thread. Then wrap over this wet glue base to secure the thread before cutting the excess thread. Make sure to use only a small drop of glue, since you want the thread to absorb it all—not soak the area or become transferred to other materials, which the glue might color or stain.

307 WHEN A THREAD BREAKS

Every flytier has times when the thread breaks when tying a fly. Rather than throw out the fly, you can usually save it with some quick steps. First, do not touch the fly or materials. If there is a tag end to the broken thread, hold that, and with the same two fingers of your left hand, grab the end of the thread still hanging from the bobbin. Then use the bobbin thread to wrap around the area where the thread broke to tie and secure any loose materials. If there is no hanging tag end of thread, just use the bobbin to wrap over the tying area to secure materials. If the thread broke in the bobbin, leave the fly alone for a moment and re-thread the bobbin.

308 CAPPING THREAD SPOOLS

Small plastic end caps that fit over standard thread spools are available from craft, fabric, and sewing supply stores. Keep your fly-tying thread from unraveling by slipping on a cap and then catching the thread end between the plastic cap and the spool.

309 FINE THREAD

If you're not sure what thread to use, use one that is finer than you think you need. If you break the thread when tying the first fly, you might have to go to a larger size. Thin-diameter threads are best, since they are less bulky when adding materials and make a neater fly.

310 HEAVY THREAD

Use heavy thread when tying bass bugs to create enough pressure to secure the materials and make a sturdy bug. A lot of experienced flytiers use size "A" thread that is more often used for rod wrappings. Other possibilities are the various Kevlar threads and the gel-spun threads that are now available.

311 FLATTENING THREAD

One way to reduce bulk in flies is to flatten the thread. To do this, untwist the thread so that it lies flat on the hook shank. This also broadens the thread as it untwists, which is often a help in holding and securing materials.

Unfortunately, there is no industry standard as to twist direction, so you must check each manufacturer for their twist. One easy way to check this is to tie on and hang the bobbin, then wait until the bobbin starts untwisting. This is the direction you need to turn to further flatten the tying thread. If you need the thread tight in a tight twist, reverse the direction in which the thread is unwinding.

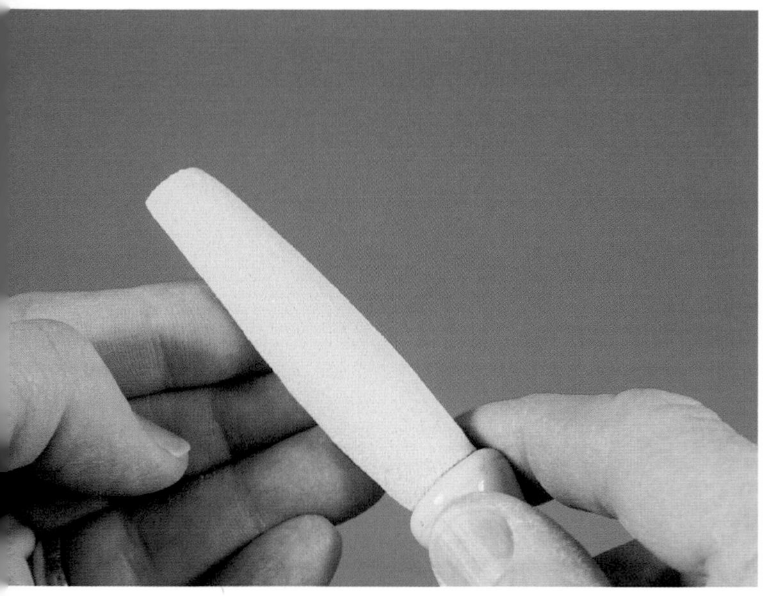

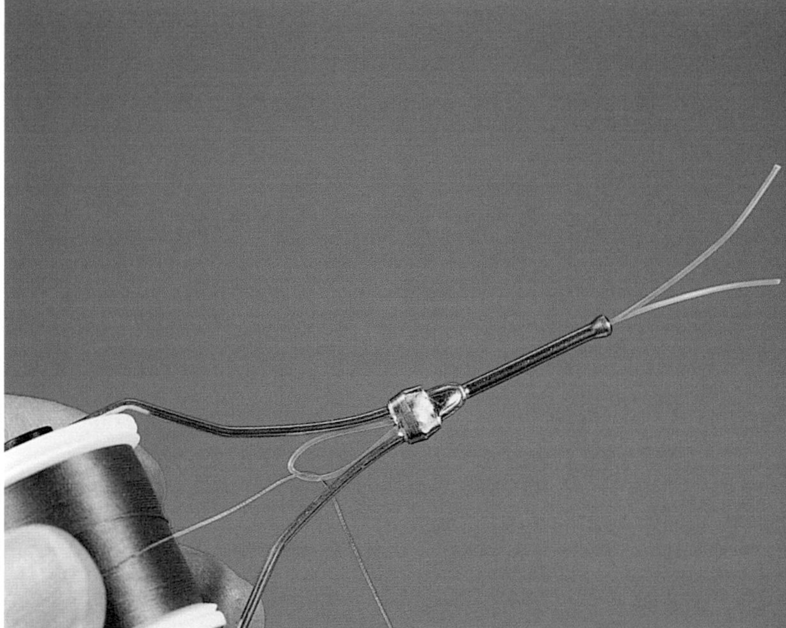

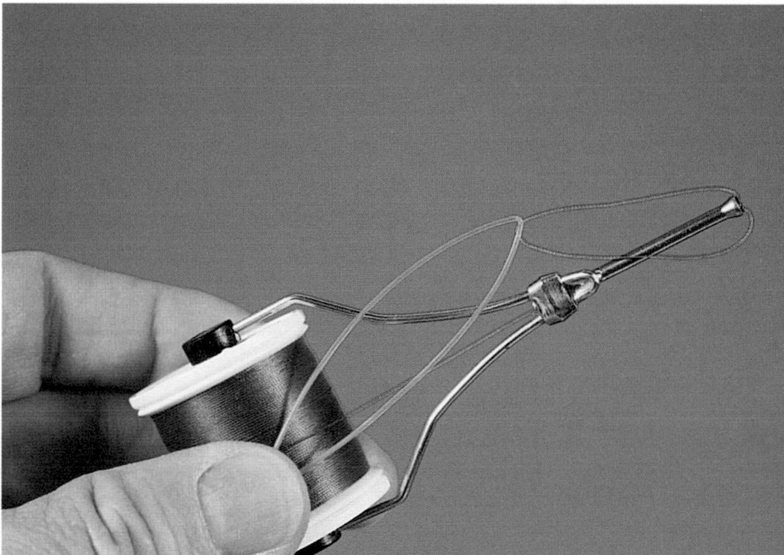

312 PUMICE STONE

Use a pumice stone to smooth your fingertips before handling fly-tying materials. This prevents snagging and tearing the working thread or other fly materials. It is particularly important when handling fine-body materials such as floss and fine threads. Many professional and commercial flytiers keep a pumice stone on their fly-tying bench to keep their fingers smooth.

313 RIGHT SIZE THREAD

Too fine a thread will break when adding coarse materials on larger flies. Too coarse a thread on a small hook bulks up the fly too much and might bend the hook. Use the right size thread for the fly.

For flies 18 and smaller use size 10/0. For flies 16 to 12, use size 8/0 to 6/0; for flies 10 to 4, use size 3/0; and for flies of size 2 and larger, use size 3/0 to size A or G (Gudebrod).

These recommendations can be adjusted to your fly standards, since some flies in a given size require more thread tension (and heavier thread) than others. A prime example would be the heavy tension required to spin deer hair versus the minimal tension required to tie a thread-wrapped midge pattern.

314 MORE ON THREADING BOBBINS

To pull thread through the shaft or tube of a bobbin, double a fine monofilament strand (no more than 8-pound-/3.6-kg-test), push the double end down through the end of the bobbin, run the thread end through the resulting loop, and pull the thread out through the tube or shaft.

This works like a longer version of a needle threader, which is available from sewing stores for threading needles of all types.

315 SECURING WINGS

To easily tie down fly wings, hold the wing over the hook with the left hand. With the middle finger of the bobbin hand supporting the thread, bring the thread up on the near side of the fly. Then drop the thread on the far side of the fly so that the thread captures the wing. The result is a centered wing, beautifully positioned.

316 TRIMMING DEER HAIR BUGS

Instead of scissors, use a razor blade (preferably double-edge), broken in half and with the back taped for protection, to trim your deer hair bugs, muddlers, or any deer hair fly or bug. All flytiers agree that the double-edge blades are far sharper than the safer single-edge blades that are readily available in industrial packs.

317 TYING CORRECTLY

When wrapping material on a hook shank when thread is to be tied over the material (as when wrapping a yarn or chenille body after wrapping the thread forward to tie off), use the correct hand for each stage of the wrap.

Assuming right-handed tying with a right-hand-positioned vise, bring the material up and over the hook shank with the right hand, catching it with the left hand when hitting the hanging thread, and switching to the right hand again in front of the hanging working thread. The opposite of this—wrapping up and over with the left hand—may hit the vise, while the right hand may hit the working thread on each wrap.

The first method is better, quicker, and surer, and with less risk of a problem.

318 BULLET-HEAD FLIES

Carrie Stevens (and later Keith Fulsher in his Thunder Creek series of patterns) first popularized bullet-head flies. To make these more lifelike, use red thread. The reason is that you can easily tie in the body and the forward-facing wing fibers with this thread hidden when you fold over and tie down the bullet head. After tying down the body and head, fold these wing fibers (usually bucktail) back over the hook. Secure these wing fibers with the red working thread to make this wrap look like gills on a small minnow, thus attracting more gamefish. When finished, complete with a whip finish and then seal the thread with head cement.

319 "SOFT LOOPS"

Use the "soft loop" method to keep materials in proper place on the hook. To do this with a streamer wing, for example, hold the wing in place on the hook shank with your left thumb and forefinger. Bring the thread straight up to where you can pinch it between your thumb and index finger to hold it, and then bring it straight down on the back side of the fly. Pull the thread straight down to tighten the thread and secure the wing in line and on top of the hook shank.

You can use this method for adding streamer wings, dry fly wings, tails, body material, throats, or almost anything you wish on the fly hook.

320 SPIN DEER HAIR OVER A THREAD-WRAPPED SHANK

Most experts agree that spinning (flaring) deer or other body hair around a hook shank to make bass bugs is easier to do over a thread-wrapped body. There is less of a tendency for the hair and thread to slip than there would be on a bare hook shank.

Wrap the thread forward neatly around the hook shank, a little at a time, as you work on the bug body. Then wrap the thread back from the front to completely cover the hook shank before beginning to spin the deer hair.

321 TAPER STREAMER HEADS

When finishing a large fly such as a streamer, don't build up a big block of a head. Instead, taper the thread wrap so that it is small in the front and then tapers back to the area of the thread holding the wing in place. Doing so makes the streamer fly look more fishlike and natural.

322 GAP CLEARANCE WITH BASS BUGS

When making deer hair bass bugs, place the hook shank in the body as close to the belly as you can to maintain a wide hook gap. This is necessary for sure hooking of any fish.

CHAPTER 13 HANDLING HOOKS AND MAKING WEED GUARDS

323 STORING SMALL HOOKS

It is best to keep small hooks (size 16 and smaller) in their original container or in a pillbox with a tight-fitting lid to prevent loss or mix-up. You can also keep very small hooks in a labeled 35mm film canister. Just be careful not to spill the hook contents when opening the snap lids of these containers.

324 STRAIGHT-EYE HOOKS

If tying large flies, such as those for barracuda or pike that are attached to the leader with a braided wire bite tippet, you must use a straight-eye hook for the fly to work properly in the water. For best results, use a figure-eight knot for attaching braided wire to the hook. The straight-eye hooks keep the fly working in a straight line, thus appearing natural, rather than working at an up or down angle as would occur with a turned-up or turned-down eye hook.

325 TURLE KNOT HOOK CHOICES

If you use a Turle knot to tie on flies when fishing, you must tie all of your flies on a turned-up or turned-down eye hook. Otherwise, the knot will not work, as the mono tippet will be at an angle to the hook shank.

This is only true for the Turle knot. You can tie all other knots, such as the improved clinch knot and palomar knot, using a hook with any type of eye.

326 CORROSION-RESISTANT HOOKS

If tying saltwater flies, it is best to tie only on stainless steel, tin, or other hooks with finishes designed to resist the corrosive effects of saltwater. Most hook companies now design hooks for saltwater use, so you should be able to find regular, long shank, circle, and specialty hooks made of materials to resist corrosion.

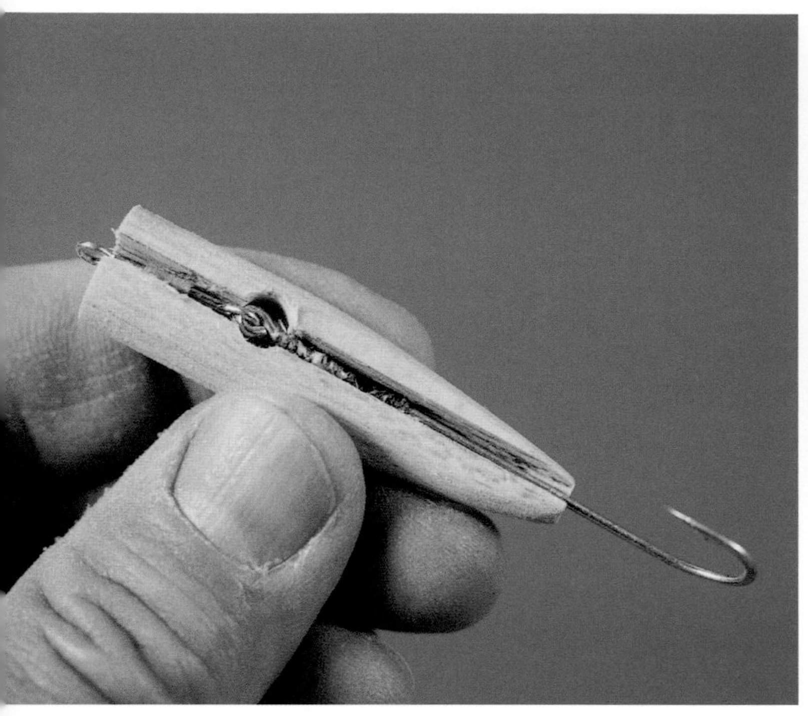

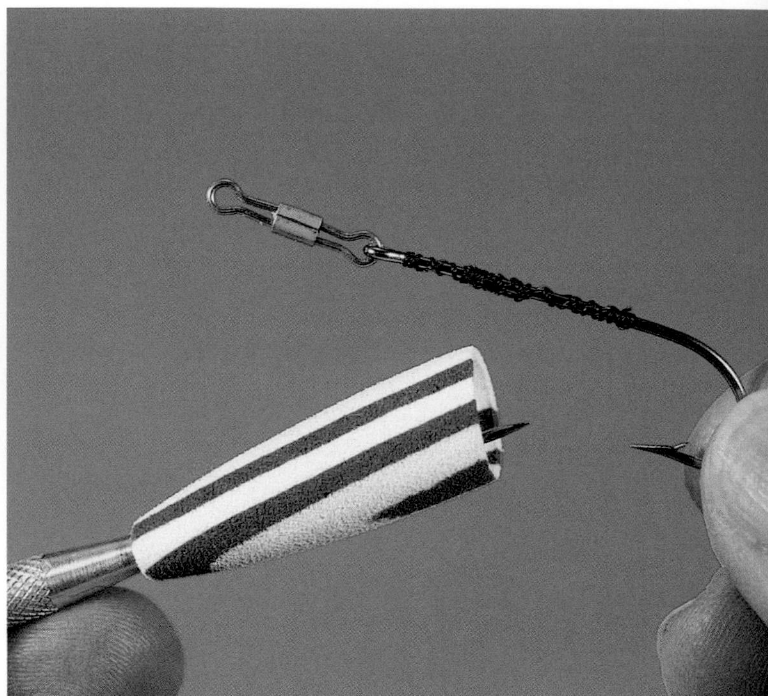

327 HOOK EXTENSIONS FOR LONG MINNOW POPPERS

To make very long flies for some streamers and many poppers, extend the hook shank by cutting off the bend and point of a hook, then bending the shank to easily make a sharp "J" bend in the end to slip over the straight eye of the hook to be used. Clamp this "J" end down with pliers and then wrap it with thread to secure it. For a fly, tie over this extended shank. For a cork or balsa popper, cut a slot with a hack saw for the shank and then enlarge an area where the eye of the rear hook joins the forward hook shank. Put in place and glue securely.

Another way to make an extended hook shank is to use a standard fishing connector link. These come in several sizes and are designed with a sliding sleeve to make connection at either end possible. Slip this over the hook shank to be used and glued into a popper body, tied into a fly, or pulled through a foam popper body using heavy monofilament.

328 CHECKING FLY HOOKS FOR SHARPNESS

Most fly hooks are sharp as they come out of the box. However, it does help to check each hook for sharpness by touching the point to your thumbnail to see if it catches. If it does, it is sharp; if not, sharpen it.

To sharpen fly hooks, place the fly in the vise, then use a very fine hook hone or sharpening file on the hook. Sharpen by running the sharpening instrument at an angle over the point, running the file between the point and hook shank. Do this at an angle, touching both the point and the barb. Then lightly touch the outside of the hook point to triangulate the hook.

You cannot do this if using circle hooks. For sharpening them, use a hook hone with a groove in it and run the hook point in the sharpening groove along the outside of the hook.

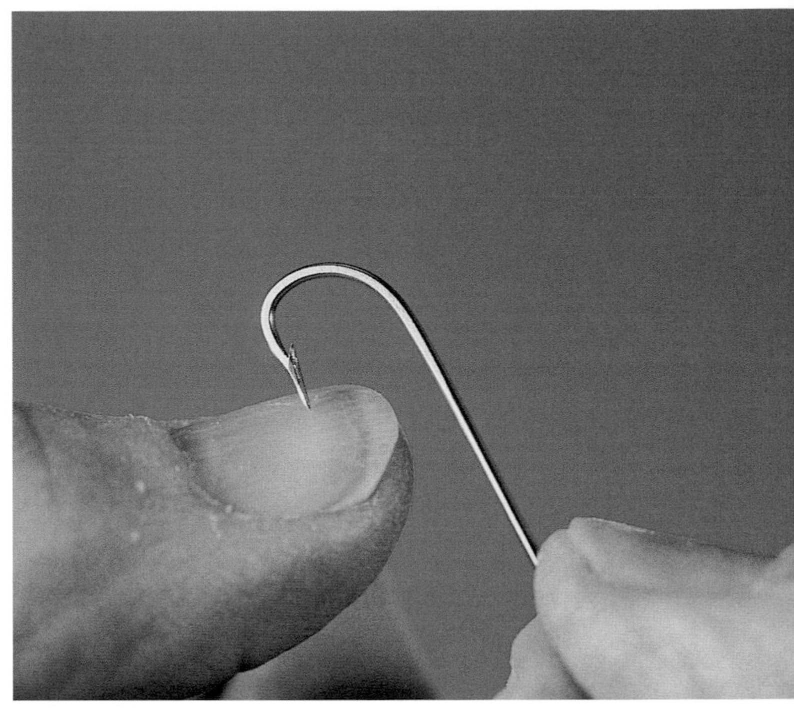

329 OPEN HOOK GAPS

To make a fly hook fish easier, use pliers to slightly open the hook gap. Do this before tying the fly, so that if the hook breaks, you will not have ruined the fly. Make this change very slight; you want to increase the gap for surer hooking, not open the hook to the point where you might lose a fish.

330 BENDING HOOK BARBS

There are two ways to bend down the barb of a hook. One is to hold the pliers at a right angle to the hook shank and bend the barb down. The second way is to hold the pliers jaws parallel to the hook point and bend. The second way is usually best, since it lessens the possibility of the hook breaking or bending.

331 REMOVING HOOK BARBS

One way to remove the barb from a fly hook to make a barbless hook or for adding a bead is to use a fine file or hook hone to file off the barb.

To do this, place the fly hook in a vise and hold the hook by the "heel" (the bend of the hook) with the point and barb protruding from the vise. Then use a fine file or diamond-dust hook hone to file down the barb. This takes longer than using pliers to bend down the barb, but it is safer since there is less likelihood that the point will break.

Do this before tying the fly and consider preparing a number of hooks this way at once so that they are ready for tying later.

332 SNELLING TANDEM FLY HOOKS ▲

One easy way to add a rear hook to a main hook to make a tandem fly is to snell the rear hook, using heavy mono for durability. Snelling is like a nail knot on the hook shank.

You can then secure the mono to the front hook by laying it alongside the hook shank and wrapping tightly with the tying thread.

One way to keep the mono from slipping out is to use a flame to make a melted ball at the end that can't slide under the wrapped shank. If your hook has a large eye, you can also run the mono along the hook shank, up through and over the eye, and back parallel to the hook shank. Then wrap over both of these strands of mono with the tying thread. Since you run the mono through the hook eye, there is no way that the two hooks can pull apart. Tie the fly after making this hook connection to the rear-tied fly.

333 THE RIGHT HOOK FOR SNELLING FLIES

If you are snelling a rear hook to make a tandem rig and plan to run the mono through the hook eye, you must use a hook with a turned-up or turned-down eye. (On the forward hook, you can use a turned-up eye, turned-down eye, or the commonly available straight ball eye.)

You can snell also to a straight eye hook without running the mono through the eye, since the eye serves as a "stopper" to prevent the mono from coming loose. To do this, lay the mono alongside the hook shank and eye as you snell mono to the hook.

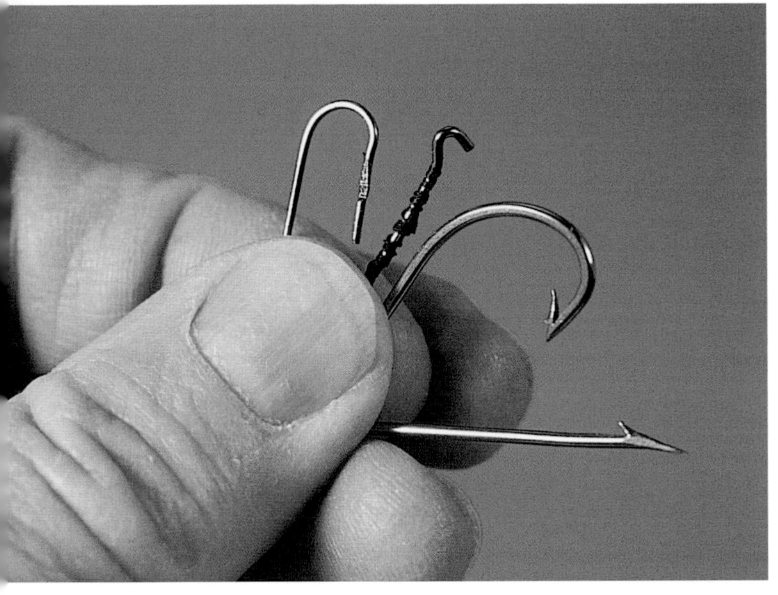

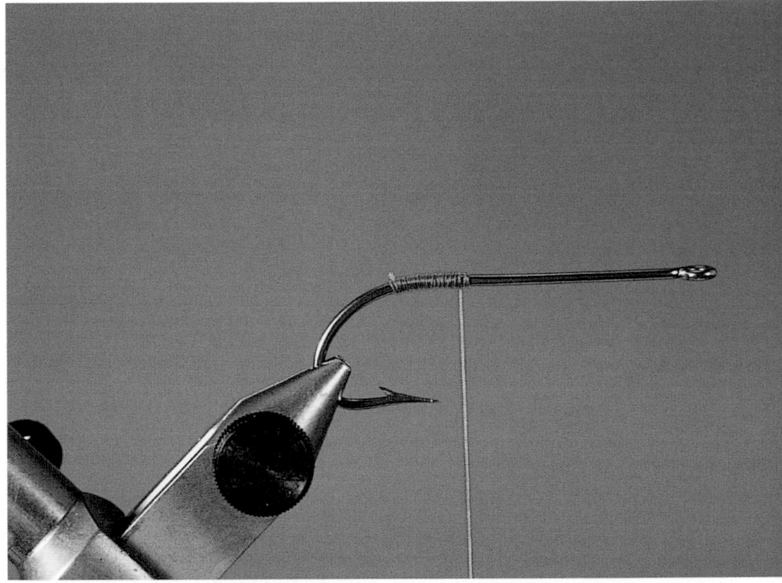

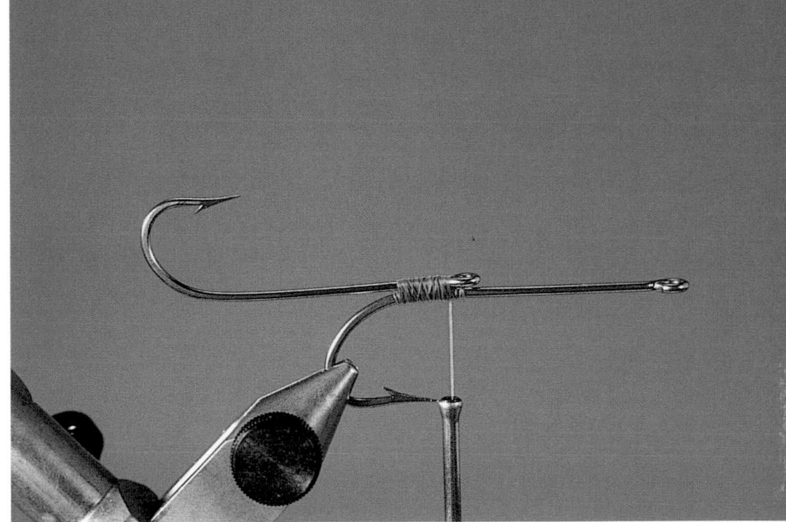

334 CHECKING FOR HOOK FLAWS

Check hooks for flaws before tying. While modern hook manufacturers have strict quality controls, sometimes a bad hook does sneak through and end up in a box. Though uncommon, flaws can include bent shanks, poor or bent points, damaged barbs, and incomplete eyes. You certainly want to discover any flaws before tying a fly on that particular hook.

335 CIRCLE HOOKS

Try tying some of your larger flies for saltwater and warm-water fishing on circle hooks. These are now available for fly tying in both standard and long shank lengths, and are ideal for catch-and-release fishing. Usually when fishing with these, the fly ends up in the corner of the mouth of the fish, and is more likely to result in a positive strike and solid hooking, along with easy unhooking.

336 MAKING FIXED TANDEM RIGS

You can make a hook with a fixed tandem rig by wrapping a hook, point up, to the main hook on which you tie the fly. With the main hook in the fly-tying vise, first tie on with the tying thread. Then place the second hook on top of the first with the point up. Wrap over the two hook shanks with the tying thread, spiral wrap all along the shank, and then tightly wrap the hook shank.

Seal with head cement or five-minute epoxy before continuing and finishing the fly. Or use shrink tubing to fasten the two hook shanks together. Then wrap the bound hooks with heavy tying thread to make sure that they will not come apart.

First make sure that such tandem or double-hook flies are legal in your area.

337 PREVENTING CUT THREAD

If you sometimes cut your thread on the point of the hook protruding from the jaws of the vise, consider clamping the hook to hide the point in the vise jaws. This way, the thread will only slide over the smooth and polished vise jaws, preventing thread breaks.

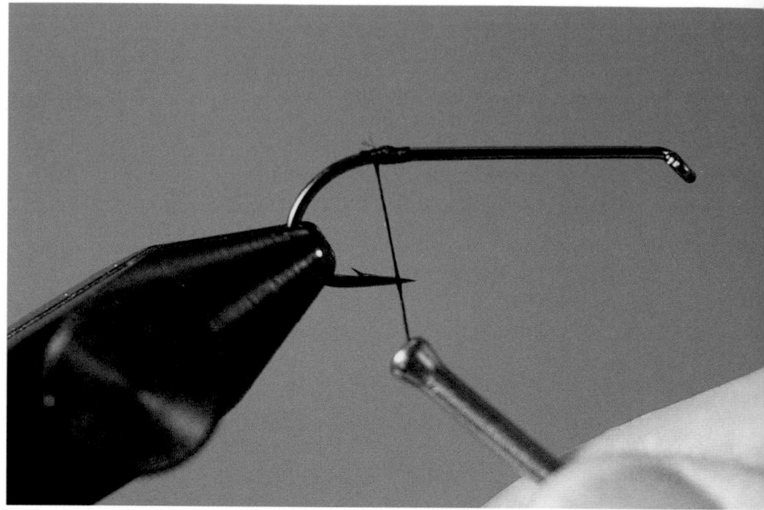

338 STORING THREAD SPOOLS

An easy way to store thread spools is on a thread spool rack sold in craft and sewing stores. These hold up to about 40 spools in a wood rack, which you can hang on the wall or prop easel-like on the fly-tying bench. You can also store other spooled materials, such as spools of wire, lead wire, braided materials, etc.

339 WEIGHTING HOOKS WITH LEAD WIRE

One of the best ways to weight a hook is to wrap lead or non-lead wire around the hook shank. You can also control the sink pattern of the fly by tying the lead along the entire shank (sinks evenly), at the rear (sinks tail first), or in back of the hook eye (sinks head first).

Of these three methods, usually the head-weighted method is best, since on a twitch retrieve, the fly gets jerked up and then falls down, creating more action and a lifelike look.

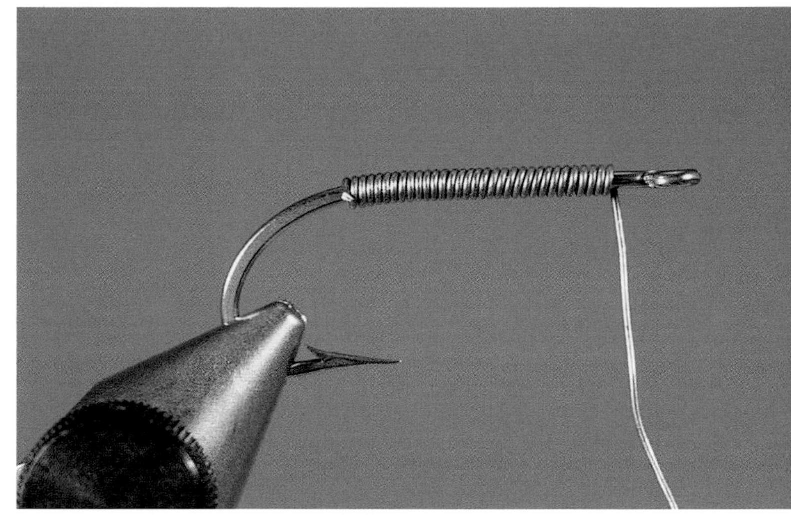

340 CONTROLLING FLY SINK RATE

You can control the sink rate of a fly with a wrapped lead or non-lead underbody by using different-size wire. Lead wire, for example, comes in sizes from 0.010- to 0.035-inch (0.254- to 0.889-mm) diameter. This is also important for adjusting the weight and size of the lead wire to the size of the hook.

341 ANOTHER WAY TO ADD NON-LEAD WIRE

If adding non-lead wire to a fly hook by tying it parallel with the hook shank, it is often best to use one length or three lengths, with the three lengths spread evenly around the hookshank diameter.

Two lengths, often described as best tied on each side of the hook, are difficult to keep in place and often loosen to slide around the hook shank. If you wish to tie in two parallel lengths of lead wire, one on each side of the hook shank, it is best to do this over a shank wrapped with a layer of thread. This tends to keep the lead from slipping. Add a drop of glue to the wrapped shank to help keep the lead or non-lead wire in place as you wrap it to the hook shank.

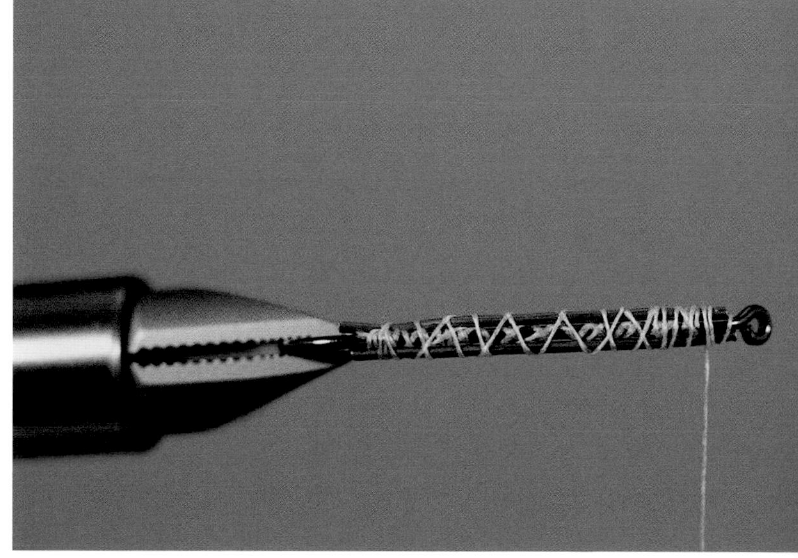

342 HOOK STORAGE SYSTEMS

Use a system to store your hooks. Some flytiers store hooks by size, regardless of type; others separate hooks by type (scud, shrimp, nymph, streamer, wet fly, dry fly, stainless-steel saltwater, etc.). Pick the system that works best for you so that you can find hooks easily.

One way to separate hooks is to use one of the small many-drawer compartments, such as those sold for storing nuts and bolts. You can label each drawer by size, brand, and type of hook. Storage racks are available from general and hardware stores in a variety of sizes and numbers of compartments. You can get these with anywhere from about a dozen to four dozen compartments.

343 MAKING FLAT NYMPH BODIES

Many nymphal forms of insects have flat bodies, the better to survive in fast currents. One way to make a flat body for a nymph pattern is to first wrap the hook shank with lead wire and then use pliers to flatten the lead wrap. Continue to tie the fly, following other tips for using lead and creating lifelike flies. For these nymph patterns, the lead helps to sink the fly to where the trout are located, and the shape helps to fool the trout into thinking the fly is a live insect—a typical flat-bodied nymph.

344 POPPER HOOK

Some popper hooks come in both regular- and long-shank styles. For almost all fishing, you get more and deeper strikes by using the long-shank popper hooks. This allows more of the hook point to extend in back of the bug and keeps the bug at a more pronounced angle in the water for better hooking. It also allows more room when tying on tails and collars.

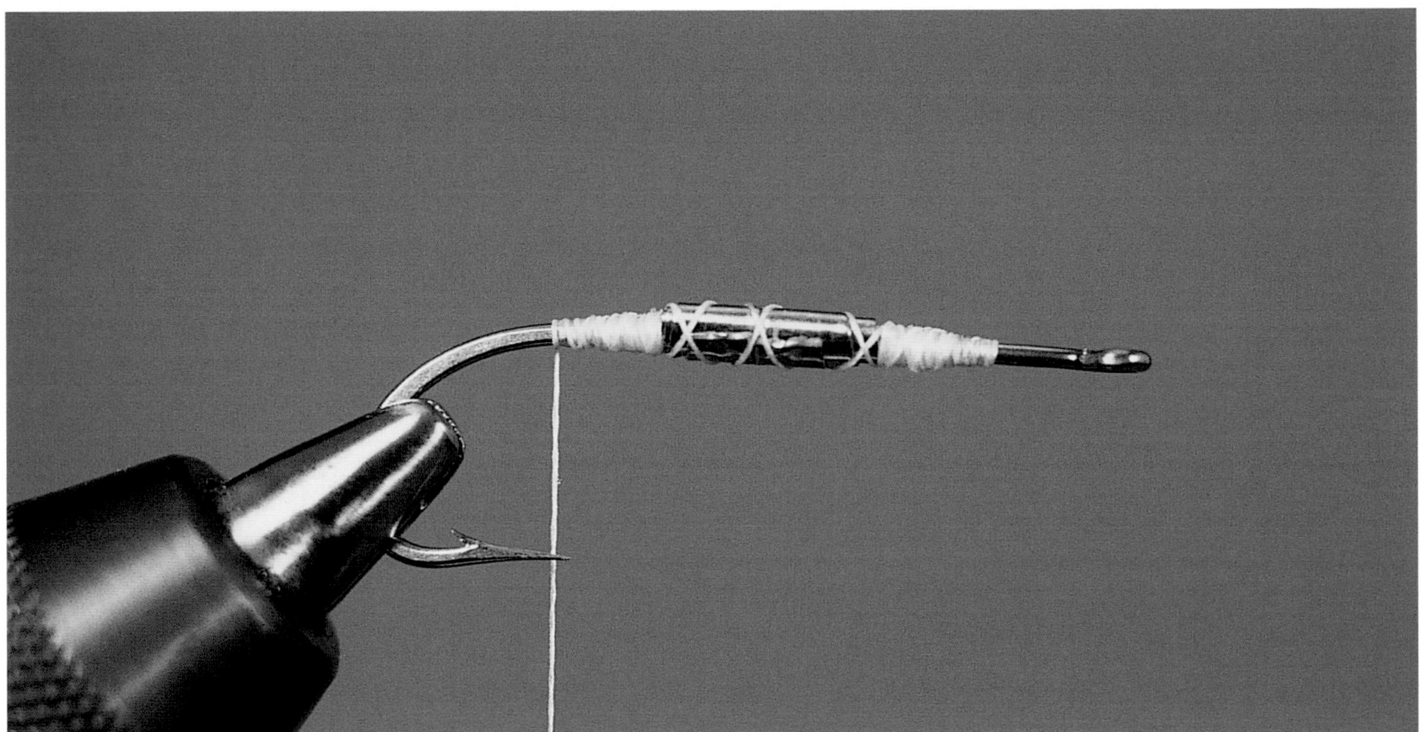

345 PICKING THE RIGHT SIZE WIRE

One simple way to pick the right size lead or non-lead wire for your fly is to choose wire that approximates the hook diameter. You can do this by sight or feel, with the best way holding the wire against the shank of the chosen hook to see if both feel about the same diameter. While hooks of various model numbers within a manufacturer's line and definitely between manufacturers do vary, a rough chart that you might use follows:

Lead Wire Diameter	Approx. Hook Size Standard Hooks
0.010 inch/0.254 mm	16 and smaller
0.015 inch/0.381 mm	14
0.020 inch/0.508 mm	10, 12
0.025 inch/0.635 mm	8
0.030 inch/0.762 mm	6, 4
0.035 inch/0.889 mm	2 and larger

346 RAMPING

Make a "ramp" of thread when tying in a wrap of non-lead wire to a hook shank for weight. To make a smoothly tapered body on a fly tied with wraps of wire around the hook shank, use the tying thread first to crisscross and spiral wrap over the lead wrap to help secure it. Then use the tying thread at each end of the wrapped lead wire to make a tapered "ramp." This allows you to wrap the body material over the lead wire without the over-body making a "jump" or creating a gap as it goes from the hook shank to the wire wrap.

347 WORKING WITH MONO WEED GUARDS FOR FLIES

When adding a weed guard to a fly, tie down the end of the weed guard on the shank at the tail of the fly before adding any materials. Then tie the fly before finishing the weed guard at the head of the fly. Once the fly is finished, bring the end of the weed guard up to the head and tie it down and clip the end before tying off and finishing the fly.

When wrapping down the end of the mono to complete the weed guard, it helps to partly pull out the end of the weed guard and then use a flame (match or lighter) to make a ball on the end of the mono weed guard. Then pull the mono back until the formed ball seats against the head of the fly. Continue wrapping and finishing the fly. The ball on the end of the mono prevents the weed guard from pulling loose.

For more protection in really weedy waters, you can do the same thing with double mono weed guards. Tie in the end of the weed guard on both sides of the hook shank using tying thread. Then tie the rest of the fly. Once finished with the fly, pull the two mono loops forward, making sure that both are identical, and have equal size loops. Tie off as before. And then finish the fly with a whip finish and sealer.

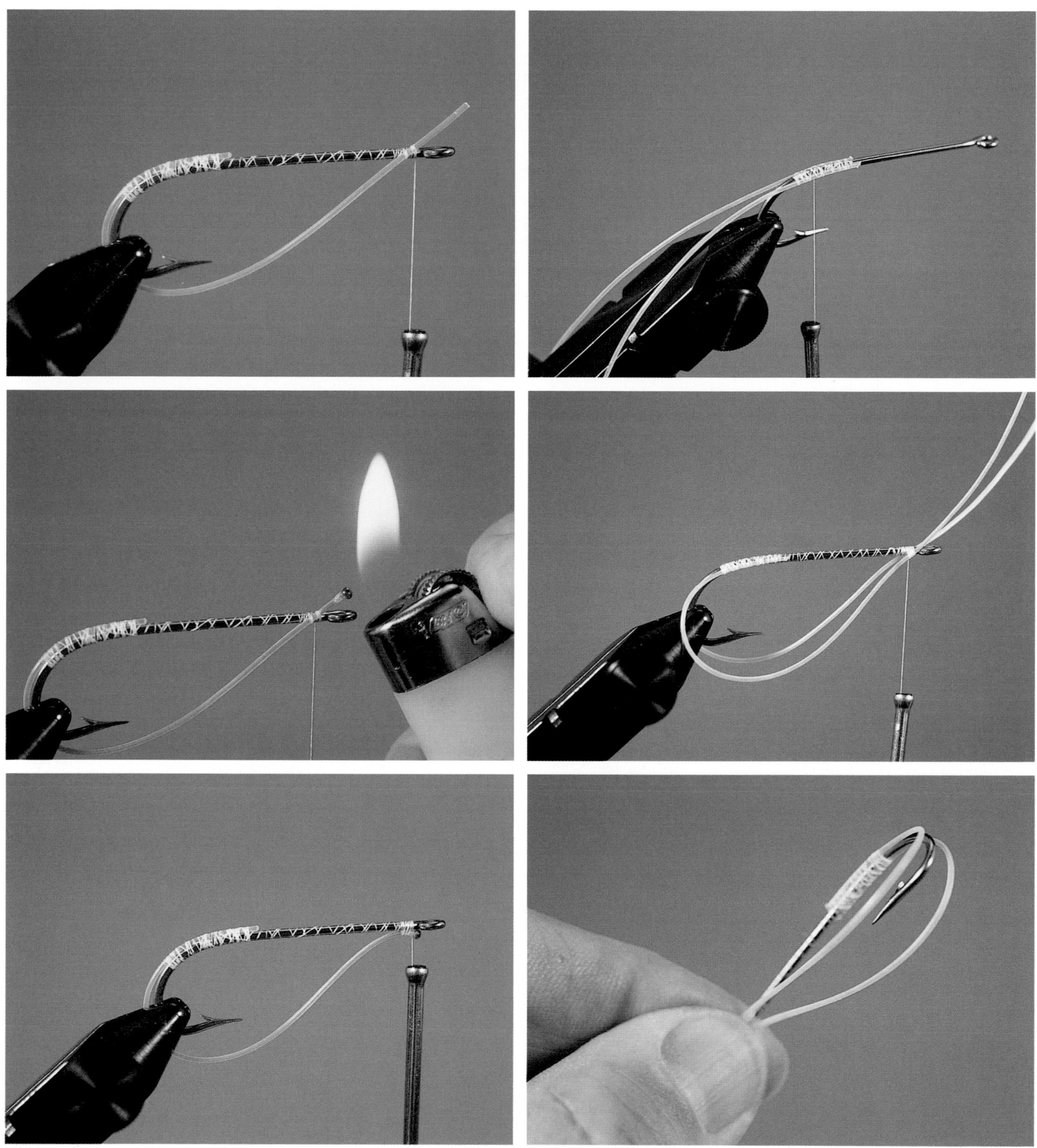

348 WIRE WEED GUARDS, TIP ONE

For durable weed guards, use plastic-coated braided wire, bent into a slight "Z" or "S" shape, tied in at the head of the fly and then bent down to protect the hook point. For best results, use 30-pound-test (13.6-kg) for flies size 2 and smaller, and 40-pound-test (18.1-kg) for flies size 1 and larger.

If you are fishing really heavy weeds, use a double-point (prong) weed guard. Use epoxy when seating this weed guard so that it will not come loose.

349 WIRE WEED GUARDS, TIP TWO

One way to make a wire weed guard on a fly is to use light monel (single strand) wire such as 12-pound-test (5.4-kg), fold it in half, and then bend a slight angle into the folded end. If you are used to trolling wire sizes, use size 5 for flies size 1/0 and smaller and use size 7 for flies 2/0 and larger. Tie this folded end to the hook under the fly head, secure tightly, and then finish the fly. Use wire cutters (wear safety glasses) to trim the two ends of the wire to protect and extend on either side of the hook point.

"Many go fishing all their lives without knowing that it is not fish they are after."

—*Henry David Thoreau*

350 FINISHING MONO-LOOP WEED GUARDS

To finish a mono-loop weed guard after tying the rest of the fly, position the loop of mono so that it is big enough to protect the hook point without being so big as to be unwieldy. Note that you might be positioning or changing the loop position depending upon how you tie it down, so take care that you configure the loop for the final position that it makes on the completed fly.

351 FITTING BEADS TO HOOKS

If a metal bead does not quite fit onto a forged shank hook, you can often make it fit. To do this, place the bead in a shop vise and just barely tighten the vise so that the bead slightly flattens to make the hole oval. Then slip the bead onto the hook point after bending down the barb. Since you have flattened the bead, you can adjust it so that the flat hole lines up with the forged shank and bend of the hook to slide around the bend easily. Then move the bead up to the eye of the hook and tie in place with working thread.

352 WEIGHTED-WIRE NYMPHS

Tie simple, weighted nymph imitations with a wrap of brass or copper wire, and a head of peacock herl. These are very similar to the so-called Brassie patterns used to get deep to trout.

On some waters prohibiting lead, flies with brass wire may not be legal. Brass does contain small amounts of lead, so check before fishing.

353 IDENTIFYING WEIGHTED FLIES

You can't tell by looking at a fly whether or not it is weighted. One way to mark flies to indicate whether they are weighted is to use different head colors.

You could tie non-weighted flies with white thread and weighted flies with black thread. You can even go further by marking non-weighted, lightly weighted, and heavily weighted flies by using three different colors of thread. White, red, and black heads are good examples.

You can also indicate fully-weighted, rear-weighted, and front-weighted flies the same way. Red, orange, and pink are favorite colors for this system. Just don't make too complicated a system that you have trouble remembering.

354 FLY-TYING WIRE SOURCES

Electronics stores are a good source of inexpensive wire for fly tying. Try to buy the least amount of wire possible, or get an assorted pack of wire sizes and colors. Often very fine wire is best for tying bodies or ribbing.

355 ADDING BEADS AND CONES TO FLY HOOKS

When adding beads or cone heads to a fly, use hooks with a symmetrical round bend, sometimes known as a Perfect Bend. This prevents a sharp radius of the bend as might occur with an Aberdeen, an O'Shaughnessy, a Limerick, or other similar fly hook styles from stopping or restricting the bead.

356 MAKING BEAD CHAIN EYES

To make bead chain eyes with more weight, action, and flash, use four or six beads, which places two to three eyes on each side of the fly. These also help the fly to stay upright with the point up when the fly scoots along the bottom.

Another advantage is that the two or three beads on each side of the fly add both flash and rattle noise as they move around.

357 WEIGHTING FLIES

Bead chain makes ideal eyes for flies, particularly when you want a large eye without the weight of lead or non-lead dumbbell or hourglass eyes. Bead chain is available from hardware stores or home supply stores, and comes in several sizes in both brass and bright nickel. Some fly shops also carry this, where it is also available in several sizes of stainless steel for saltwater flies.

To use, cut off two of the beads with wire cutters (use safety glasses). Wrap them into the head of the fly with thread as you would dumbbell or hourglass eyes, wrapping around the wire joint between the two beads as you hold the bead chain eyes crosswise on the hook shank.

358 WEIGHTING LEECHES

Tie leech patterns with a weight, dumbbell eye, or hourglass eye in the front, since they are retrieved in an up/down fashion, which is close to the swimming action of a real leech.

To get the fly to swim this way, use slight twitches to cause it to fall on the pause, jerking it back up with each twitch.

359 WEIGHTING METAL AND OTHER BEADS

You can make metal bead heads even heavier by a simple trick. Most metal beads have a tapered hole, with the larger open end of the hole designed to fit toward the rear of the fly and the small hole to fit against the hook eye. Slide the bead onto the hook shank and around to the hook eye. Make a wrap of one or two turns of lead or non-lead wire around the hook shank in back of the bead. Then push the wrap of lead wire forward and into the hole to hide it. Use pliers to push the lead forward if necessary. Tie on the thread in back of the bead and wrap around the hook shank in back of the bead and lead wire to keep the lead wrap in place.

You can do this with any size fly, since lead and non-lead wire comes in 0.010- to 0.035-inch (0.254- to 0.889-mm) diameters.

360 ADDING TUNGSTEN TO FLY HEADS FOR WEIGHT

To add weight to the head of a fly, add tungsten or lead powder to the head sealer. This works best with the thicker epoxy coatings on large flies, but you can also add it to head cement and fingernail polish. Lead or tungsten powder is available in golf shops. Some fly-tying stores (at this writing) are starting to sell it also.

To add it to epoxy, first squeeze out equal parts of the resin and hardener and then add the powder to one of these two parts. When you have stirred the weighted powder into one part, mix the two parts completely and add to the fly. Stir frequently to keep the tungsten powder suspended in the fluid.

You can do the same thing by adding the powder to a small puddle of head cement or clear nail polish. Because of the added weight of this material, place the fly on a rotator for curing.

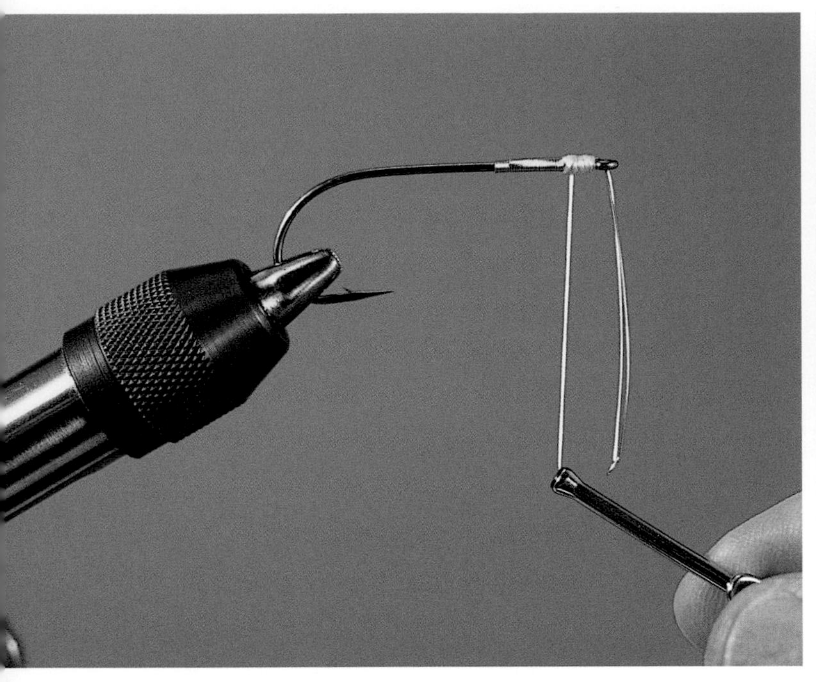

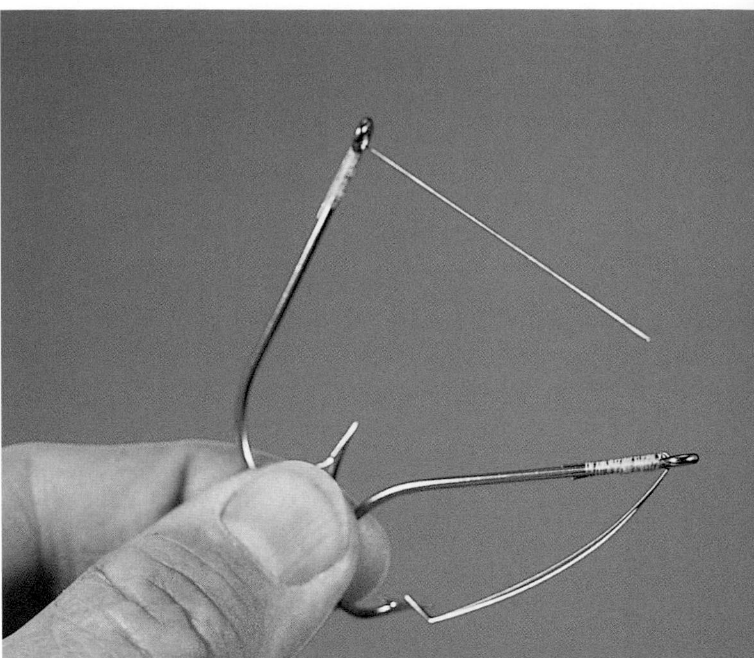

361 WIRE AND HACKLE WEED GUARD TIPS

To make a single-strand wire weed guard, clip the wire about one-and-a-half times the length of the hook shank. Use pliers to bend at a right angle the end of the wire about ¼ inch (6 mm) from the end of the wire. Tie this short end into the fly hook right behind the hook eye. Then tie the rest of the fly. (Alternatively, tie the fly up to this point and then tie in the wire end.)

Finish tying the fly and seal with head cement. Bend the wire weed guard back close to the hook point and trim it with wire cutters if required. You can also double this wire, tying down the two ends and using pliers to make a slight bend in the wire fold to fit over the end of the hook point.

An alternative way to make a weed guard when a heavy one is not needed is to tie in a heavier, wider, and thicker than normal hackle. This will tend to protect the hook point and prevent hang-ups or snags.

362 MONO SIZE FOR WEED GUARDS

The best size mono for tying mono-loop weed guards is about 20-pound-test (9.1-kg) for most flies (about size 1 through 2/0). Go as light as 12-pound-test (5.4-kg) for flies size 2 and smaller, and go as heavy as 30-pound-test (13.6-kg) for flies size 3/0 and larger.

A good guide to making a mono weed guard is to use regular fishing monofilament that is about half the diameter as that of the hook shank. This ensures the right stiffness and protection, without it being too stiff to prevent strikes or too weak and collapsing to catch a weed. Below is a rough guide. Realize that the wire diameters of hooks vary with model, manufacturer, and style of hook (2X fine for dry flies; 3X stout for nymphs). Mono diameters for a given pound-test also vary with the manufacturer and type of mono. Use the chart below as a starting point for experimentation and develop a system for your tying.

363 MAKING BONEFISH FLIES SNAGPROOF

Mix in a few strands of monofilament with the wing of a bonefish fly to make it even more snag resistant. These flies, tied point up with the wing flared over the hook point, are semi-snagproof anyway. By adding a little mono, or a single strand of 20-pound-mono (9.1-kg) hidden and veiled in the regular materials wing, you can make them completely snagproof while hiding the mono weed guard.

Hook Size	Hook Diameter	Mono Pound-Test
14	approx. 0.0177 inch/0.45 mm	6 (approx. 0.009 inch/0.228 mm 2X)
12	approx. 0.020 inch/0.508 mm	8 (approx. 0.010 inch/0.254 mm 1X)
10	approx. 0.0225 inch/0.571 mm	10 (approx. 0.0120 inch/0.305 0X)
8	approx. 0.025 inch/0.635 mm	12 (approx. 0.013 inch/0.330 mm)
6	approx. 0.028 inch/0.711 mm	15 (approx. 0.015 inch/0.381 mm)
4	approx. 0.033 inch/0.838 mm	15 (approx. 0.015 inch/0.381 mm)
2	approx. 0.035 inch/0.889 mm	15 (approx. 0.015 inch/0.381 mm)
1 and larger	approx. 0.040 inch/1.016 mm	20 (0.018 inch/0.457 mm) 30 (0.026 inch/0.660 mm)

364 BRUSH GUARD MONO WEED GUARDS

To make a stiff weed guard for a large fly, use a few strands of monofilament line, bundled to make a brush-style weed guard. Use light, 8- to 12-pound-test (3.6- to 5.4-kg) mono for flies to size 2; and use 12- to 20-pound-test (5.4- to 9.1-kg) for larger flies. If possible, pick stiff mono rather than limp, cold-water styles.

Clip a few strands, arrange them into a small bundle, even the ends, and then fold the ends into a right angle with a pair of needle-nose pliers. Then tie in the short end under the head of the fly, clip any excess, and finish the head. Trim the free ends of the nylon with scissors short enough to reduce visibility, but long enough to protect the hook point.

366 MAKING WORM FLIES

It is easy to make a bass fly that resembles the plastic worm used by spinning and casting bass anglers. To do this, use cactus chenille. Tie a length (about three times the length of the worm desired) to the rear of the hook shank. Then hold the cactus chenille at about two-thirds the length from the hook and twist in the same direction that the material was twisted to create the chenille.

After a few turns, hold a bodkin in the middle of this twisted length and fold the chenille over on itself to tie down at the rear of the hook shank. Release the bodkin and the cactus chenille will twist on itself. Tie down well and wrap the thread forward. Use the remainder of the cactus chenille to wrap around the hook shank and tie off at the head.

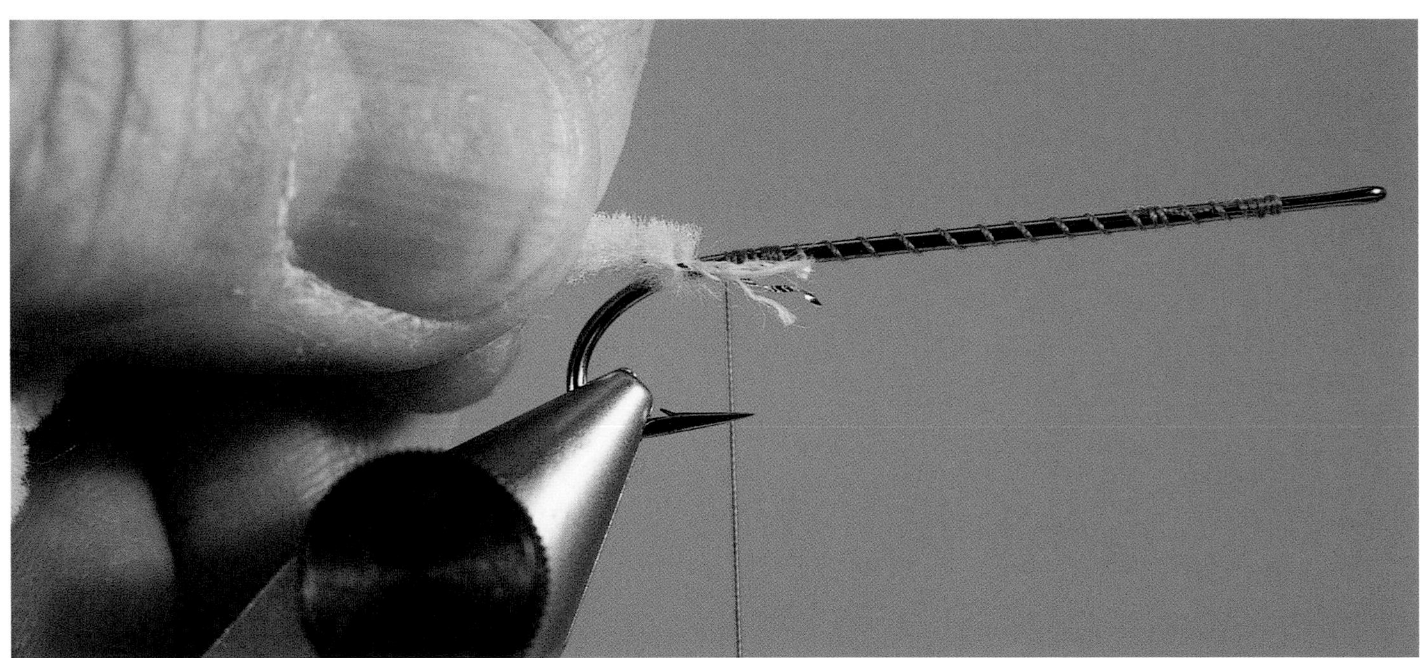

365 CHENILLE TYING TIPS

If you do not want to lay down a length of chenille along the hook shank when tying on at the rear of the hook to prevent lumps, use your thumbnail and index fingernail to pull fibers from the tag end. This exposes the thin core of two or three threads that have little bulk and are easy to tie down. Use these threads to tie down chenille to prevent any bulk buildup that would mar the appearance of the finished fly.

367 FOAM BEETLE BODIES

The best way to get a natural-looking beetle body of foam is to tie in a short length of flat foam at the rear of the hook shank with the foam facing the rear. Then wrap the thread forward, fold the foam over, and tie down with the thread. Add legs or fold over previously wrapped legs to complete this simple bug.

Make segments wrapping the thread forward to the point where you want the segmentation, then fold over the foam and segment the body at that point with the tying thread. Tie off with a whip finish at the head of the fly.

368 MAKING TAPERED WORM ENDS

To make a tapered end to a worm fly, such as a San Juan worm, use a lighter or butane grill starter to lightly burn/melt the end of the chenille. Then carefully use your fingers to twist and taper it. The chenille is hot, but it should not burn you. By doing this and creating a taper in the ends of the worm, you make it more lifelike and natural.

369 TYING WORM FLIES WITH CHENILLE

When tying worm flies where the chenille ends are exposed, make sure that you use Ultra Chenille, Vernille, or similar products that will not fray like standard tying chenille. This is important with small flies, such as the popular San Juan worm for trout fishing.

370 MAKING A CADDIS CASE NYMPH

▲

Make a simple caddis imitation by wrapping a few turns of peacock herl onto a hook directly behind the eye and tying off. Coat the fly with a waterproof glue (five-minute epoxy, Ultra Flex, Duco, etc.) and roll the result in sand. Then use your fingers to roll the sand around the hook to make it like a mini sandy cigar. The result is a fly that imitates the caddis sand cases, with the peacock herl suggesting the head of the larvae peeking out of the case. These sink well, fish great, and are easy to make. If not illegal, bring home some sand from places you trout fish to duplicate the cases these insects make.

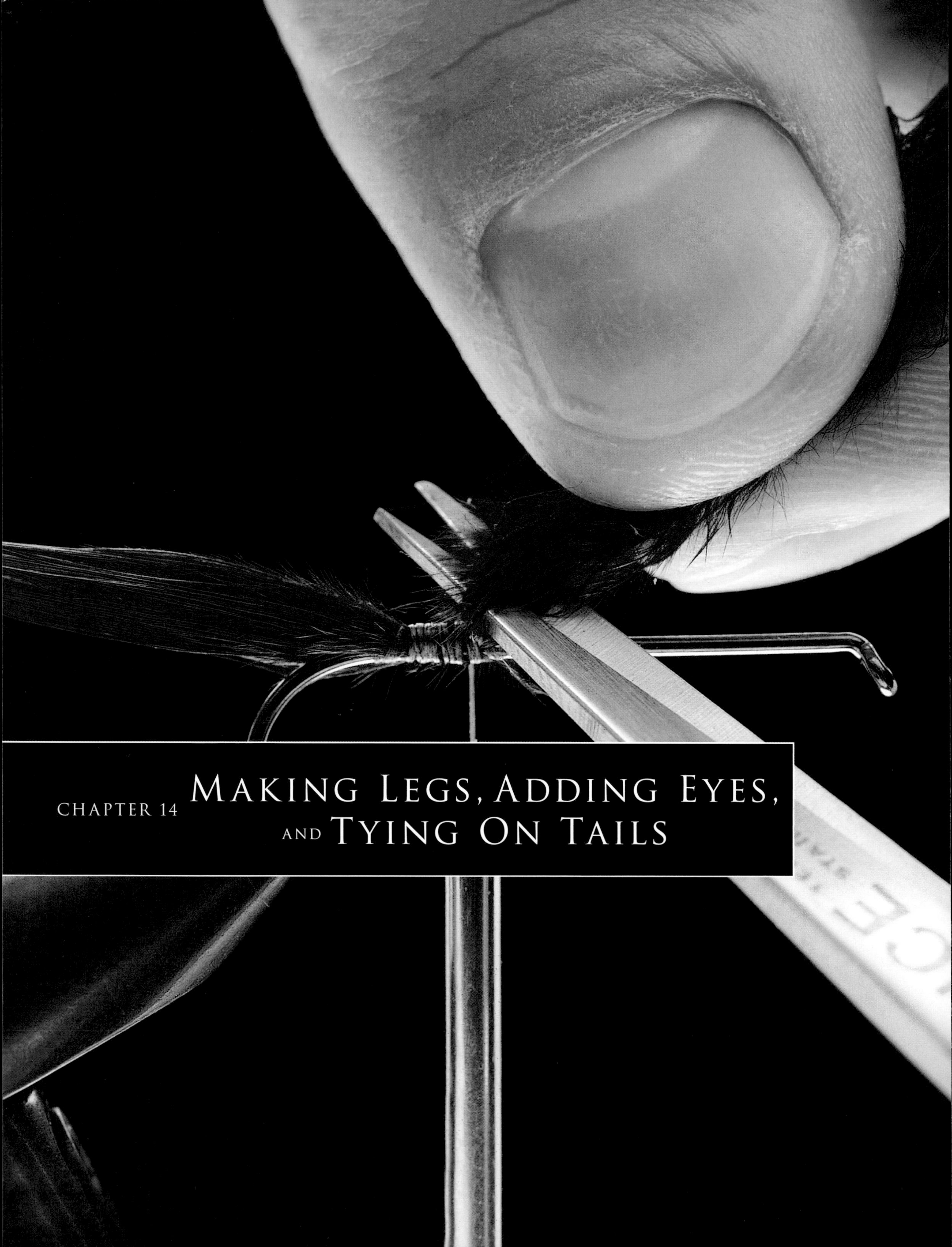

CHAPTER 14 Making Legs, Adding Eyes, and Tying On Tails

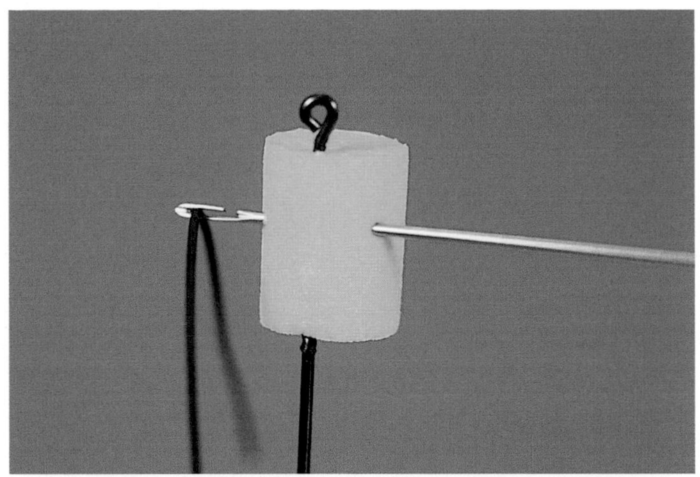

371 THREADING RUBBER LEGS

An easy way to thread rubber legs through a cork, balsa, or foam bug body is to file a notch in the eye of a large (darning style) needle, then hook the rubber legs into this open notch, and run the needle with the legs through the body as desired. Once you have the needle and the legs through the body, you can pull on one side of the legs through the hole. If using a double length of leg material for a full leg look, remove the legs from the needle-notched eye and cut the legs at this point with scissors.

372 MAKING CHENILLE NYMPH LEGS

If you are making large nymphs, such as some Western stonefly nymphs, use fine-diameter Vernille or Ultra Chenille for the legs. These materials are excellent-grade chenilles that you can taper at the ends by heating in a flame and rolling between your fingers. If you want the legs a little stiffer, add some clear flexible sealer to them. Softex is good for this, along with some of the soft epoxies like Soft Head Cement made by Loon Outdoors.

373 RUNNING PILOT HOLES

To run legs through a cork, balsa, or foam body, first make a pilot hole through the side of the bug body with a needle or bodkin. If using a plain needle, first grip the needle in a vise and then run the cork up and down on the needle. Follow this by running a notched-eye needle holding the rubber legs through the cork, foam, or balsa body.

374 MAKING HOPPER AND FLY LEGS

Use a small latch-hook tool (they are sold for fly tying in small sizes by fly shops exclusively) to make overhand knots in small bundles of feathers and fibers to make legs for hoppers and other insects. For best results, do this with the fibers still on the central vane. Make up a bunch of these and you can later clip off what you need when you need it.

375 DRESSMAKER'S PINS FOR EYES

You can make easy eyes for foam, cork, and balsa bugs from plastic-head dressmaker's pins. These come in several sizes and in assorted basic colors including white, black, blue, red, yellow, and green. They are also easy to dress up with an additional dot of paint to make a pupil on each bulging eye.

Cut the stem to a short length with wire cutters (wear safety glasses), and use pliers to insert the eye into the bug body. To keep them in place, add a small dot of glue to the metal stem to glue the stem and the base of the eye in place on the bug.

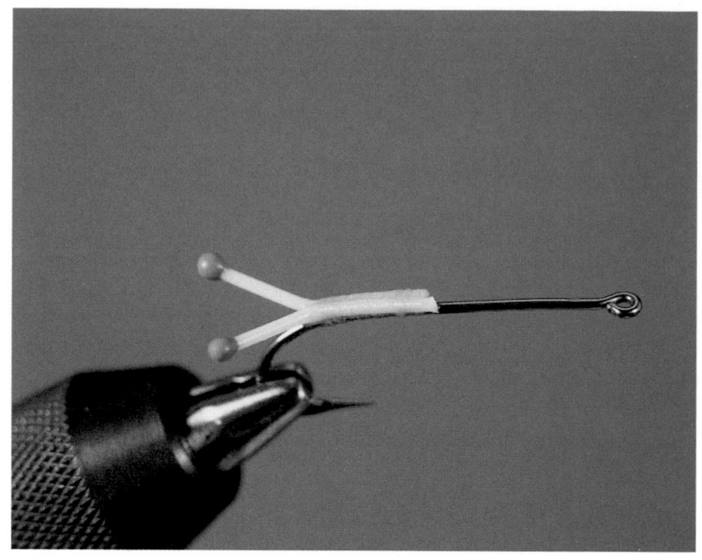

376 MAKING TANDEM FLIES

One way to make a tandem fly is to tie a few tail materials onto a separate hook and then secure it by means of a mono or wire connector to the main hook. By tying tail materials to the separate tail hook, you essentially extend the length of the fly and also the hooking ability of the fly with this second hook. You can position this hook point up or point down, as preferred.

To do this, add the mono or wire extension to the hook, place it in a vise, and tie on the materials desired. Complete with a whip finish and seal with head cement or epoxy. Place the second hook (forward) in the vise. Then tie the extended wire or mono to the forward hook before adding the materials to complete the fly.

377 MAKING HAIRBRUSH EYES

To make simple eyes for saltwater flies such as shrimp and crabs, use plastic bristles from a hairbrush. These are usually in black, but you can also find other colors. The advantage of these is that they protrude like the eyes of a real shrimp or crab, making the fly more lifelike.

Use wire cutters to cut off two bristles, tie them to the hook shank, and bend or flare out the shanks to make the eyes protrude as desired. Bend the plastic bristle at a slight angle or a sharp and right angle, depending upon the position you want for the eyes.

378 BENDING MONOFILAMENT FOR LEGS

To make bent legs from mono for tying some nymphs and realistic imitations, use a flame, soldering iron, or heated cauterizing tool. Hold the mono next to the side of a flame such as you get from a grill starter. (Lighters get too hot to hold.) Do not let the mono touch the flame, since that will melt it. Within a few seconds, the mono will bend from the heat softening the mono at that point.

You can also do this with a hot rod such as a cauterizing tool or electric soldering iron. These tools make a sharper bend in the mono. Make sure that you hold the mono horizontal so that the melted spot causes the extended part of the mono to drop from gravity and make the desired bend.

379 MAKING LEGS IN RUBBER MATERIALS

Use the same small latch-hook tool noted previously to make overhand knots for joints in the rubber legs used for some fly patterns and many bass and panfish bugs. For best results, do this after you have inserted the legs through the bug body. Otherwise, the knot makes pulling the leg through the body difficult. Do this carefully so that the overhand knot makes a neat bent leg right where you want it in the fly.

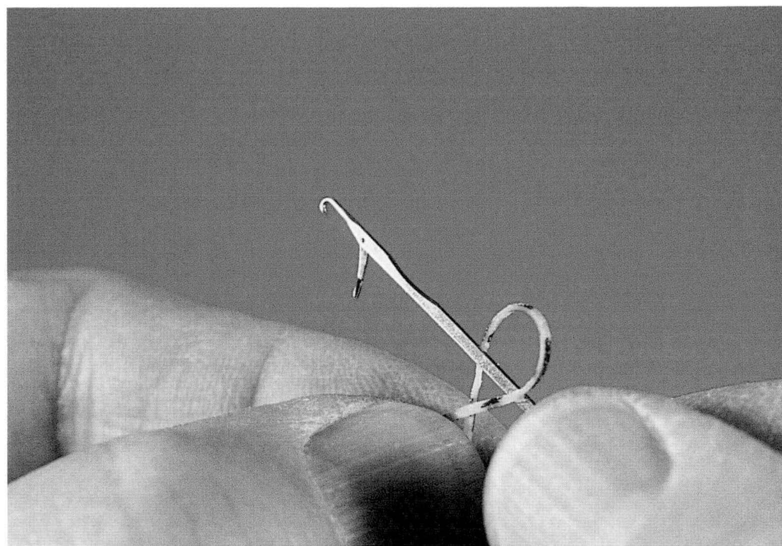

380 QUICK AND EASY LEGS

For a quick, easy, and professional way to run rubber legs through a bug body, get a sewing machine needle and cut a notch in the side of the eye with a file or Dremel tool. Then, place the needle in a small bench vise with the point up.

To run rubber legs through a foam, cork, or balsa bug, hold the bug sideways over the needle and push down (be careful to keep your fingers out of the way) until the point and notched eye are exposed. Then place the rubber legs in the notch and pull the bug straight up. Do this slowly so that you do not tear or break the rubber legs. Once free of the needle, slip the rubber legs out of the needle notch, and adjust for length. Trim if necessary.

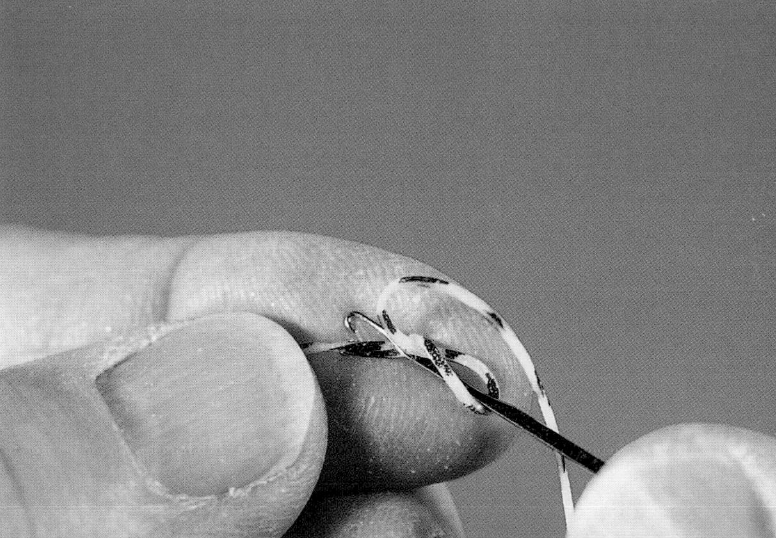

381 ADDING SELF-STICK EYES PERMANENTLY

Since self-stick eyes seldom stick permanently to the head of any fly, add the self-stick eyes and then protect them with several coatings of fly-head cement or a single coating of epoxy. You most frequently add eyes to large flies, so the epoxy coating is often the best.

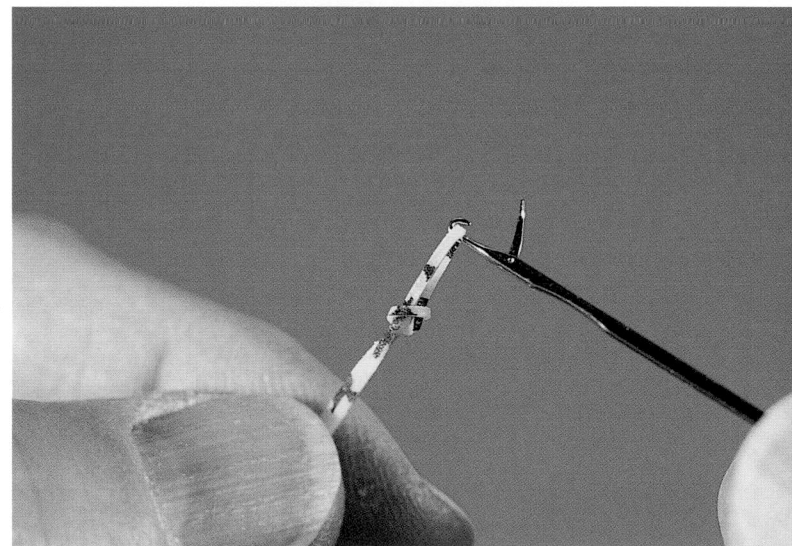

382 MAKING DUMBBELL GLASS/PLASTIC EYES

Make bright plastic or glass bead eyes for flies by placing them on mono. This makes a plastic or glass lightweight equivalent of lead dumbbell eyes or bead chain eyes. You can use any color and size bead for this.

You can get beads in transparent or opaque colors, in red, pink, yellow, green, orange, purple, and other colors. Popular sizes available from tackle supply shops and catalogs include 0.12 inch (3.00 mm), 0.16 inch (4.00 mm), 0.20 inch (5.00 mm), 0.24 inch (6.00 mm), and 0.31 inch (8.00 mm). Beads in other sizes and colors are also available from craft stores.

To do this, first string bright plastic beads onto heavy mono. Use an iron or low-heat soldering iron to melt the end of the mono. Slide two beads against this ball on the end of the mono, grip the mono with needle-nose pliers or tweezers, and cut the mono about 1/16 inch (2 mm) from the pliers. Heat and melt the end of the mono. It is a little more risky, but you can also use an open flame, such as a butane grill lighter.

The result is two beads, with a tying space in the center and the beads held in place with the melted ball on each end of the mono. Repeat as above to make more eyes.

These are ideal as eyes on flies for salmon, steelhead, shad, and similar coastal and anadromous species.

383 MAKING SPLIT TAILS

Charles Meck, in his book on fly-tying tips, notes an easy way to make split tails on dry flies and nymphs.

To do this, tie in the tail materials and then make a loop of a separate length of tying thread around the bend/shank area of the hook, immediately in back of the tail. Then pull the loop forward, using the joined strands of the loop to split the tail into two or three parts.

To split the tail into two parts, twist the loop strands and bring this between the center of the tail bundle. To make three tails, keep the strands separate and bring them up so that a center part of the tail stays between the loop, and the two split tails angle to the side.

You can adjust the angle of the split tails by the tension on the loop, which pulls forward and is tied down. Then complete the rest of the fly, tying in or wrapping on body materials.

384 SEALING AND PAINTING BULLET-HEAD FLIES

When making bullet heads on flies, such as those in the Thunder Creek series designed by Keith Fulsher (and previously developed as a method of tying by Maine flytier and Gray Ghost originator Carrie Stevens), make sure that you seal the head if you are going to paint eyes on the head. Just as with feather shoulders on flies, you must add some clear sealer to the head so that the painted eye will not bleed when applied to the bunched and folded bucktail head.

385 RECESSING EYES

Eyes on deer-hair bugs always look best if they are recessed. To do this, use a red-hot nail head to burn a recess to hold an eye in the clipped deer-hair body. Once you have burned the recess into the deer hair, add a small amount of glue (Ultra Flex, Ambroid, Duco, etc.) to the recess, and add the chosen eye to the bug.

To make these recess tools, use common nails with the right-size head for the eyes on the flies that you are tying.

Ideal eyes include plastic eyes, movable doll eyes, and bright beads.

386 ADDING SELF-STICK PRISM EYES

To add self-stick prism eyes to fly heads, use a bodkin to remove the eye from the backing sheet and add it to the head of the fly. Allow the self-stick side of the eye to stick to the bodkin point. Use the bodkin to position the eye on the head of the fly.

"Skill at the riverside, or at the fly-table, never came, nor ever will come to us by any road than that of practice."

—*George M. Kelson,* The Salmon Fly *(1895)*

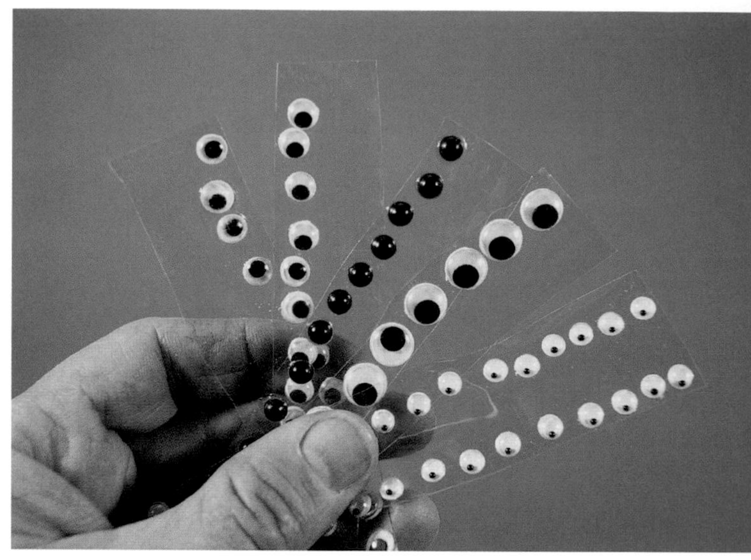

387 MAKING FABRIC PAINT EYES ON VINYL

Make painted eyes on vinyl for larger flies. These are tied in place rather than glued to the head. These position the eyes a little farther back on the fly, making a more lifelike appearance.

To do this, buy some clear vinyl from a fabric store. Different thicknesses are available to suit your fly tying and fly size. Then cut this into rectangles about the size of a dollar bill.

From a craft store, get some fabric paint but make sure to buy a brand that has a pointed spout. Get colors for both the eye and pupil color. Make a spot of eye color in two rows on the vinyl patch, followed by a smaller centered dot for the pupil. Good combinations for eye/pupil colors are yellow/black, white/black, orange/black, green/white, blue/white, red/white, and red/black.

Once the paints are cured, cut out a pair of eyes by cutting partway around the eye to leave a "tag end" to make a teardrop shape. Tie the eyes by the tag end on each side of the fly so that the eye extends back on the shoulder.

388 MAKING MONO-FILAMENT CRAB AND SHRIMP EYES

One easy way to make eyes for crab and shrimp flies is to use thick monofilament and burn one end to create a ball or "eye." You can make up a number of these in advance and have them ready for your fly tying.

Use 20- to 100-pound-test (9.1- to 45.4-kg) mono for this, depending upon the size of the fly and the size of the ball eye desired. Use a cigarette lighter or fireplace/grill lighter to create them. Color the ball eyes with a black, permanent felt-tip marker.

389 PAINTING DUMB-BELL EYES

One way to paint a lot of dumb-bell eyes for flies is to place the eyes between the teeth of a comb for easy holding and quick painting. This also makes it easy to paint both sides of each eye at once. Allow the paint to cure before removing from the comb teeth.

Another way to paint dumb-bell or hour-glass eyes is to cut a series of slits in a sheet of cardboard. Corrugated cardboard is best for this since it holds the eyes straight out for easy painting and little possibility that the eyes will fall out. Insert a dumb-bell eye into each slit and paint both sides as desired.

390 MAKING ANGLED EYES

To make angled eyes for shrimp and other saltwater patterns, wrap 50- to 100-pound (22.7- to 45.4-kg) mono around a square board or square aluminum stock. Use stock that is about 1 to 2 inches (2.5 to 5 cm) square. Secure one end of the mono, then wrap evenly and soak for a few minutes in a pot of boiling water. Remove the wrapped stock from the boiling water and "set" the mono by dipping it in ice water. Once complete, cut the mono down the middle of each stock to make for a lot of mono pieces bent into sharp bends or "elbows." Use a flame to form a ball on one end of this bent mono to make a ball eye. Color the ball with black permanent felt-tip marker. Tie these on the hook shank at the mono elbow to make eyes.

391 TYING RUBBER LEGS

To add rubber legs to a fly or bug (but not through a solid-body bug) center the legs on the hook shank and then crisscross the tying thread over the rubber legs and hook to hold them in place. The problem with this method is that the pressure on the rubber legs often twists the legs to an odd position on the hook.

A better way is to take the length of rubber leg (or legs), fold it over the tying thread, and then pull the tying thread into the hook shank to position the legs on one side of the fly. Then repeat this on the opposite side of the fly. This is quick and allows more exact placement of the rubber legs.

If you want a bunch of legs in one spot, as when tying a Calcasieu Pig Boat bass fly, you can fold a lot of legs over the thread and pull all into place at once.

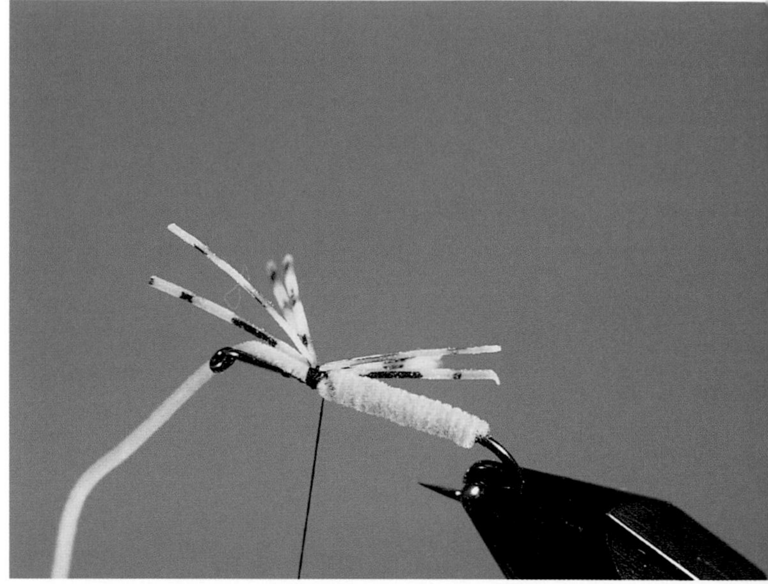

392 ADDING DOLL EYES TO FLIES

If using doll eyes that are not self-stick, use a tiny drop of glue to cement the eyes to the head of the fly. Glue both eyes in place, and then lay the fly on a flat area. Do not place the fly on a fly rotator, since this causes the eyes to slightly slide as the glue cures, positioning one eye high on the head and the other eye low.

Once you've glued and cured the eyes, coat the whole head with epoxy. Finally, place the fly on a fly rotator to allow the glue to cure without sagging.

393 USING A TAPERED-FIBER PAINTBRUSH

Some artist's and household synthetic paintbrushes contain tapered fibers that make excellent, inexpensive tails on dry flies and nymphs. Check hardware, artists supply, and paint stores for these synthetic paintbrushes and buy those that have springy tapered fibers. Most of these are nylon, so you can dye them using Rit or Tintex dyes.

394 ADDING PRISM EYES

To add prism eyes to flies, first crease and fold the eyes in half while they are still on the backing sheet. This is easy to do, since you can fold an entire row of eyes at once. This fold in each eye makes it easier for the eye to conform to the round contour of the fly head.

395 LEGS THAT ANGLE DOWN

If you want rubber legs on a bug to extend at an angle down into the water instead of out at the sides, run a needle with the legs up through the side of the belly and out the center of the back, then from this point in the back down through the bug to exit on the other side of the bug belly.

The result is rubber legs that hang down into the water instead of sticking out from the sides. The effect is different, and also helps create more action in the bug each time you twitch it.

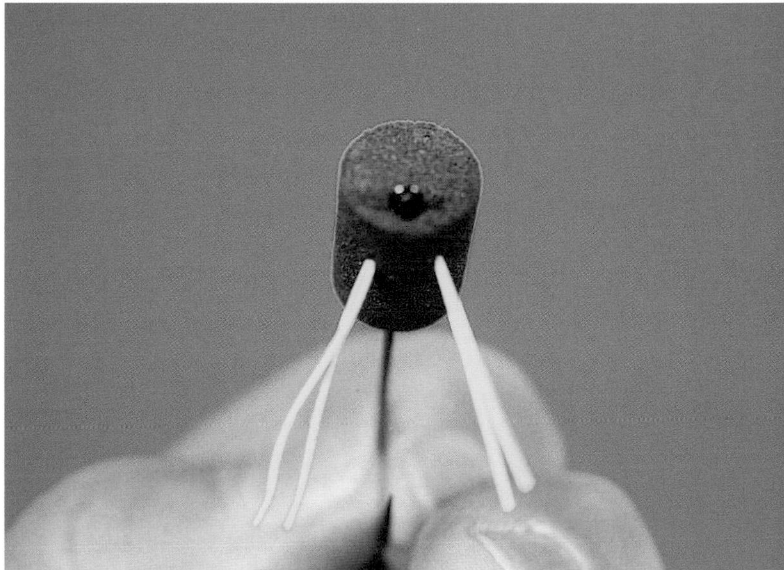

396 TYING SEPARATE BODIES AND TAILS

One way to get extra wiggle in any fly, such as the many large nymph or leech patterns possible, is to tie in a separate tail or body on a separate wire frame, which attaches to the hook with a hinge loop. There are several ways to do this.

One is to tie tail material to a separate ball-eye hook, then cut off (use safety glasses) the hook bend, and attach this tail to a forward fly that you are tying. Do this by first tying down a length of mono, threading the mono through the hook eye of the tail, and then wrapping over the mono loop to make a hinge with the articulated tail.

You can also use any wire for the tail articulated section, using mono loops on both the hook and the tail wire. It is also possible to not remove the hook from the tail so that you have, in essence, a two-hook fly.

Just make sure that any such hook is legal on your waters before using it.

CHAPTER 15

TYING BODIES, HEADS, AND RIBBING

397 DETACHED BODIES

There are very thin foam sheeting materials available today, some as thin as 0.02 or 0.04 inches (0.50 or 1.00 mm). The 0.02-inch size is ideal for making detached bodies for flies, typically imitations of mayflies.

For this, cut a long tapered section of foam that you can fold over to make a detached body. To tie these, fold over the thicker end of the foam, attach to the hook shank, and then begin to wrap only around the detached body as you progress toward the tail of the foam. Before you reach it, fold in some tail fibers and wrap over the foam to enclose them. Then reverse the wrap back toward the body of the fly and the hook shank and complete the fly.

The result is a detached body mayfly imitation that floats high as a result of the foam body. These are best to tie when making large imitations.

398 BEAD HANDLING MADE EASY

You can handle beads more easily with a small finger-cot bead holder, available from any craft or sewing store. This fits on the end of a finger and has rough finger-like projections to allow picking up several beads at once. This makes it easy to thread the hook into the bead without having to pick up one bead at a time.

399 AVOIDING LUMPS

When tying on thick materials, such as leather or chamois to make leeches or vinyl to make crayfish or crabs, the thick material can make a lump at the tie-down point. To prevent this, taper the materials to a point and tie this point in before wrapping the material around the hook shank or folding it over the body.

400 CUTTING VINYL FOR CRAB FLIES

To cut out oblong shapes of cloth-backed vinyl for crab bodies, use a plastic elliptical template, available from art supply and drafting/engineering stores. These templates include many sizes and shapes of various ellipses that simulate the shape of a crab shell.

Pick the size and shape that you need, trace the shape on the vinyl, and then cut out the shapes for use when tying crab flies. Trace the shape on the underside of the vinyl so that you do not mar the top part that is the back of the crab.

401 CLOTH-BACKED VINYL

Cloth-backed vinyl, available from fabric stores, makes great carapace material when tying imitations of crayfish, hellgrammites, large stoneflies, and others. Good colors of vinyl include brown, tan, orange, black, maroon, chocolate, and gray.

You can also make neat saltwater crabs by making a glued "sandwich" of light tan or brown for the carapace and cream for the abdomen.

402 HOT GLUING FLY BODIES

When making flies with large bodies, hot glue is a good option. Doug Brewer first developed and popularized this method of making hot-glue bodies. He uses mini glue guns and colored glue (available through his shop) to make hot-glue-body flies for bonefish, steelhead, panfish, and other species. The basic technique for this is to tie the tail of the fly and then use the hot glue gun to add a round or flattened body to the fly to seal the wraps and the tail in place.

403 ANOTHER WAY TO DUB FLIES

Flytier Chuck Edghill has figured out another way to add dubbing to hooks. To avoid making a loop in the tying thread for adding dubbing when making a dubbed body, you can use the tag end of the working thread left from tying on, along with the working thread.

To do this, leave a long tag end when you first tie the thread to the hook and position this tag end at the end or bend of the hook if not tying down there. Then work on the rest of the fly up to the point of adding the dubbing at the rear. For this, wrap the working thread back to the rear of the hook shank, and then wax this working thread and the tag end of thread.

Add the dubbing between the two threads and then grip the two threads with hackle pliers. Twist or spin to capture the dubbing material. Wrap the dubbing with the two threads around the body, strip the excess dubbing from the thread when complete, tie down the tag end thread, and then clip all excess. Do not clip the working thread, which is necessary to complete the fly.

> "I chose my cast, a march brown and a dun, and ran down to the river, chasing hope."
>
> —*Wilfred S. Blunt,* A New Pilgrimage *(1889)*

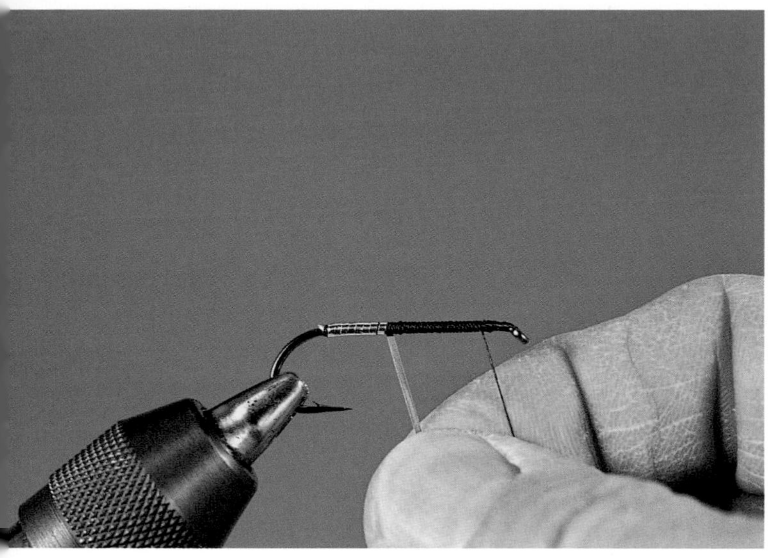

404 GETTING TIGHT WRAPS WITH TINSEL

When adding metallic tinsel, make each wrap so that it starts to slightly overlap the previous wrap. Then pull down so that the tinsel slides off of the previous wrap and falls into perfect position.

You can both hear and feel this "snap" of tinsel as it seats into place on the hook shank as you make each turn. This ensures that each wrap of the tinsel is tight against the previous wrap to make a smooth, shiny tinsel body.

405 METAL TINSEL

While Mylar tinsel and other plastic wraps are gaining more and more favor with flytiers, there is a place for the old-time metallic tinsel. This is tougher and a fish is less likely to cut through it than the Mylar or plastic wraps. If tying flies exclusively for toothy fish, or if your flies might be used for toothy critters, make sure that you use the tougher metallic tinsel in place of Mylar or plastic.

406 DOUBLE WRAP TINSEL

To make an easy tinsel body, double wrap it after tying on at the head of the fly. For this, tie the working thread down in back of the hook eye and then tie down a length of tinsel. Wrap the tinsel down the hook shank to the bend and then reverse it to wrap the tinsel back up the hook shank. Tie off at the head. Then you can tie on a wing, shoulders, and other fly parts to make a simple streamer.

You can only do this if you do not include a tail in the fly. If you do include a tail or oval tinsel ribbing, you will have to wrap over these materials with thread after tying them down.

407 MAKING STREAMLINED TINSEL BODIES

To keep from making a lump when adding metallic tinsel, cut the tinsel at a sharp angle, and tie this angled end down in place. This makes for smooth winding of the tinsel without a lump at the tie-down point. This is particularly important on small and delicate dry flies.

408 PROTECTING OVERBODIES

If tying with lead or non-lead wire on the hook shank to weight the fly, the wire may discolor any overwrap of floss or yarn. To prevent this, wrap over the wire with the tying thread and seal with head cement or nail polish to protect overlying body materials. For a quicker step in doing this, avoid the tying thread wrap and coat the wire with head cement before continuing. Allow the cement to cure before adding any overwrap body materials.

409 MAKING RIBBING

To make an easy body ribbing on any fly, leave a long tag end of the tying thread when tying on. Allow for a tag end about 8 inches (20.3 cm) long. Do not cut it. Then tie in the tail and body, and wind the thread forward. Wind the body forward and tie off with the thread. Then use the tag end of thread to spiral around the body to create a ribbed effect.

This looks best if the body and thread (ribbing) are of contrasting colors.

410 COUNTER-WRAPPING RIBS

To prevent fragile body materials from becoming frayed and undone when fished, add a rib. But instead of wrapping the rib in the same direction as the body material, counter-wrap it by going around the hook shank in the opposite direction of that used for wrapping the body. Fine wire is especially good as a reinforcement rib for fragile bodies.

411 TWISTING YARN

To get a more ribbed or segmented look in a small fly, tightly twist two or more strands of very fine yarn and wrap this around the hook shank for a body.

The two different colors of yarn make a ribbed look, without the necessity of tying the body and then tying a separate ribbing over the body. You can also vary this by how tight you twist the two colors of yarn.

412 THREAD-BODIED MIDGES

To tie a tiny fly, tie a thread-bodied midge. Pick a tying thread the color of the midge body you want, tie on, and then wrap evenly to the rear and then back to the front of the fly. Finish with a wrap or two of peacock herl or dubbing material of your choice.

Another way is to first add a bead to the fly hook (glass, plastic, or metal) and then tie the thread body.

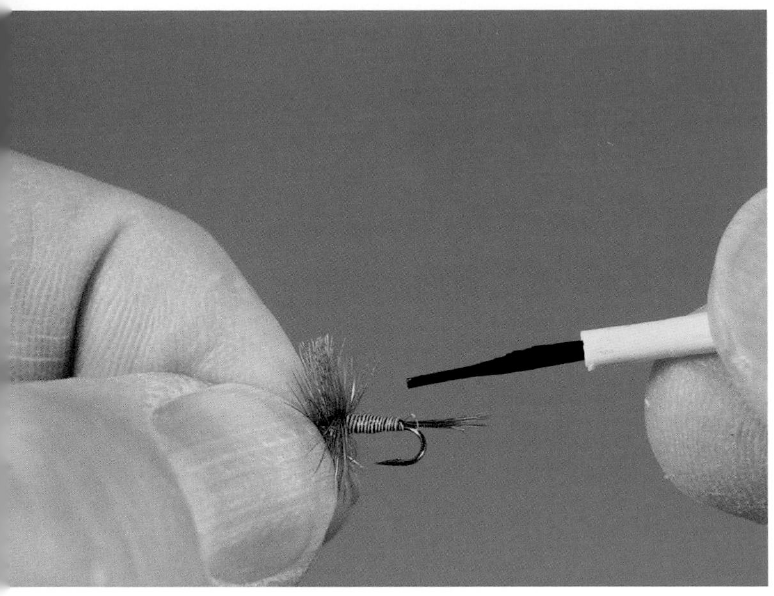

413 QUILL-BODIED FLIES

Quill bodies such as those stripped from peacock herl are very fragile. To protect them while tying and fishing, take your finished quill-bodied flies and coat the bodies with head cement to seal and protect the wrapped quill.

Another way to protect and work with quill bodies is to first coat the hook shank with glue or head cement. With the glue or cement still wet, wrap the quill body on the hook shank to seal it in place before tying off the head of the fly.

A third way to protect quill bodies is to first tie on the hook shank a length of one-pound test mono at the same time that you tie down the quill. Wrap the thread forward, followed by the quill, and then tie off with the thread. Counter wrap the body (spiral wrap in the opposite direction) with the light mono to protect the quill body.

414 SOFTENING QUILLS

To keep the quill bodies of your dry flies from breaking and cracking, soak them in warm water first. This softens the quill body so that you can wrap it around the hook shank without risking the quill breaking.

If you are going to use a number of quills for a lot of tying, you can soak them together and then place them in a zipper-sealed plastic sandwich bag. That way you can remove a few at a time to use while the remainder stay moist.

415 REMOVING FUZZ FROM PEACOCK

Use an eraser to remove the fuzz from peacock herl to make quill bodies for flies such as the Quill Gordon. Try an "ink" eraser, which is a little harder and usually works better than a pencil eraser.

Lay the peacock herl fiber out on a flat surface, hold one end, and use the eraser to rub in one direction only (away from the end you are holding). Do this gently so as to not break the fiber.

416 LARGE PEACOCK QUILL BODIES

To make large bodies of peacock quills, use two or more to completely cover the hook shank. For best results, tie in both together and then wrap the two together around the hook shank. Since you are using two fibers, you cover more hook shank with each wrap, thus covering the hook shank rapidly.

417 WORKING WITH FRAGILE PEACOCK HERL

Peacock herl is a wonderful material for flies, but fragile and sometimes difficult to use. One way to strengthen a bundle of this before wrapping it as a body is to tie down peacock strands and then wrap them with the tying thread. Use this twisted thread and herl to wrap around the hook shank to the tie-off point. Then separate the thread from the peacock herl and tie down the herl with the thread, clip the excess peacock, and tie off.

Another way to make peacock herl more durable on a fly before wrapping it down as a body material is to coat the hook shank or fly underbody with glue or head cement and then rapidly tie in the herl to cement it to the fly hook. This will not affect the iridescence of the fly or the peacock, but it will help to prevent the herl from loosening or unraveling.

A final way to reinforce peacock herl is to tie down a bundle for a body, then wrap the thread forward to the tie-off place. Twist the bundle of peacock strands into a thicker bundle and wrap around the hook shank forward. Then tie off the herl with the thread.

418 MAKING MINNOW BODIES

You can use a lot of different materials to make "skeletons" for minnow shapes covered by braided Mylar or other tubing materials designed to make minnow bodies. Some possibilities for this include flat, stiff, foam materials such as is used for packaging and sheet plastic. You can use stiff, thick cardboard if you cover it with a sealer such as waterproof glue, epoxy, or a few layers of head cement.

Cut the material into the desired minnow shape and length, position it on the hook, and spiral wrap and crisscross with the tying thread to secure it until you can cover it with the tubing material. Often this is best wrapped and secured to the top of the hook shank so that you do not reduce the gap of the hook. If you wrap it underneath the hook shank, make sure you taper it in the back to provide good hook gap.

After securing and sealing the body shape, cover the skeleton with a length of tubing tied in place at both ends. Long-shank hooks are best for these minnow imitations.

419 TYING EMERGERS AND SHUCKS

Of recent interest in fly tying is the tying of emerger insect imitations, which have a trailing shuck (the leftover skin or casing from their days underwater as a nymph, and from which they have emerged as an adult winged insect). One good way to make this and still keep the fly afloat in the surface film is to tie in a tiny piece of foam at the rear of the hook shank, then veil it with a few light-colored, soft hackle fibers. This makes it appear broken and discarded as with a real shuck. Then tie the rest of the fly as normal, concentrating on a surface floating or comparadun style that floats in the surface film.

Good foam material includes the tiny beads of foam that are part of polyfoam packaging material. These "beads" of foam are easily broken or rubbed off of blocks of packaging material foam.

420 HACKLE CONTROL, TIP ONE

Use a short length of a plastic straw to push back the hackle of a wet or dry fly to make it easier to finish the head and make a whip finish. You can also use a small strip or sheet of plastic, formed into a funnel shape by folding it around itself. Because of the angled shape, this is usually best for wet fly hackle.

To do this without slitting the material for the thread, slip the material onto the bobbin before tying down. Then slide the straw or material into place when tying off.

421 HACKLE CONTROL, TIP TWO

Another way to hold back hackle of wet flies or dry flies when finishing the head or tying a whip finish is to cut a slit in a small piece of paper, and then slide this over the eye and head to hold the hackle back. The slit in the paper is necessary to pull the thread forward to tie off the fly.

Then form the paper into a slight cone by overlapping the cut edges of the paper and pulling back the hackle. Wrap with the thread to secure and position the hackle in a tapered position. Form the head with the thread, tie off with a whip finish, and cut the thread to complete.

422 MAKING FUZZY BODIES

To make a fuzzy body that has the undulating and moving lifelike appearance of a nymph insect, use the blood feather from marabou. The blood feather on any bird is the feather that grows from the base of each feather stem and is very fluffy and webby. By tying this down and wrapping around the body, it is easy to create a soft, buggy-looking fly.

To make this a little less buggy and to protect the marabou blood feathers, leave a long tag end of thread, and after wrapping the marabou forward, follow by a wrap or counterwrap of the thread, spiral wrapped around the marabou blood feather body.

423 SHAD OR SMELT BODIES

Flies that imitate smelt, menhaden, sunfish, or shad must have deep bodies that closely resemble these baitfish. One way to do this (and to weight the fly at the same time) is to use lead or non-lead tape cut into a small rectangle. Most of this tape is self-stick. Center the metal tape on top of the hook shank, then fold the tape over the hook shank so that the two parts of the tape touch (stick together). Cut the front and rear of the tape at an angle so that the body resembles a deep shad shape. Cover this body base with Mylar or similar tubing, tied off at the front and rear to make a shiny fish body.

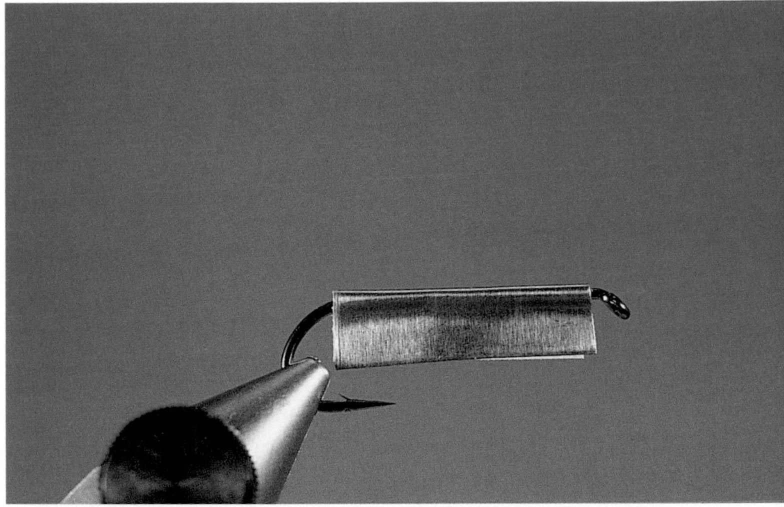

424 SMOOTH AND TAPERED BODIES

Bodies on flies should be neat and smooth, or at least not lumpy at the rear. This is especially important when tying a fly designed to imitate a natural insect, such as a mayfly, stonefly, or caddis fly in either adult or nymph form. Sometimes, this can be a problem if tying on tail and body material at this same point. The thread wrap, lump of body material tied down, and tail material can increase the body diameter at the rear. To prevent this, make the tail material the full length of the hook shank. When tying down the body material, leave enough tag end of body material that you can wrap over both the forward part of the tail material and the tag end of the body material when wrapping the thread forward. This makes a smooth body and minimal thread wraps at the end of the hook shank where these two materials combine.

425 TRANSLUCENT LOOK

To get a translucent look to a fly body, wrap the hook shank with a base-color thread or tinsel and then overwrap with a thin layer of floss, yarn, or dubbing. Experiment by placing your flies in water to see which material combination works well for this look. A good combination is Gudebrod EZ-Dub over a solid thread body. White EZ-Dub is designed so that it becomes translucent when wet to allow underlying materials to show through.

426 NON-WEIGHTED SMELT BODIES

An easy way to make a non-weighted body for a smelt pattern is to use one that Maine tyer Charlie Mann developed. To do this, cut a length of a tapered Stim-U-Dent toothpick, cut and taper the blunt end, and then glue it under the hook shank and wrap with thread. Cover this with a wrap of tinsel or shiny braid tubing or slide a length of Mylar tubing over the body base. Tie off the tubing at both ends to make a body, and finish the fly.

"Quite possibly this is the key to fishing: the ability to see glamour in whatever species one may fish for."

—*Harold Blaisdell,* The Philosophical Fisherman *(1969)*

427 ISOLATING DRY-FLY WINGS

To isolate wings when tying divided wing or spent wing mayflies, wind a few turns of thread around the base of each wing after separating the wing with crisscross and figure-eight wraps. The individual turns of thread around each wing help support it, hold it erect, divide it, and maintain the upright, divided wing.

428 FOLDING HACKLE

To make some flies, you need to fold the hackle, using the stem as a fold point. Such tying methods are ideal for salmon flies, some wet flies, flies palmered with hackle, and soft hackle spey-type flies. You can do this easily without one of the costly tools made for this purpose. One way is to use an old, discarded book.

Place the book in a rack with the open side (pages) up, with the pages slightly loose. Then hold the hackle by the stem at both ends (use two hands), lightly insert the hackle, and "saw" the hackle stem into and between the open pages. The result is that the pages naturally fold the hackle fibers over. Press the pages together, leave the hackle there for a while, and then remove as desired for tying onto the hook.

You can also prepare a number of hackles this way by preparing and folding the hackles between different pages of the book. This keeps each hackle separate, but folded and stored in this position.

429 SPEY FLIES

Sparse is good when tying spey and other soft hackle flies. With these longer soft hackles, you get more action and seemingly more movement and lifelike wiggles out of a sparsely dressed or palmered hackle spey/soft hackle fly.

Do this by making only one or two turns of the hackle around the hook shank before tying it off. Also be sure to use hen hackle or the soft butt fibers of a hackle stem that gives you the action desired.

430 HEN HACKLE FOR SOFT-HACKLE WET FLIES

Use hen hackle when making soft-hackle wet flies. Hen hackle is easier to get than some of the exotics such as partridge or grouse feathers, and makes for a softer, more "alive" hackle than the stiffer rooster hackles used for most dry flies.

In using this material for soft or spey hackle flies, realize that the hackle should be longer than that used in standard wet flies. For most wet flies, hackle (or throat hackle) should be only long enough to hit the point of the hook. For soft-hackle flies, the hackle is often up to twice as long as the hook shank for added movement and action in the water.

431 HEAD CEMENT SUBSTITUTE

If short of head cement for finishing and sealing the thread wraps and head of your flies, you can use clear fingernail polish. A favorite of many flytiers is Sally Hansen Hard As Nails. You can also use colored nail polish to give a different look to the fly and to make colored heads on flies.

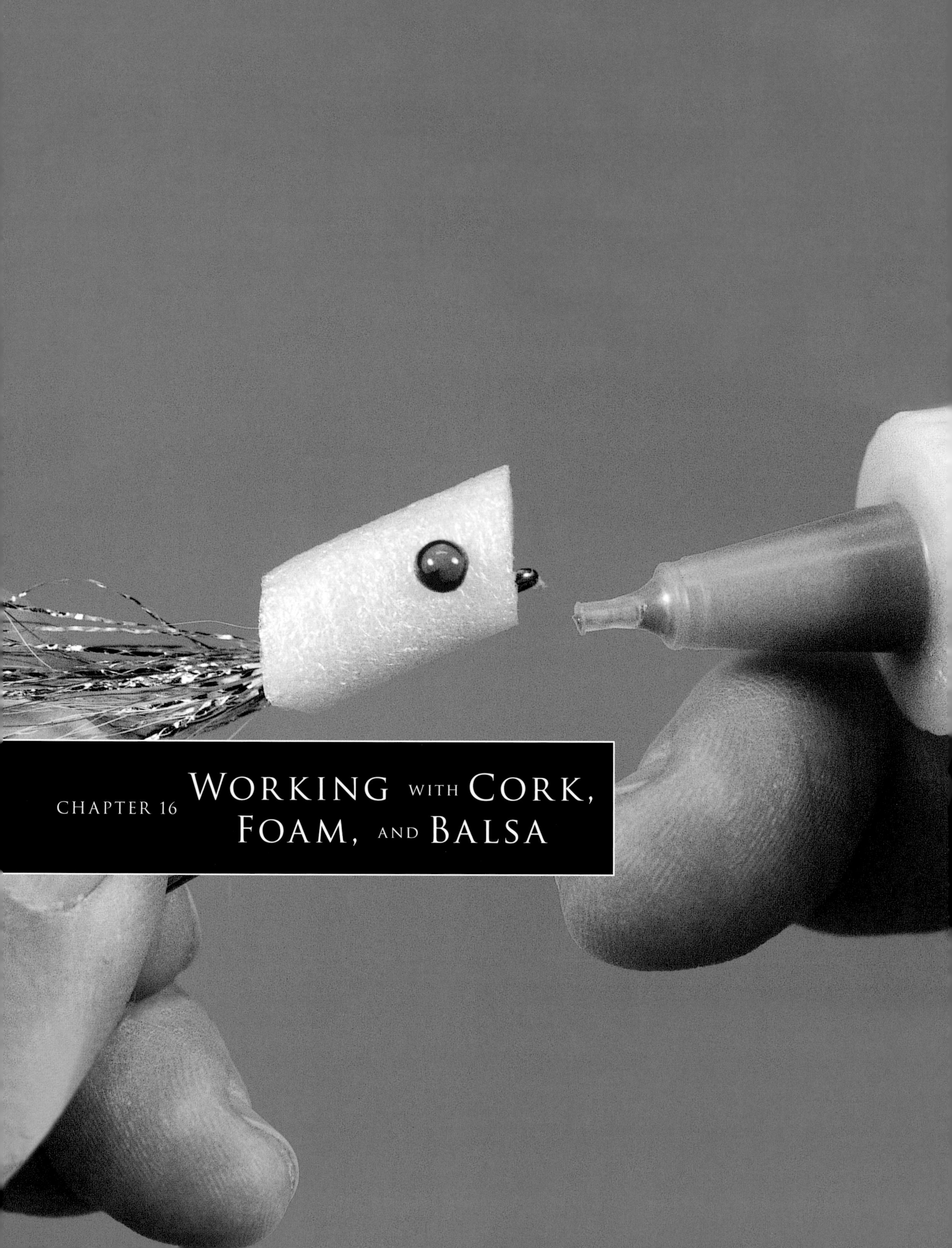

CHAPTER 16 WORKING WITH CORK, FOAM, AND BALSA

432 CHOOSING THE RIGHT DIAMETER BUG BODY

If making cork, balsa, or foam poppers or sliders, choose bodies that have a diameter approximately equal to the gap of the hook used. This creates the best proportion and balance on the finished bug. In some cases, you might even want to make bugs that have a body smaller than the gap of the hook, such as making bugs specifically for panfish and bluegills. These fish have very small mouths, so the smallest possible body that will still wake or pop, yet tied on a hook that hooks the fish, makes it easier to unhook the fish.

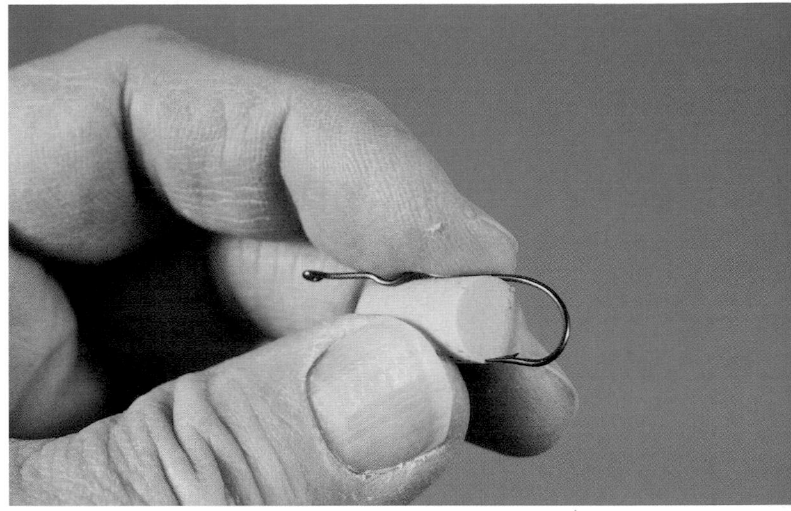

433 SHAPING FOAM BODIES

Onc way to shape foam bodies is to use a flame (lighter or grill-starter) to slightly heat the foam, and then roll it with your fingers (be careful to not burn yourself) to form the foam into a tapered or rounded shape. This works best with lightweight foam bodies or pre-cut foams used to make beetles, ants, jassids, hoppers, crickets, termites, and other terrestrial fly patterns. This tapering and rounding makes a more natural body appearance in any fly.

434 HIDING TAIL WRAPS

To hide the wrap of tail material on a foam bug body, use a triangle tapered cutter in a Dremel-type tool to make a tapered opening in the rear of the bug. Tie the tail, flash, collar, etc., on the hook so that the bug body buries these wraps.

Soak the hook and the tail thread wrap with CA glue (cyanoacrylate cement) and force the hook into the pilot hole in the bug until seated properly. Done properly, the foam body completely hides the wrap used to hold the tail.

435 GLUING HOOKS IN BUG BODIES

When tying bass bugs, the simplest way to make a tight glue bond of the hook into the cork or balsa body is to wrap the hook shank with heavy, coarse thread. Use size "D," "E," or "EE" thread (used for rod wrapping). Spiral wrap the thread up and down the hook shank and tie off with a whip finish. This is important even when using kink- or hump-shank hooks designed for bass bugs.

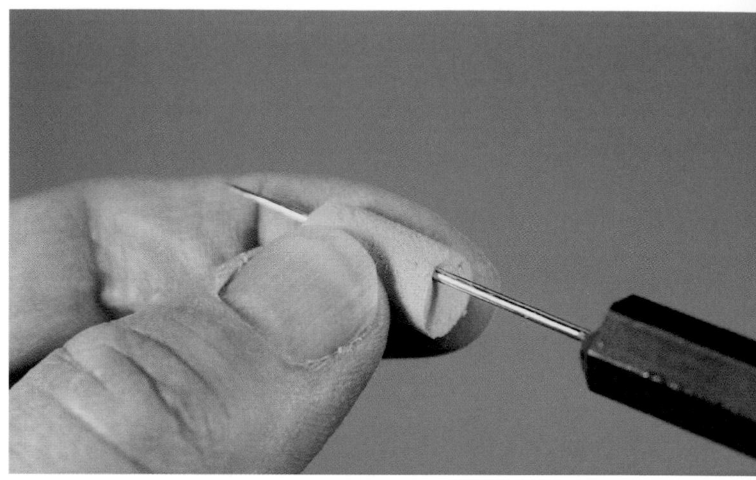

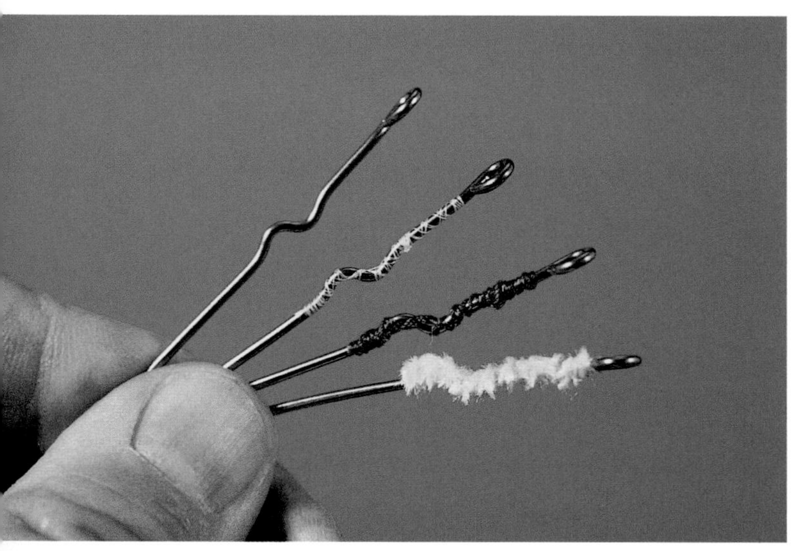

437 MAKING HOLES FOR GLUING HOOKS

You do not need to make a slot to hold a hook in a closed-cell foam bug body. To secure the hook, use a bodkin to make a hole through the belly of the bug body to serve as a pilot hole for the hook shank. Make the hole as close to the skin as possible to preserve the hook gap of the fly.

436 THE STRONGEST BONDS FOR BUG BODIES

For the strongest bond of a hook in a cork or balsa body, first tie on regular fly-tying thread and then tie on and wrap the hook with chenille or yarn. Tie off with the thread.

Make a large slot in the cork or balsa body, and then soak the chenille/yarn-wrapped hook with five-minute epoxy, add some epoxy in the wide slot, and insert the hook. Add a little more epoxy on top of this and remove any epoxy that seeps from the two ends.

Tests have shown that this is the strongest of all possible methods of gluing a hook into a cork or balsa body, even though it takes a little more time to complete. This works well for both plain- and hump-shank hooks.

438 GLUING INTO FOAM

To glue a hook shank into a foam bug body, spiral wrap the hook shank with thread and tie off. Coat the hook shank with CA glue (cyanoacrylate cement) and force the hook, eye first, through the pilot hole previously formed and into the rear of the bug. Align the hook with the bug body before the glue sets up.

439 SLOTTING CORK BODIES WHEN MAKING POPPERS

The best way to make a slot in a cork popper body is with a hacksaw blade—not a knife or razor. Use a fine-tooth hacksaw blade to cut a blade-width slot into which you can glue (with waterproof cement) a thread-wrapped popper hook shank. This leaves adequate room for gluing, does not strain the cut slot, and makes for a more durable popper.

For even more strength in a popper, tape together several (three or four) fine-tooth hacksaw blades and cut a wide slot in the belly of the popper. Then wrap the popper hook with thread and tie in a wrap of chenille. Tie off and soak the chenille wrap with glue, and then glue and seal it into the wide body slot. Tests have shown that this is the strongest and most durable of the possible bonds of a hook into a cork body.

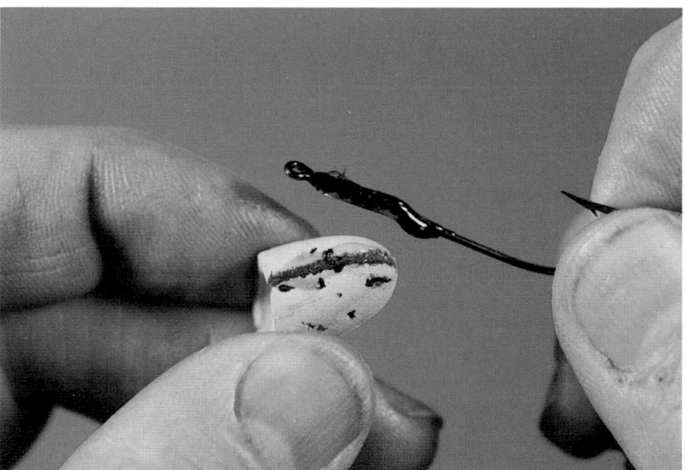

440 AEROSOL PAINTING OF BASS BUGS

The best way to get a good, smooth coat of paint on cork or balsa bass bugs is to spray them using an aerosol spray can or a professional-style airbrush. However, this often sprays paint on the hook as well. To prevent this, you can "mask" the hook and hook shank area with a fold of cardboard that fits around the hook shank as you hold it.

If you wish to paint bug bodies in an assembly line, you can use a long strip of corrugated cardboard and slip a number of hook shanks into the corrugated cardboard where you can spray them all at once. You can also spray them from both sides with the hook point and shank completely protected.

Another option is to make up a slotted corkboard to hold the hook shanks for repeated assembly-line operations.

441 PAINTING FRAMES

An ideal frame for holding the tulle or scale netting for spraying scales on bugs is one of the spray frames used to hold needlepoint work. These are available from craft and sewing stores in a number of sizes and shapes.

442 PAINTING BUGS

If gluing or painting cork, foam, or other materials to a hook shank to which you have already added rubber legs, do not let the paint or glue touch the legs. Often synthetic legs curl and bend from contact with liquid paint or glue, making them unnatural or unusable afterward.

443 SPRAY PAINTING BUG BODIES

When spray painting cork- or balsa-body bugs, use an inexpensive pair of needle-nose pliers to hold the hook. Best are long needle-nose pliers to hold the bug by the hook and allow spray painting without the risk of painting your hand. You can also use wide-jaw pliers to hold bugs by the hook, since the wider jaws help mask the hook and protect it from paint.

An alternative way to handle cork- and balsa-body bugs for spray painting is to wear inexpensive latex gloves. These are disposable and available in packs of ten or a hundred from discount or drug stores. Hold the hook while spraying to prevent getting paint on your skin and discard the gloves after each painting session.

444 PAINTING STEPS FOR BUGS

When painting cork- or balsa-body bass bugs, it is always best to use a coat of primer and then two coats of white paint. This is absolutely necessary if painting a top or final coat that is pale, pastel, or fluorescent. Without the undercoat of white, lighter colors will appear muddy, dull, and unnatural.

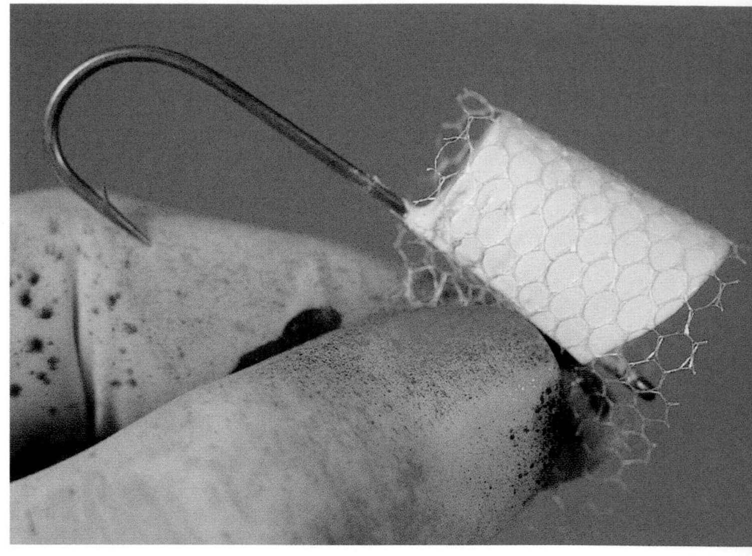

445 SCALE FINISH ON BUGS ▲

Want scales painted onto your cork or balsa bug body? This is easy. Get some scale netting from a fly or tackle shop or buy tulle (a type of netting material) from a craft or fabric store.

First paint a base coat of the scale color desired. Then stretch and hold the netting over the bug, and spray a second time with a contrasting color of paint. The result is a scale finish.

If you want light scales, use a light or white base coat and then spray through the netting with a dark color. For dark scales, use a dark undercoat and spray through the netting with a light or white aerosol paint.

Since most bugs and lures are spray painted with scale finishes only on the sides (not the top or belly), the best way to do this is to mount the scale netting in a frame and hold it tight against the bug body when spraying.

446 FOAM COLOR

When tying foam terrestrials, the color of the foam may not matter much. A trout or panfish looking at a bug from underneath almost always sees the bug in silhouette. Up close, they can distinguish colors if they take time to closely examine a bug. It is best to keep foam bugs to basic colors—black, white, yellow, brown, and green are popular.

447 ADDING COLOR TO FOAM TERRESTRIALS

Although the color of your foam terrestrials might not make much difference to the trout or panfish, adding a square of color to the top of the foam allows you to track the fly better in rough water or where there is a lot of detritus on the surface. Consider adding a final wrap to secure a small square of bright red, orange, or yellow foam on top. The square of color does not affect your fishing, since the fish only see the underside or side of the fly, not the top.

448 EYE-BUSTING PAINT IN HOOK EYES

To get the paint out of the eye of a painted bug body, use an "eye-buster" tool, designed to remove the paint from jig heads. These are available from most tackle shops.

For best results, do this shortly after the paint has cured, since it becomes harder and more difficult to remove with time. Also, the harder and older paint gets, the more likely it is to chip or flake.

449 LEAVING CLEARANCE FOR PAINT ON BUGS

If you add several coats of paint or enamel to your cork or balsa popping bugs, leave about 1⁄16 inch (2 mm) of bare shank in back of the eye as clearance for the paint buildup. If you seat and glue the popping cork to the hook with the head touching or right in back of the hook eye, subsequent coats of paint will clog the eye, making it impossible to clean without damaging the paint on the bug face. This 1⁄16-inch clearance allows for paint buildup on the face of the bug without clogging the hook eye.

450 MAKING SEGMENTED BODIES

You can make segmented tails of large insects, such as dragonflies, using a neat trick I first learned from creative flytier Bill Skilton. By this method, you can make segmented extended bodies or tails formed by wraps of thread around lengths of foam. This is not just spiral wrapping the thread around the body as is done on bodies formed on a hook shank.

To do this, prepare a long, thin strip of foam twice the length of the desired tail. Tie the working thread in the middle. Then fold the foam strip in half at the point where you tied in the tying thread. To make this step and following steps easy, fold the foam over a long needle placed in your fly-tying vise, with the fold/tied part next to the vise jaws. Then run the thread between the two foam strips, followed by making two wraps around both foam strips and the central hidden needle. Do this where you want the first segment.

Following this, again run the thread between the two foam strips and repeat the above at the junction of the next two segments. When you achieve the desired segmented length, pull the extended body from the needle. Remove the needle from the vise and add a hook. Tie the extended body to the hook shank. Continue the body and finish the fly. The end result is a beautiful body with clearly separated segments extending from the rear of the fly hook, as would the body on a dragonfly or damselfly.

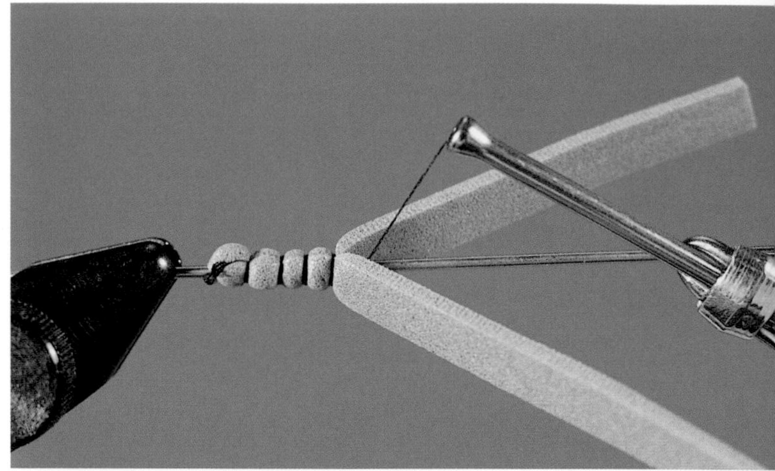

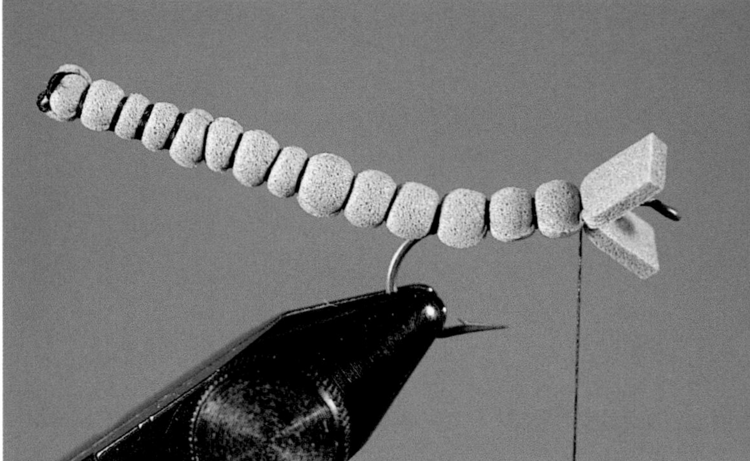

451 "SANDWICH" FLIES AND BUGS

You can make bugs by forming a "sandwich" of flat foam materials. These foam sheets are available from fly-tying shops as well as craft stores. If making sandwich bugs, glue the parts of the foam sheeting together using contact cement or a spray adhesive, such as 3M Super 77.

452 WAXING HOOK EYES

If you don't like the idea of scraping or punching out paint from the eye of painted cork and balsa bugs, there is another way to solve this vexing problem. It adds another step, but many flytiers like the convenience it affords.

For this, coat the hook eye of the bug hook with wax before painting. To do this, first complete the bug body by gluing, sealing, and preparing the body for painting. Then dip only the hook eye into molten candle wax to coat the eye. Make sure that you cover only the hook eye, since you do not want wax on the cork or balsa body.

Next, paint the bug body by dipping, spraying, or brushing. The wax on the hook eye prevents any paint from adhering. You can easily scrape off any leftover paint with a fingernail. Then finish the bug by tying on the tail, collar, adding rubber legs, etc.

Another way to accomplish this is to use petroleum jelly on the eye of the hook. Test both systems first to make sure that they work with the paint formula that you are using, since different paints have different reactions with various products.

453 CRUDE CORKS CATCH FISH

If you are tying cork bass bugs for your own use and only care about catching fish, you do not have to fill in the pits before painting them. You should still paint with primer, undercoat, and final coats, but the pits won't bother the fish or keep them from hitting. Some very excellent fly anglers do not even paint their bugs, but only fish natural cork bodies glued on a hook and tied with simple tails.

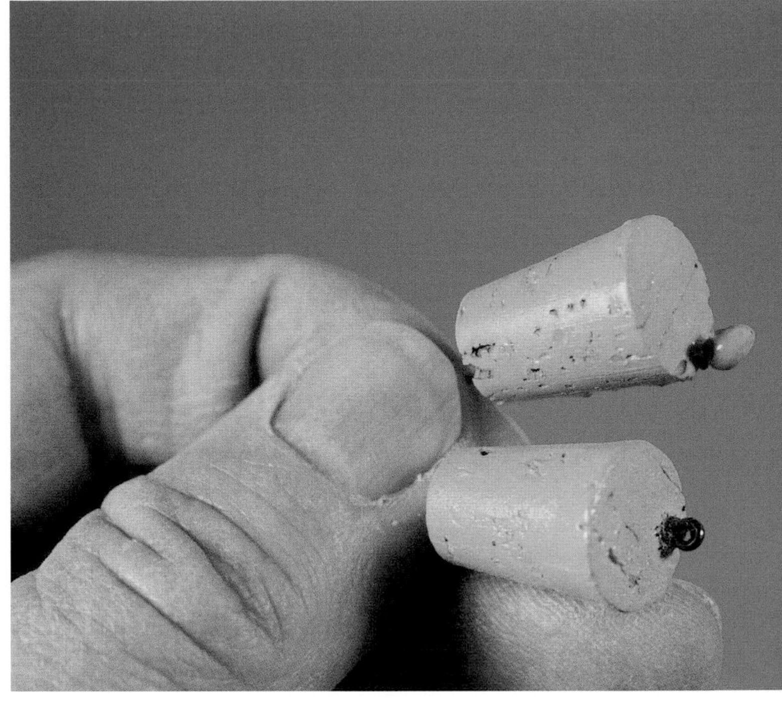

454 MAKING PROFESSIONAL-LOOKING BUGS

If you wish to make cork bugs that look professional and do not have pits in them, first seal the bugs with Dap filler that is easy to wipe on with your finger. You can do this before or after you glue the bug onto the hook. It is easier after gluing, since the hook makes a little "handle" by which to hold the cork. Make sure that the body is smooth and allow the Dap to cure as per the directions before painting with a primer.

CHAPTER 17 TYING FLY WINGS

Wet, Dry, Streamer, Saltwater, Bass

455 TYING ON DRY FLY WINGS

When tying on dry fly wings, tie them down with the tips facing forward. Then wrap the thread to the rear, tie on the tail and body material, and wrap the thread forward.

Wrap the body up the hook shank toward the eye of the hook, wrapping over the butt of the wings tied to the hook shank. This also builds up the body diameter slightly at this point to make a more natural tapered look.

Then wrap the thread forward, raise the wings with a bump of thread in front of the wings, and tie in the hackle.

The result makes a very lifelike look. It does not create the problems or lumpy look that would occur if tying on the wings butts forward.

456 MAKING WINGS

To make sure that you have even wings on flies when you make them from waterfowl wing quills, take matched sections from the longer or outside edge of each of the matched quills from the two wings. Pick the wing sections from the same part of each quill, and make sure that each wing section is the same width before joining them to the hook shank.

457 PROTECTING DRY FLY HACKLE

To protect dry fly hackle, run a few turns of working thread through the wound hackle. Work the thread in a zigzag path to prevent the thread from catching or binding down any of the hackle fibers while protecting and binding over the base of the wrapped hackle. Two or three turns of thread are about right and provide protection to keep the hackle from damage and becoming undone.

458 DIVIDING UPRIGHT WINGS

Use a bodkin to evenly separate the upright wing in a dry fly when making a divided wing. This allows you to look at the two wings and make sure that they are equal before you crisscross the thread between them to divide the wing permanently.

459 TYING STREAMER WINGS

To get a streamer wing of bucktail or synthetics tied correctly to the top of the hook shank, hold the butts at an angle to and in front of the hook shank when wrapping the thread over the shank and wing.

Pulling down on the thread slides the wing up into the proper position on top of, and parallel to, the hook shank where you can secure it with subsequent wraps. The result is a properly positioned wing on top of and in line with the hook shank.

460 TYING DOWN SYNTHETIC STREAMER WINGS

Synthetic streamer wing material is often slipperier than natural materials, making it difficult to get a good bond and secure tying. To avoid this, tie down synthetic materials in several small bundles rather than one large bundle. The result is that several wraps of thread are holding each small bundle, making for a more secure binding. You can also coat each bundle with head cement as you tie for a more permanent bond.

An alternative to the above is to tie the bundle of synthetic material down in one bunch after soaking the end to be tied in head cement or glue. By wrapping over the soaked bundle with tying thread, you both glue the synthetics together and also soak the thread to glue the synthetics to the fly hook.

A third way to secure synthetics is to lightly heat the end of the bundle with a flame. You want to just melt the strands together—not make a molten mess. Immediately tie down the bundle with thread to seal it and secure it to the hook shank. You may get a slight lump of the molten ends of the synthetics. This helps hold it in place, but it is also best to use only on larger flies.

461 POSITIONING STREAMER WINGS

To position a streamer wing, make two loose wraps over the wing as you hold it in place on top of the hook shank. Then pull the thread tight and straight down to secure the wing in position on top of the hook shank.

462 VEILING STREAMER WINGS

To make a streamer wing that encircles or "veils" the body, first position the wing on top of the hook shank with two or three light-pressure wraps of thread. Then use your left thumbnail to push down on the top of the wing base to spread the wing fibers around the hook shank and to veil the body. Check that the veiling is even, then wrap tightly.

463 HOLDING STREAMER WINGS

To secure a streamer wing of bucktail or synthetics to the top of a hook shank and keep it in position, make a "reverse" loop wrap. To do this, bring the thread up in front of the hook shank, and then in back, up, over, and around the wing. Finish by bringing the thread in back of the hook shank (far side of the hook) and pulling tight.

This wraps like a figure-eight, or infinity sign, to secure the wing on top of the hook shank. Because of the figure-eight loop, the wing is not able to creep down onto the side of the fly and thus destroy the appearance of classic streamer flies.

Finish by making several more wraps of thread around the hook shank and base so that the wing will not twist from its position on top of the hook.

464 DIVIDING WINGS WITH THREAD HARNESS

To divide upright wings when tying dry flies, use a thread harness, as I first learned from the writings of flytier Charles Meck.

For this, first tie down the wings by the butt end with the tips extending forward. Tie them to the upright position. Then take a separate length of tying thread, make a loop around the hook shank in back of the wings, and pull the ends straight up. Pull this thread harness forward and between the divided wings to separate them into two equal bunches of fibers. Pull down just forward of the wings, using enough tension to create the divided look you desire. Tie off this thread harness with the working thread.

You can also make this easier by twisting the thread harness before pulling it forward to divide the wings. This prevents an errant wing fiber from sticking straight up between the thread harness.

465 MARKING HACKLES

You can "make" your own specialty hackles using permanent felt-tip markers to color as you desire.

Today, we use a lot of plain hackle and grizzly hackle, but there are special hackles that have dark center vanes and/or dark outside fibers. You can mark plain hackles the same way, as well as to make grizzly feathers.

To do this, use a permanent felt-tip marker, a ruler, and some scrap paper. Lay each hackle that you want to mark on the paper, and lay the ruler along the part you want to mark. For the center, this would be alongside the main stem, while for the edges it would be along the edge. Then dot or pat the felt-tip maker along the area to be marked. You can't stroke it, since this will only bend the hackle fibers.

For grizzly hackle, hold the ruler at right angles to the feather and mark each section in turn as you move the ruler up the feather. If you like, you can turn the feather over and mark in the same spots for a darker, more pronounced effect. You can do this with any light feather using any color of marker. Black, olive, and brown are the most favored.

466 MOISTENED MARABOU

Marabou is a great, soft attractor material for wings and tails in flies, but also difficult to handle. To make it easier to tie down, moisten the marabou slightly and then bundle the butt ends.

One way to handle the butt ends is to twist the butt end of the moistened marabou to make a tight, skinny bundle for easy tying. Don't wet or soak it if you only want to control the marabou—adding water will rust the hook or make it difficult to handle.

467 USING MARABOU BLOOD FEATHERS

The blood feathers from the stem of marabou (turkey underfeathers) are generally uniformly the same length and thus easy to tie in as a streamer wing. When they are available, most flytiers prefer these to working with the longer marabou feathers where you have to cut the plumy part from the main stem and then carefully fold it into a bundle. To use marabou bloods, trim the butt end and then stroke the feather back as you tie the butt end into the fly.

468 MAKING MARABOU BUNDLES

More marabou is available as stems and feathers than as the smaller and easier-to-use blood plumes. These are harder to handle, since you must cut from the main stem and then craft it into a bundle.

To make these bundles for tying down as a streamer wing, first cut a section from one side of the main stem. Then carefully fold the section over once or twice, creating a bundle—or at least a more easily handled batch of marabou that you can twist or roll into a bundle.

This bundle is then easy to tie onto the hook to make a wing. If necessary, this can be done several times to create a large bundle for tying down one time, or several small bundles that can be tied on one at a time to make a thicker wing.

469 MIXING MARABOU

To keep marabou from tangling around the hook bend or hook shank, mix the marabou with stiffer material such as bucktail, calf tail, or synthetics to give it some structure while still retaining the fluffy movement of the marabou. Do this to create a mixed wing bundle before tying it down on the hook.

Good stiffening materials for this include calf tail or any of the stiffer synthetics such as Super Hair, Ultra Hair, and Fish Hair.

470 ADDING FLASH MATERIAL TO WINGS

Add flash material (Krystal Flash, Crystal Splash, etc.) to the sides of a streamer fly wing by using one bundle that is double the length of the bundle you want on each side. Tie this down on the hook at the middle of the bundle on one side of the fly wing. Then cross the bundle of flash over the top of the hook to the opposite side and wrap with thread again to tie down this side. If necessary, trim the two sides to an equal length.

This method requires less time in preparing the flash on the wing for tying, and creates equal flash bundles for the two sides of the fly.

471 EASIER "EVENING" OF BUCKTAIL

To make it easy to stack, or make even, bucktail fibers and similar materials when making streamer wings, add a little talcum powder to the bucktail bundle when adding it to the stacker. The talcum powder makes it easier for the fibers to slide against other fibers when using the stacker.

The best way to do this is to pour a tiny amount of talcum powder into your hand and brush the bucktail or other fur in this puddle of powder. This coats the fibers before adding them to the stacker to make it easy to even the ends.

472 SYNTHETIC STREAMER WINGS

To get a tapered look to a streamer wing of synthetic material (such as Super Hair, Ultra Hair, Unique, and others), use barber thinning scissors to thin the material to make the wing fibers different lengths. This will not taper the individual fibers, but makes the whole wing look tapered and thus more natural and lifelike.

CHAPTER 18 A Few Miscellaneous Tips

473 PROPER PROPORTIONS FOR TYING FLIES

Getting a fly to look professional and "right" involves getting all the parts properly proportioned for each fly and fly type of each size. Following is a handy chart that has been used for years by fly tiers for getting their flies to look right. Note that the proportions for streamers are from the author, since no single standard exists for these flies.

Dry Fly
Height of wings = shank length of hook
Height (radius) of hackle = ¾ shank length of hook
Tail = length of entire hook, less eyes (shank length plus head)
Body length (tail to hackle) = ¾ shank length of hook

Wet Fly
Body = shank length of hook, less wrapped head
Wings = shank length of hook + bend of hook, less wrapped fly head
Tail = body length (shank length of hook, less wrapped fly head)
Hackle = distance from wrapped fly head to point of hook

Streamer Fly
Wing = 1¼ to 2 times the shank length of the hook
Tail = ⅓ the shank length of the hook, less the wrapped fly head, or to meet the end of the wing
Body = shank length of the hook, less the wrapped eye
Shoulders = ⅓ of the shank length of the hook, less the wrapped fly head
Cheek = ¼ the shank length of the hook, less the wrapped fly head
Throat = ½ the length of the hook, less the wrapped fly head

474 SPACING DRY FLIES

Beginners often have trouble making the head on a dry fly. One reason is not leaving enough room to make the head properly without impeding the hook eye or damaging the dry fly hackle.

Older fly books suggested that you leave a small amount of space (about the width of a fly hook eye) between the eye and the front of the wrapped head.

To make a wrapped head properly, tie in the wings at about one-quarter to one-third of the hook shank length in back of the hook eye. This leaves room for the body, along with ample room for the wings and hackle, while providing space for finishing the small tapered head.

475 USING CASSETTE TAPE FOR BACKING

You can tie on simple scud and shrimp carapaces from cassette tape. Cassettes come in both the standard and the mini-tape, with all measuring about ⅛ inch (3 mm) across. Most vary from brown to gray in color. Cut into a convenient length for use, tie down, and segment with spiral wraps of tying thread.

476 MAKING TEMPLATES FOR TYING IDENTICAL FLIES

Tying different sizes of the same fly pattern? One way to get consistent results is to make up a simple template or chart that indicates the correct length of tails, wings, hackle, etc. You can do this for dry flies, wet flies, and even for proper wing and tail length on streamers and bucktails. You can get these measurements from some books on fly tying, tools that attach to the fly-tying vise that are made for measuring hackle and tails, or from the chart shown here.

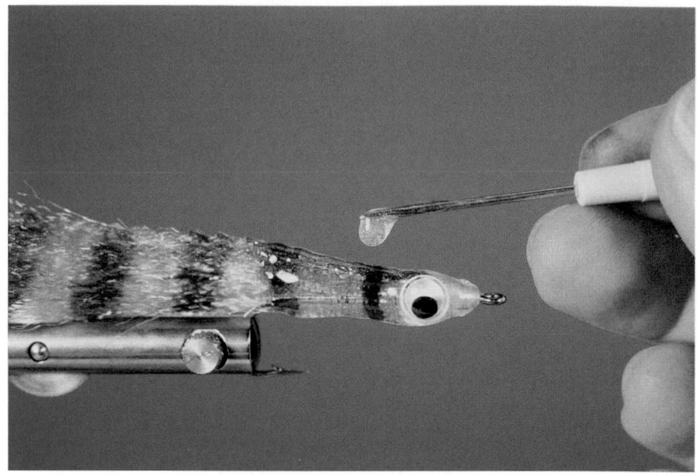

477 CLEARING HEAD CEMENT

It is not uncommon to have head cement clog the eye of a fly, which is why all anglers should carry safety pins or a nipper with a built-in needle to clear the eyes of flies. One way to prevent this is to run a scrap feather or hackle through the eye after tying and sealing to clear out any excess wet sealer. You can use a feather several times for this before the glue makes it ineffective.

478 MIXING EPOXY

Mix epoxy on a white card or paper, stirring the two parts evenly to eliminate the visible swirls in the glue, and apply to the head of the fly with a bodkin.

479 ELIMINATING BUBBLES IN EPOXY

Mixing epoxy glue for coating fly heads or other fly-tying purposes can cause bubbles. To eliminate the bubbles, spread and mix the epoxy and breathe on the epoxy puddle. Your breath will break any bubbles that have formed.

480 USING EPOXY FINISH

Epoxy finish is best for large flies, flies with larger heads, or where you want a very durable fly when fishing for tough or toothy fish. To make an epoxy head, best results are from clear, five-minute epoxy glue, mixed thoroughly and applied evenly to the fly head. Most epoxies turn slightly yellow in time, so don't make up too many flies in advance.

481 PREVENTING EPOXY SAGGING

To prevent epoxy heads on flies from sagging, place the fly on a fly rotator that slowly (five to twenty turns per minute) rotates flies as the epoxy cures. These fly rotators are available in AC or battery styles from any fly shop or catalog house. You can also make your own.

To make your own, rig a low-rpm motor on a stand and add a large foam ring or disk into which you can hook flies. Good motors for the purpose are those for hobbies or used for turning a barbecue spit.

482 ANT IMITATIONS

When tying ants, make sure to maintain a thin, distinct "waist" on the fly and keep separate the thorax and abdomen parts. In some flies, such as the McMurray's Ant, this is pretty obvious, but use care when tying ants built up on the hook shank with thread, yarn, or floss. The separation of both parts and a wide waist helps the trout recognize this as an ant and not a beetle—not that beetles won't catch fish!

483 CATERPILLARS

If palmering hackle to make surface- or subsurface-caterpillar fly imitations, consider using larger-than-normal hackle and then trimming it all around. The result is a blunter, more visible hackle that closely resembles the short, fuzzy projections found on most caterpillars. You can also trim it in different ways, such as leaving it long on the sides and short on the top and bottom, or long at one or both ends and short in the middle. These more closely approximate the appearance of a live caterpillar.

484 PROTECTING PALMERED HACKLES

To protect palmered hackle and make a fly more durable, wind a spiral wrap of tying thread through the hackle. Leave a long tag end of tying thread when starting the fly, add other materials/hackle, and wrap the thread and hackle forward. Follow this by a spiral wrap of thread over and through the palmered hackle. For best results, make this wrap in the opposite direction (from back to front, rather than from front to back around the hook), over the previously palmered hackle.

485 VARYING YOUR PALMERING

When palmering a fly body with a spiral wrap of hackle, you can vary the look of the fly. To make a very bushy fly, use close spirals to build up hackle bulk. To make a spare, straggly body, use wide turns of the hackle.

Realize that if you make a very bushy palmering wrap, you might have to use more than one hackle feather. You can do this by tying two or more hackle feathers to the hook shank, then wrap up the hook shank.

A second way to do this is to tie on one hackle and wrap it to the end of the hackle, then tie in a second hackle as you tie off the first. Continue this way to create a bushy palmering until you reach the head of the fly.

Regardless of how you do it, the several hackles make a bushy palmering, even if not wrapped in a tight spiral.

If you want a very sparse palmering for a different look, space the spirals of the hackle far apart.

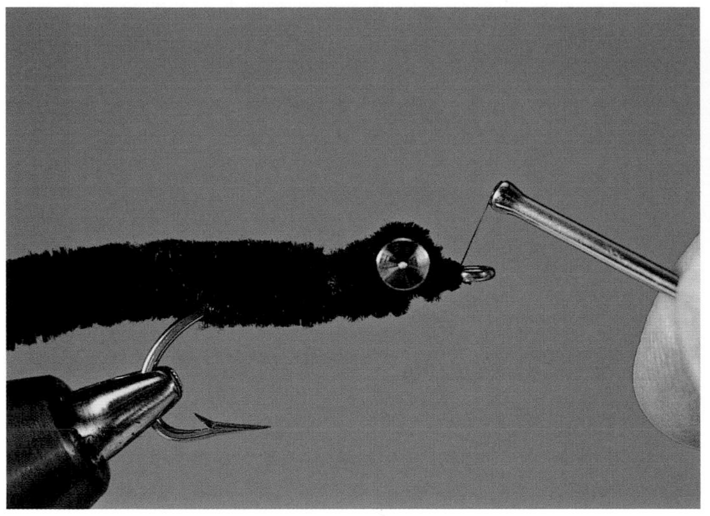

486 MAKING TUBING EELS

Eels are a staple food for a lot of inshore saltwater and larger freshwater gamefish. To make a simple eel, Brian Owens of Connecticut came up with the idea of using velvet tubing available from sewing and fabric stores. The thin-wall cloth tubing, about ½ inch (13 mm) thick, is available in black, white, red, and maroon. You can color the back of white eels with permanent felt-tip markers to make them more eel-like. Good colors are black for the back and olive for the upper sides.

To "tie" these, cut several inches of tubing and remove the internal cord. Run the hook through the open end and then out the side. Place the hook in a vise, tie on the thread, and tie down the open end to finish the eel. Complete by sealing the tail end with fabric glue. You can make similar smaller eels using bolo cord also available from sewing stores or white parachute cord, available from outdoor stores.

487 FLATTENED FLY SKELETONS

Nymphs are often flat to best resist water pressure and currents. This is true for both small nymphs and the larger nymphs such as hellgrammites and western stoneflies.

For larger flies, make them by tying down a flat "skeleton" board to the hook, and then gluing the flat skeleton to the hook for stability. With this skeleton tied and glued in place, wrap over the skeleton with body material to make the desired nymph pattern.

Good skeleton material for wrapping onto a hook includes the plastic used in flexible hook boxes (such as Mustad), strips of strapping material used to pack and ship boxes, and any suitable flat, clear plastic from blister-packed products.

An easy way to tie this on is to cut a notch on both sides of each end. This leaves a small nib in the center of each end to tie onto the hook before the thread is spiral wrapped around the rest of the skeleton and before you epoxy it in place.

488 TYING SIMPLE CHUM FLIES

You can tie simple chum flies to catch saltwater fish when chumming, by using a single wrap of crosscut rabbit strip, then tying off with a neat head and sealing with epoxy. Make the fly more durable for toothy fish, such as bluefish, by tying down the tag end of the rabbit strip, then coating the hook shank with epoxy glue, wrapping the thread up the hook shank, and then following with the crosscut rabbit strip. Then make the head, and finish and seal it with epoxy.

This method seals the wrapped rabbit strip into a bed of epoxy so that no toothy fish can cut it off or damage it. Toothy species can still fray the fur, but they can't cut the fly apart.

> "When dressing dry-flies, we must always keep in mind the fish's point of view rather than our own."
>
> —*Romilly Fedden,* Golden Days *(1919)*

489 PLASTIC TUBING MINNOWS

A neat way to make minnow-like flies for warm water and saltwater use is to use synthetic plastic tubing material such as E-Z Body or Corsair. Both of these are braided, open tubing materials that come in a variety of sizes and colors for making all types of streamer flies.

Slide them over the body of the fly with the wing or tail materials extending from the rear. To make these materials flat to simulate the flat side of minnows such as silversides, dace, anchovies, etc., iron the material before using it. Do this on a hard surface such as a kitchen counter, not a soft ironing board. When doing this, make sure that you set the iron to a medium setting and that the iron does not harm the countertop. Hold the tubing at both ends (you might need help in holding one end) and then iron a length of the tubing, which you can later cut into short lengths for individual flies.

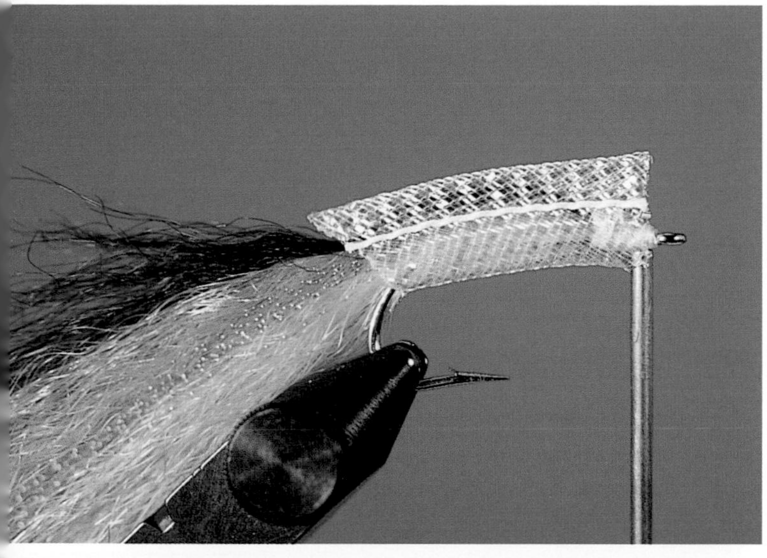

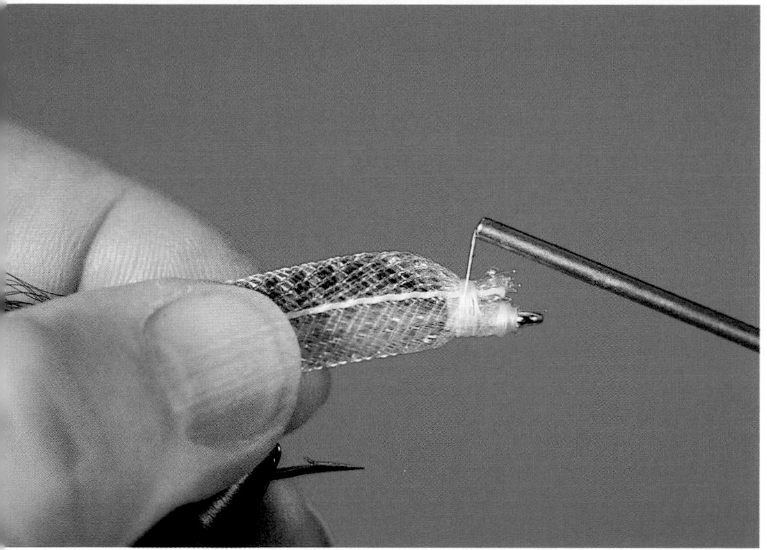

490 TYING PLASTIC TUBE MINNOWS

Many minnow patterns are possible by using a body of plastic tubing (E-Z Body, Corsair, Gudebrod G-Tubing). A simple way to tie these is to cut a length of the tubing, slide it onto a long-shaft bobbin, and then tie on the thread and a wing/tail of bucktail or synthetics. Then slide the body tubing up onto the hook shank, covering the forward part of the wing/tail, and tie down with the bobbin. This prevents tying off and tying back on again.

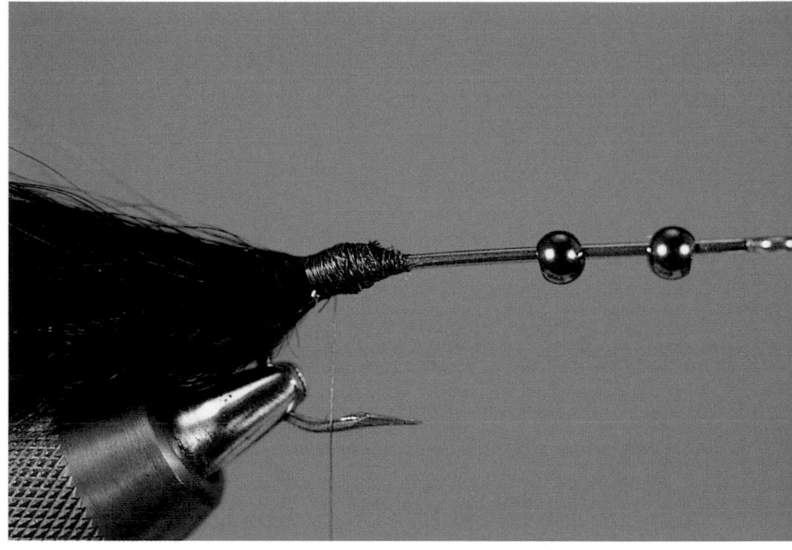

491 RATTLING BEADS ON A FLY

Rattles help fish find flies, particularly in stained or murky water. Rattles of plastic, glass, or aluminum are available for tying into flies, but you can also use sliding beads, in a suggestion from flytier George Liros.

For this, first slide two loose metal beads onto a long shank hook (bend the barb down first). Then begin to tie, but start the fly about halfway down the hook shank. Tie the fly you want (usually a streamer fly) and finish the fly, gluing the rear bead to the hook shank and the wrapped head. Allow the forward bead to slide free.

When fishing, use twitches so that the fly falls head first, while a twitch pulls it up to cause the forward bead to slide back and strike the rear bead to make noise.

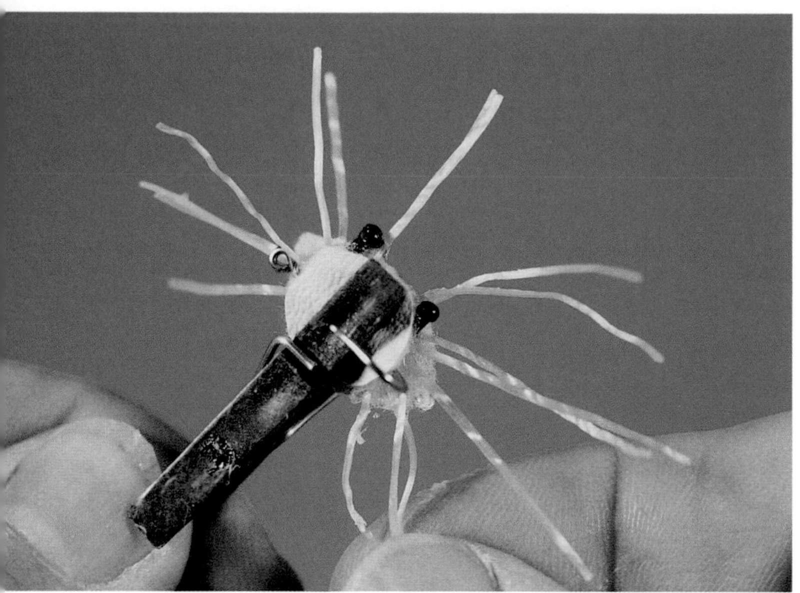

492 GLUING CRABS

Crabs can be made by gluing together two parts (carapace and abdomen) with the hook and legs between the two parts. Often the best carapace and abdomen includes foam, fuzzy foam, vinyl, and similar flat waterproof materials.

To make sure that these materials glue well, use small doll-size clothespins to hold the two body parts tightly together while the glue cures. Doll-size clothespins are available from toy stores.

493 ADDING GLITTER TO FLY HEADS

For a little more flash on your large warm water or saltwater flies, add standard or micro glitter to the epoxy when making the epoxy head.

To do this, first add the glitter to either the "A" or "B" (catalyst/hardener or resin) portion of the epoxy, mix thoroughly, and then mix with the other part. This step is particularly important if using a five-minute epoxy. Note that you will dilute the glitter you add to just one part when you mix it with the second equal part of the glue. Mix thoroughly and add to the fly, then place the fly on a rotator.

Craft shops carry glitter.

494 REINFORCING FLY SHOULDERS

Anglers use feathers such as those from guinea fowl to make shoulders on some flies. These shoulders are further dressed with a painted-on eye. This is a traditional method of tying some streamers in a Northeast style.

To make this easy to do, first coat the shoulder feathers with a clear sealer such as Softex, Flexament, or Loon Soft Head Cement. This also reinforces the shoulder to make it more durable. Then paint the eyes on the shoulder using different-size nail or pin heads to dot the eye and the pupil on the feather. The clear coating protects the feather from damage and prevents the paint of the eye from running or bleeding into the feather.

495 CRANE FLY IMITATIONS

Tie in a short body and then a very large hackle to simulate the long legs of these ungainly insects to create a simple crane fly imitation.

These large crane flies are a lesser, but still important, food source for trout, and a few of these can work wonders when fishing in the evening hours during the summer months. In essence, these are like the variant patterns of flies that are tied with extended tails and oversize hackles.

496 MAKING POM-POM GLO BUGS

You can make great glo bugs for trout, salmon, and steelhead fishing without tying and cutting material as is called for in most fly-tying books. For this, visit a craft store and buy some pom-poms in the right size and color. If you cannot get pom-poms in the color desired, you can buy white pom-poms and dye them pink or orange with Rit or Tintex.

To use these pom-poms, impale the center of the pompom with the hook point and then force the pom-pom around the hook bend and shank. To avoid sticking yourself, use care when doing this.

Place the pom-pom on a scrap of wood and then push the hook point down on the center of the pom-pom. Once the hook point and barb are through the pom-pom, then you can slide the pom-pom around on the hook shank.

To keep the pom-pom in place on the hook, first wrap the hook shank center with tying thread, tie off, and soak the thread with epoxy or CA glue before finally sliding the pom-pom into place on the center of the hook.

497 HANDLING BULLET HEADS ON FLIES

The Thunder Creek series of flies have a bullet head in which the wing (usually bucktail) is tied forward and then reversed over the body. It is then tied off about one-third the shank length in back of the hook eye to make a gill pattern.

To make these easy to tie and to form the bullet head, use a large plastic straw to reverse and push the bucktail from the forward position to the rear. To tie it off, push the straw into the bucktail bundle from the side, arrange it so that the bucktail surrounds the straw, and then push the straw back over the hook.

The reason for pushing the straw into the bundle from the side is to prevent bucktail from ending up in the lumen of the straw as might happen if you pushed it on from the front end. You can leave the straw in place while you tie down the bucktail (do not tie down the straw) or hold the bucktail bundle with the fingers of your left hand as you wrap the bucktail.

If you want a more permanent bullet-head pusher, buy a length of metal tubing from a hobby shop. You can get these in aluminum, copper, brass, and PVC plastic. They are available in different diameters, from about ⅛ inch (3.2 mm) and larger, so that you can have different-diameter pushers for different-size flies.

498 MAKING BULLET-HEAD FLIES

To make the most effective bullet-head (Thunder Creek style) patterns, use some light-colored bucktail or fur for the belly of the fly and dark-colored bucktail or fur for the back of the fly.

To keep these separate for later folding over the hook shank to form the wing, use a separate length of tying thread to loosely wrap around the forward part of the bundle to keep it separate from the subsequent bundle. Thus, if first tying down the light-colored belly, wrap some thread or cord around it, and then tie down the darker-colored back fibers or bucktail.

Next, wrap the thread back to the tie-down position and fold the back fibers over the hook shank and tie them in place. This is easy since the belly fibers are separate and loosely wrapped in a thread bundle.

Then remove the thread wrap over the belly fibers, fold that back, and tie in place with the working thread at the same spot.

499 NETTING FOR FLOAT PODS, TRAILING SHUCKS

To hold a tiny float pod of foam onto a fly as a parachute post or trailing shuck, use a piece of old stocking to hold the pod into place. Use sheer stocking material, or a color that matches the color needed for your fly. Cut the stocking material into small squares. Place the foam float pod into the center of a square and then wrap the stocking material tightly around it. Then tie the "neck" of this bundle onto the hook shank, secure it with thread, and then continue with the rest of the fly. The result is a tightly secured float pod, parachute post, or trailing shuck that will not come apart.

500 GLUING JUNGLE COCK TO SHOULDERS

To add jungle cock eyes to a shoulder feather, such as silver pheasant, glue them in place to make tying easier. First assemble a number of the shoulder feathers, place them separately on your workbench, and then glue a jungle cock feather to form an eye on the shoulder. Use flexible cement for this, such as Flexament or similar flexible fly-tying glue. Do this with a bunch of feathers and jungle cocks so that you have them ready when tying a particular fly. This is particularly good when tying freshwater dace patterns.

501 MAKING SHRIMP ANTENNAE

To make antennae for shrimp flies, you can use thin monofilament, dyed black. To do this, dye a spool of 12- to 20-pound (5.4- to 9.1-kg) mono with black Rit or Tintex dye, or buy a spool of black or dark-dyed mono. To create the antennae effect on a shrimp fly, tie in a few strands of the mono and leave them long, as they are on a real shrimp. You can use more than two (the number on a live shrimp) since fish cannot count. You only want to create the impression of the antennae, so a half-dozen strands are not too many. Another possibility is to use a few strands of black Super Hair, twisted and held together with soft glue such as Ultra Flex, Flexament, or Softex.

Final Words

Angling ethics, as with any ethics in life, involve the Golden Rule: Do unto others as you would have them do unto you. Thus,

- Don't crowd other anglers.
- Don't try to "steal" a spot from another fly fisherman.
- Ask anglers sitting on the bank if they are fishing and if they mind if you try; they might just be resting before resuming fishing.
- Don't run close to another angler when boat fishing.
- Always close gates or leave a farm as you find it (if granted the right to fish).
- Don't cut through farm fields or growing crops.
- Never enter private property without permission.
- Carry out your fishing waste (line, leader tippets, damaged flies, wrappers, and containers).
- Keep only the fish that you can use if not practicing catch-and-release.

These are only a few of the commonsense "rules" of fly fishing, which revolve around respect for your fellow anglers, respect for private or public property, respect for the environment, and respect for the fish.

Remember that without water and the habitat for fish to live, we will not have any fly fishing in the future. Let's make sure that on all trips we release fish where we can, take only those we can use for one meal, and handle all fish gently.

In addition, we have to make sure that we do not litter. Littering on the water messes up the home where fish live and makes it an unsightly place to fish.

A good way to practice a conservation lifestyle is to join a fishing club. It can provide access and introduction to fellow fly fishers, have information on local streams and possible fishing water, know about the hatches and hatch schedules, help with a vexing fly tying or fly casting problem, and have interesting programs and speakers at their monthly meetings.

Finally, the best and last tip of this book comes from my wife, Brenda, a beginning fly angler who has in our few years of marriage caught on the fly bonefish, smallmouth bass, shad, trout, panfish, stripers, bluefish, and other species. Her advice is to relax and enjoy fly fishing. Great advice. Fly fishing is not, and is not supposed to be, work. Enjoy the trip. Enjoy the day. Enjoy the scenery, your companions, your catches, your challenges. And you don't have to keep the fly in the water or the rod in the air all the time. If you feel like taking a break, trying something different, watching the birds, taking a nap, eating a sandwich, watching turtles, it is all a part of the fishing experience.

Enjoy! Brenda says it's okay.

FURTHER READING

GENERAL FLY FISHING

Borger, Gary. *Presentation,* Wausau, WI, Tomorrow River Press, 1995.

Earnhardt, Tom. *Fly Fishing the Tidewaters,* New York, NY, Lyons & Burford, 1995.

Humphreys, Joe. *Joe Humphreys's Trout Tactics,* Mechanicsburg, PA, Stackpole Books, 1981.

Jaworowski, Ed. *The Cast,* Mechanicsburg, PA, Stackpole Books, 1992.

Kreh, Lefty. *Lefty Kreh's Ultimate Guide to Fly Fishing,* New York, NY, The Lyons Press, 2003.

——. *Advanced Fly Fishing Techniques,* New York, NY, The Lyons Press, 2002.

——. *Presenting the Fly,* New York, NY, The Lyons Press, 1999.

——. *Fly Fishing in Salt Water,* New York, NY, The Lyons Press, 1997.

——. *Fly Casting with Lefty Kreh,* Philadelphia, PA, J. B. Lippincott Company, 1974.

Meck, Charles. *Patterns, Hatches, Tactics and Trout,* Williamsport, PA, Vivid Publishing, 1995.

——. *Fishing Small Streams With a Fly Rod,* Woodstock, VT, The Countryman Press, 1991.

Merwin, John. *Fly Fishing: A Trailside Guide,* New York, NY, W. W. Norton & Co., 1996.

Mitchell, Ed. *Fly Rodding the Coast,* Mechanicsburg, PA, Stackpole Books, 1995.

Murray, Harry. *Fly Fishing for Smallmouth Bass,* New York, NY, The Lyons Press, 1989.

Pfeiffer, C. Boyd. *Shad Fishing,* Mechanicsburg, PA, Stackpole Books, 2002.

——. *Fly Fishing: Saltwater Basics,* Mechanicsburg, PA, Stackpole Books, 1999.

——. *Fly Fishing: Bass Basics,* Mechanicsburg, PA, Stackpole Books, 1997.

Reynolds, Barry, and John Berryman. *Pike on the Fly,* Boulder, CO, Johnson Books, 1993.

Reynolds, Barry, Brad Befus, and John Berryman. *Carp on the Fly,* Boulder, CO, Johnson Books, 1997.

Sosin, Mark, and Lefty Kreh. *Practical Fishing Knots,* II, New York, NY, Lyons & Burford, 1991.

Tabory, Lou. *Inshore Fly Fishing,* New York, NY, The Lyons Press, 1992.

Whitlock, Dave. *L. L. Bean Fly Fishing for Bass Handbook,* New York, NY, The Lyons Press, 1988.

Wulff, Joan. *Joan Wulff's Fly Casting Techniques,* New York, NY, Nick Lyons Books, 1987.

FLY TYING

Best, A. K. *Production Fly Tying,* Boulder, CO, Pruett Publishing Co., 1989.

Borger, Gary. *Designing Trout Flies,* Wausau, WI, Tomorrow River Press, 1991.

Bruce, Joe. *Fly Design Theory & Practice,* Lisbon, MD, K & D Publishing, 2002.

Fullum, Jay "Fishy." *Fishy's Flies,* Mechanicsburg, PA, Stackpole Books, 2002.

Hughes, Dave. *Trout Flies, The Tier's Reference,* Mechanicsburg, PA, Stackpole Books, 1999.

Klausmeyer, David. *Guide Flies,* Woodstock, VT, The Countryman Press, 2003.

———. *Tying Contemporary Saltwater Flies,* Woodstock, VT The Countryman Press, 2002.

Kreh, Lefty. *Saltwater Fly Patterns,* New York, NY, Lyons & Burford, 1995.

Lafontaine, Gary. *Trout Flies, Proven Patterns,* Helena, MT, Greycliff Publishing, 1993.

Leeson, Ted, and Jim Schollmeyer. *The Fly Tier's Benchside Reference,* Portland, OR, Frank Amato Publications, 1998.

Likakis, John M. *Bass Bug Basics,* Woodstock, VT, Countryman Press, 2003.

Martin, Darrel. *Fly-Tying Methods,* New York, NY, Nick Lyons Books, 1987.

Meck, Charles. *101 Innovative Fly-Tying Tips,* Guilford, CT, The Lyons Press, 2002.

Moore, Wayne. *Fly Tying Notes,* Seattle, WA, Recreational Consultants, 1984.

Morris, Skip. *Tying Foam Flies,* Portland, OR, Frank Amato Publications, 1994.

———. *The Art of Tying the Bass Fly,* Portland, OR, Frank Amato Publications, 1996.

Pfeiffer, C. Boyd. *Bug Making,* New York, NY, Lyons and Burford, 1993.

———. *Fly Fishing Bass Basics,* Mechanicsburg, PA, Stackpole Books, 1997.

———. *Fly Fishing Saltwater Basics,* Mechanicsburg, PA, Stackpole Books, 1999.

———. *Shad Fishing,* Mechanicsburg, PA, Stackpole Books, 2002.

———. *Simple Flies,* Woodstock, VT, The Countryman Press, 2005.

———. *Tying Trout Flies,* Iola, WI, Krause Publications, 2002.

———. *Tying Warmwater Flies,* Iola, WI, Krause Publications, 2003.

Scheck, Art. *Tying Better Flies,* Woodstock, VT, The Countryman Press, 2003.

Schollmeyer, Jim. *Nymph Fly-Tying Techniques,* Portland, OR, Frank Amato Publications, 2001.

Schollmeyer, Jim, and Ted Leeson. *Tying Emergers,* Portland, OR, Frank Amato Publications, 2004.

———. *Inshore Flies,* Portland, OR, Frank Amato Publications, 2000.

Steeves, Harrison R., Jr. *Tying Flies with Foam, Fur and Feathers,* Mechanicsburg, PA, Stackpole Books, 2003.

Stewart, Dick. *Fly-Tying Tips,* Intervale, NH, Northland Press Inc. 1990.

Talleur, Dick. *The Versatile Fly Tyer,* New York, NY, Nick Lyons Books, 1990.

Tryon, Chuck and Sharon. *Figuring Out Flies,* Rolla, MO, Ozark Mountain Fly Anglers, 1990.

Veniard, John, and Donald Downs. *Fly-Tying Problems and Their Answers,* New York, NY, Crown Publishers, 1972.

Veverka, Bob. *Innovative Saltwater Flies,* Mechanicsburg, PA, Stackpole Books, 1999.

Williamson, Robert. *Creative Flies Innovative Tying Techniques,* Portland, OR. Frank Amato Publications, 2002.

INDEX

Aerial roll cast, 71
Aerosol painting, 191
Airline security, 109
Albright knot, 38
Anchors, 89
Ankle support, 45, 92
Ant imitations, 206
Antennae, shrimp, 214
Arbor knot, 38

Back braces, 47
Backcasting, 70, 71. *See also* Casting
Backing, 16, 17, 205
Baitfish, simulating, 12
Barefoot fishing, 91
Bartlett, Norm, 53, 90, 94, 108
Bass bugs, 120, 128, 139, 142, 144, 145, 192, 195
Bead-chain, 126, 127, 160
Beads
  adding, 159
  for eyes, 171
  fitting to hooks, 158
  handling, 177
  rattling, 211
  weighting, 161
Big-game, 85
Birds, 85, 86
Blaisdell, Harold, 186
Blood feathers, 201
Blood knot, 38
Blunt, Wilfred S., 178
Boat, hooked fish under, 90
Boat leader box, 93
Bobbin rest, 129
Bobbins
  adjustments, 133
  cleaning, 134
  labeling, 132
  threading, 140, 143
  uses for, 133
  See also Thread
Bodies
  beetle, 165
  bonds for, 190
  choosing diameter for, 189
  detached, 177
  flat nymph, 154
  fuzzy, 184
  hot gluing, 178
  minnow, 183
  non-weighted, 186
  segmented, 194
  separate from tails, 175
  shad or smelt, 185
  shaping foam, 189
  smooth, 185
  spray painting, 192
  tapered, 185
  tinsel, 179
Bodkins, 126, 135, 137
Boots, 45, 46
Bottle brushes, 135
Bottom-feeding fish, 85
Brewer, Doug, 178
Bubbles in epoxy, 206
Bucktail, 202
Bullet heads, 213

Cameras, 54
Carapaces, 177, 205, 212
Cars, 107
Cases, 11, 13. *See also* Storage
Cassette tape, 205
Casting
  above water surface, 69
  aerial roll, 71
  from a boat, 89
  distance, 89
  dummy, 89
  ease, 69
  false, 75
  last cast, 75
  "Lazy S," 80
  practice, 55
  from shore, 74
  side roll, 71
  sinking lines, 70
  sinking shooting heads, 70
  upstream, 79
  with the wind, 72
  See also Backcasting
Caterpillars, 208
Chenille, 164, 165, 167
Chest packs, 44
Chumming, 78, 87
Clamp and board, 125
Cleaning fishing areas, 66
Cleats, 93
Clothing, 43–45, 48–51, 91
Comfort, fly-tying, 117
Cones, 159
Controlling fish, 61
Cork, 191, 195
Count down fishing, 70
Crabs, 212
Crane fly imitations, 212
Customs slips, 110

Dangers, 77, 85
Dapping, 79
Deer hair, 120, 128, 139, 144, 145
Deren, Jim, 63
Diamond hone, 14
Double loop of, 17
Double-haul, 73
Downstream fishing, 75, 81
Drag anchors, 89
Drags, backing off, 103
Dressmaker's pins, 168
Drifting a fly to undercut bank, 79
Dubbing, 131, 135, 178
Dubbing wax, 136
Duffle bags, 105, 106
Dummy casts, 89

Edges, 63
Edghill, Chuck, 32, 47, 178
Eels, 209
Emergency kits, 109
Emergers, 183
Epoxy, 206

Ethics, 217
Expenses, travel, 110
Extension butts, 20
Eye strain, 115, 121
Eye-buster tool, 193
Eyeglasses, 47
Eyes
angled, 173
doll, 174
dressmaker's pins for, 168
dumbbell, 24, 26, 57, 140, 160, 161, 171, 173
glass/plastic, 171
hairbrush, 168
monofilament, 173
painted, 172, 173
prism, 174
recessing, 172
self-stick, 169, 172

Fabric, 118
Falling in, 65
False casting, 75
Farm ponds, 81
Fedden, Romilly, 210
Ferrules, 102, 103
Field kits, 109
Fighting big fish, 61
Figure-eight boat retrieve, 90
Fishing clubs, 217
Flash, 13, 202
Flashlights, 52
Flattened fly skeletons, 209
Flies
bag for, 95
box for, 95
bullet-head, 144, 171, 214
checking, 123
chum, 210
drifting, 79
drying, 67
examining, 120
floating, 11
leaf-hooked, 81
marking baitfish, 136
natural float, 124
point-up, 140
presoaking, 11
proportions for, 205
quill-bodied, 181
rattle, 16
removing, 63, 65
sample, 119
sandwich, 194
sinking, 70
small, 120, 121, 124
snagproof, 163
snelling, 151
spacing dry, 205
spey, 187
steamed, 99
storing small, 11
streamer, 12, 13, 123, 145, 148, 179, 202, 205, 212
tails and legs on, 119
tandem, 168
using different, 54
weedless, 12
weighted, 57, 159, 160, 161
worm, 164
Float pods, 214
Fly boxes, 11, 67, 95, 109
Fly fishing deep, 58
Foam, 189, 190, 192–193, 194, 214
Ford, Corey, 49
Fox, Charlie, 78
Frames, painting, 192
Freshwater fish, 77
Fulsher, Keith, 144, 171

Gallows tool, 126
Gap clearance, 145
Garbage bags, 51
Gel-spun lines, 16, 17
Glitter, 212
Gloves, 50, 51
Glue, 13, 178. *See also* Epoxy; Head cement
Gordon, Theodore, 54
Guides, 53, 99
Guides, fishing, 55

Hackle
control, 183
dry fly, 197
folding, 187
marking, 200
palmered, 208
pliers, 125
weed guard tip, 162
Hair packer, 128
Half hitch, handmade, 140
Half-hitch tool, 124, 139
Handling fish, 217
Hat clips, 49
Hats, 48, 49
Hawker, Col. Peter, 14
Head cement, 130, 135, 187, 206
Head gear. *See* Hats
Hemingway, Ernest, 64
Hemostats, 42
Henshall, James, 77
High backcast, 71
Hip boots, 46, 103
Holding fish, 54
Hook gap, 15, 145, 149
Hooks
barbs, 15, 149
circle, 149, 150
corrosion-resistant, 147
damage to, 15
extensions for, 148
eyes, 193, 195
flaws, 151
gluing, 190
popper, 154
sharpness, 14
snelled, 16, 150
storing, 147, 154
straight-eye, 147
weighting, 153

Ice, 53
Improved clinch knot, 38
Insect repellent, 47
Insects, collecting, 121

Jungle cock, 214

Keeping cool, 49
Kelson, George M., 172

Knee pads, 46
Knots, 32, 38–39
Kreh, Lefty, 46, 92
Kulsher, Keith, 144

Landing fish, 61, 62, 77
Lanyards, 41, 42
Last cast, 75
"Lazy S" cast, 80
Lead alternatives, 26
Leaders
  box for, 93
  braided wire, 29
  caught in reel, 57
  choosing, 28
  coils in, 22
  controlling, 22
  fluorocarbon, 28
  formula, 27
  heavy shock, 29
  length for sinking lines, 58
  looping long, 58
  preparing, 30
  sinking, 59
  storing, 30
  weighted, 57
Leeches
  bead-chain, 126
  weighting, 161
Legs, 167–169, 174, 175
Leisenring, Jim, 79
Light, tying and, 115
Light levels, 52
Line
  camouflaging, 34
  coils in, 23
  control, 22, 74
  damage to, 28
  double-taper, 27
  floating, 24
  marking, 33, 34
  mending, 73
  numbering, 33
  retrieving, 74
  sinking, 58, 70
  spare, 13
  spooling, 23
  tangles, 92
  tangles in, 57
  washing, 101
  weight-forward, 27
Line slip, 24
Line-stripping baskets, 90, 91
Lip landing, 62
Liros, George, 211
Littering, 217
Loop control, 58, 69
Loop-to-loop connection, 13, 17, 31, 39
Lumps, 177

Mann, Charlie, 186
Marabou, 201
Marinaro, Vince, 78
Marking materials, 136
McGuane, Thomas, 105
Meck, Charles, 171, 200
Midges, thread-bodied, 180
Mini lead heads, 26
Minnows, 210, 211
Mono, cutting, 22
Mothballs, 117, 118
Motor controls, electric, 93

Nail knot, 39
Natural materials, protecting, 117
Necks, storing, 120
Nets, 44, 62
Netting (material), 192, 214
Netting fish, 62
Night fishing, 52
Night light, 108
Nymphs
  cases, 165
  flat-bodied, 154
  weighted-wire, 159

Overbodies, 179
Owens, Brian, 209

Paintbrushes, 174
Painting, 172, 173, 191–192, 193
Palmering, 208
Passports, 110
Peacock herl, 159, 165, 180, 181, 182
Penn, Robert, 28
Perfection loop, 39
Personal floatation device (PFD), 65
Pertwee, Roland, 35
Photocopying documents, 110
Photographing fish, 54
Pike, landing, 61
Pilot holes, 167
Pliers, 42, 125
Pom-pom glo bugs, 213
Poppers, 191
Popping and swapping, 86
Practice, 55
Pumice stone, 143
Pushing to breaking fish, 89
PVC fly rod holders, 94

Quill wing dividers, 137
Quills, 181, 197

Racks, 126, 127
Rain parka, 51
Ramping, 155
Ransome, Arthur, 41, 121
Rattle flies, 16
Rattling beads, 211
Reading the water, 77–78
Reels
  anti-reverse, 20
  cleaning, 100
  conventional, 20
  direct-drive, 20
  drag, 19
  large-arbor, 20
  leaders caught in, 57
  loose, 21
  protecting, 95
  retractable, 41
  seats, 19, 21
  washing, 101
Releasing fish, 62
Retrieves, 19, 90
Ribbing, 180
Rods
  bags, 36
  carrying, 66

grips, 35
holders, 94
length, 69
marking, 35
protecting, 94
pumping, 63
storing, 99, 108
threading, 24
travel, 108
tubes, 34
washing, 102

Saltwater fish, 85
Samples, 119
Scale finish, 192
Sealers, 31
Seams, 63
Shank, thread-wrapped, 144
Sharpening hooks, 14
Sharpness, 14, 149
Shoes, 92
Shooting heads, sinking, 24
Shot
small, 12
split, 12
Shoulders, 212, 214
Shrimp antennae, 214
Shucks, 183
Side roll cast, 71
Sink rate, 153
Skeletons, 209
Skilton, Bill, 194
Sliding hoods, 21
Slip strike, 29
Snagproof bonefish flies, 163
Snags, 81
Snelled hook holders, 16
Snelling, 150, 151
Soft loops, 144
Spills, 130
Spools
capping, 142
extra, 21
marking, 22
storing, 152
Stacker protection, 116
Stevens, Carrie, 144, 171
Storage
hooks, 154
natural materials, 117
necks, 120
small hooks, 147
thread spools, 152
tying supplies, 116, 118, 119, 135
Stranded materials, 119
Streamer heads, tapering, 145
Strike, timing, 75
Strike indicator, 81
Sun safety, 47, 48, 51, 52, 91
Swinging the fly, 74

Tail wraps, 189
Tails, 171, 175
Talcum powder, 202
Tandem rigs, 69, 151
Tapply, H. G., 103
Temperature gauges, 53
Templates, 205
Terrestrials, 69, 192
Thread
breakage, 142, 152
changing, 140
fine, 142
flattening, 142
harness, 200
heavy, 142
labeling bobbins, 132
pressure, 133
size, 143
slipping of, 142
storing, 152
See also Bobbins
Throats, 123
Tides, 86
Tinsel, 179
Tippets, 28, 29, 59, 66
Tip-tops, 13
Tool racks, 126
Trailing shucks, 214
Translucent look, 185
Travel, 105, 108, 110–111
Tubing eels, 209
Tungston, 161
Turtle knot, 32, 147
Twain, Mark, 99
Tying correctly, 144

Underfur, 120

Vests, 43, 44
Vinyl, 177
Vises, 123, 125

Waders, 45, 46, 103, 105
Wading, 64, 87
Wading staffs, 41, 64
Walkie-talkies, 54
Walton, Izaak, 139
Weak backcast, 71
Weed guards
alternative, 12
brush-style, 164
improving, 59
mono, 156–157, 158, 163
wire, 158
Weighting, 57
Whip finish, 141
Wind, 72
Wind knots, 32
Wings
dividing, 197, 200
dry fly, 197
isolating, 187
securing, 144
streamer, 197, 198, 199, 202
Wire
braided, 29
lead, 153
non-lead, 153
size, 155
sources for, 159
weed guards, 158, 162
Worm flies, 164, 165

Yarn, 116, 180
Yo-yo lift, 79

Zem, Ed, 69

ACKNOWLEDGMENTS

Many of my friends over several decades have helped me in all aspects of fishing and its related hobbies and activities. These include friends such as Chuck Edghill, Lefty Kreh, Mark Sosin, Norm Bartlett, Ed Russell, Art Scheck, Dave Klausmeyer, Bill May, Jim Heim, Gary Neitzey, Joe Zimmer, George Reiger, Irv Swope, Jack Goellner, and so many others. To all these fly anglers—close buddies and casual acquaintances—along with those I may have forgotten with a memory dimmed by the years—I say thank you.

In addition, I have picked up ideas from a number of publications over the years, including *Fly Fisherman, Fly Tyer, American Angler* in particular, but also a host of other magazines in the fly fishing/fly-tying genre or general fishing magazines with fly fishing/tying coverage or columns. Books, too, have always been an interest of mine, and there is a plethora of books on all aspects of fly fishing, fly tying, and tying for particular geographic regions and specific species. Seminars, too, have led to an influx of ideas and techniques from which I have gained much.

I also give credit to an old man who 50-odd years ago took a boy under his wing to teach him about the fishing of which the boy's parents and family knew nothing. Fred Klemcke was about 60 and I was about 11 when my parents moved to a home adjoining his property. Fred's friendship and help over the several years before he retired and moved to Maine taught me about fishing, fly fishing and fly casting, trout fishing, and fly tying.

Lastly, thank you to Brenda, my wife, who photographed specific shots for the book. She also gave me the time for this project and encouraged me with this, as she does with all of my efforts, and indeed with life.

Boyd Pfeiffer